Latest Trends In AI Ethics

Practical Advances in Artificial Intelligence and Machine Learning

Dr. Lance B. Eliot, MBA, PhD

ISBN: 978-1-95-738608-9

DEDICATION

To my incredible daughter, Lauren, and my incredible son, Michael.

Forest fortuna adiuvat (from the Latin; good fortune favors the brave).

CONTENTS

ACKNOWLEDGMENTS

I have been the beneficiary of advice and counsel by many friends, colleagues, family, investors, and many others. I want to thank everyone that has aided me throughout my career. I write from the heart and the head, having experienced first-hand what it means to have others around you that support you during the good times and the tough times.

To Warren Bennis, one of my doctoral advisors and ultimately a colleague, I offer my deepest thanks and appreciation, especially for his calm and insightful wisdom and support.

To Mark Stevens and his generous efforts toward funding and supporting the USC Stevens Center for Innovation.

To Lloyd Greif and the USC Lloyd Greif Center for Entrepreneurial Studies for their ongoing encouragement of founders and entrepreneurs.

To Peter Drucker, William Wang, Aaron Levie, Peter Kim, Jon Kraft, Cindy Crawford, Jenny Ming, Steve Milligan, Chis Underwood, Frank Gehry, Buzz Aldrin, Steve Forbes, Bill Thompson, Dave Dillon, Alan Fuerstman, Larry Ellison, Jim Sinegal, John Sperling, Mark Stevenson, Anand Nallathambi, Thomas Barrack, Jr., and many other innovators and leaders that I have met and gained mightily from doing so.

Thanks to Ed Trainor, Kevin Anderson, James Hickey, Wendell Jones, Ken Harris, DuWayne Peterson, Mike Brown, Jim Thornton, Abhi Beniwal, Al Biland, John Nomura, Eliot Weinman, John Desmond, and many others for their unwavering support during my career.

And most of all thanks as always to Lauren and Michael, for their ongoing support and for having seen me writing and heard much of this material during the many months involved in writing it. To their patience and willingness to listen.

CHAPTER 1
INTRODUCTION TO AI ETHICS

There is an urgently rising societal interest in the field of AI Ethics.

Thankfully so.

As Artificial Intelligence (AI) continues to advance and increasingly become part of our daily lives, we need to be on our toes about AI that diverges from ethical behavior and crosses over into unethical behavior. The field of AI Ethics seeks to apply ethical precepts and theories of ethical conduct to the devising and usage of AI systems, doing so to try and steer AI into sufficient ethical mores and avert unethical actions by AI.

Formal definitions of AI Ethics tend to vary somewhat. All told, the notion is to combine what we know or believe about ethics as a guiding tool toward the mounting advent of AI-based intelligent systems.

Some would argue that the AI horse is seemingly getting out of the barn and doing so without needed ethical boundaries. In a headline-grabbing worst-case scenario envisioned by AI futurists, AI systems are predicted to become mightier than we can adequately control and end up as an existential risk to the fate of humanity. Dire catastrophic outcomes are being painted.

You don't though need to look solely at the far future to get concerned about the ethical actions of AI. As will be discussed, there are plenty of AI systems of today that already have made known the adverse consequences of not taking into account the importance of AI Ethics.

As a particularly succinct and insightful definition of AI Ethics, consider this one by The Alan Turing Institute: "AI ethics is a set of values, principles, and techniques that employ widely accepted standards of right and wrong to guide moral conduct in the development and use of AI technologies" (as published in *Understanding Artificial Intelligence Ethics And Safety: A Guide For The Responsible Design And Implementation Of AI Systems In The Public Sector* by David Leslie, 2019).

Notice that there is an important dual-element consisting of both the development of AI systems and the usage of AI systems.

AI Ethics comes to play as a guiding light throughout the development process when devising AI. The entirety of the AI development life cycle must encompass AI Ethics principles. From the moment that an AI system is first initially conceived of, and then during the design, building, testing, fielding, and upkeep, all stakeholders involved in producing the AI are to be giving due consideration to AI Ethics. In addition, once an AI system has been placed into active use, you still must be on alert to watch for, detect, and potentially correct AI that verges from ethical conduct into unethical actions.

I mention the aspect of remaining aware once AI has been placed into use because there is often a faulty notion of fire-and-forget mindset that some developers of AI get caught up in. They believe that if they tried to develop the AI in an ethically minded fashion, there is no need to continue any AI Ethics forays once the AI is released into use.

This belies the real and frequent possibility that the AI will veer from its earlier ethics-oriented groundings and sway into unethical territory while in use.

AI Ethics And The Entire AI Development Life Cycle

Keep in mind then that we will want to ensure that both conditions of development and of use are being met, namely:

a) Apply AI Ethics throughout the AI development process from start to "finish"

b) Continue to apply AI Ethics even once the AI is placed into use

The AI development life cycle must be viewed as ranging from the initial conceiving of the AI to the entire time that it is available for use. Do not shortchange that range. Some AI developers do not consider the initial conceiving stage as within the scope of AI Ethics and think that just the building or coding stage is where AI Ethics first arises. In a similar mistaken belief, some AI developers assume that after the AI has been released into production and put into use that they can wash their hands of any residual or newly emerging AI Ethics qualms about the AI system. Nope, trying to narrowly confine where AI Ethics is needed will undoubtedly lead to ethical problems, one way or another, and sooner or later.

Another quick point is to realize that AI Ethics is something that all stakeholders amidst an AI system must be cognizant of. The normal assumption is that the software engineers alone are the caretakers of any AI Ethics considerations. Not so. Management that oversees the crafting of an AI system is part-and-parcel of the AI Ethics matters. If the organizational leaders are shortchanging the value of applying AI Ethics, you can bet that this same persona will permeate and undercut the AI life cycle. Budgets for devising the AI won't include set-asides for incorporating AI Ethics considerations. Schedules and deadlines won't either. In the end, a pell-mell rush to get the AI out the door will take top priority and AI Ethics will barely get a word in edgewise.

All stakeholders have a stake in enduring that AI Ethics is sufficiently incorporated into the full life-cycle of an AI system.

When an AI system exhibits unethical activity, this can be traced not just to the coding and the software developers, but also tracked to the leaders that oversaw the AI life cycle, the business and systems analysts involved, and even those that are operating or responsible for the final deployment of the AI.

The usual escape hatch entails those other stakeholders claiming that they weren't the ones that churned out the code that underlies the AI system. This is a convenient and at times nearly convincing argument for those that do not fully grasp how an AI system came to be. Overall, all stakeholders have both an ethical responsibility for the AI and are likely to have legal accountability too.

Making Sense Of What AI Is

When I refer to Artificial Intelligence, the AI moniker can be a bit confusing as to what AI entails.

Welcome to the club in the sense that the meaning of Artificial Intelligence continues to be bandied around and there is no single comprehensive and all-agreed definition for AI. One of the issues facing the latest efforts to regulate AI systems has been how to appropriately define AI within our laws. If the legal definition is overly broad, new laws seeking to better govern AI systems can inadvertently encroach on all manner of software applications and computer systems. If the legal definition of AI is excessively restrictive, the odds are that AI systems that should have been encompassed will wiggle out from being bound by those laws.

The easiest way to define AI consists of saying that any computer or machine that exhibits seemingly intelligent behavior is in the realm of AI.

This notion dates back to 1956 when Professor John McCarthy coined the name Artificial Intelligence as part of a proposal to bring together many luminaries of math and computer science for a research project: "The study is to proceed on the basis of the conjecture that every aspect of learning or any other feature of intelligence can in principle be so precisely described that a machine can be made to simulate it" (in his co-authored proposal entitled *Proposal For The Dartmouth Summer Research Project On Artificial Intelligence*).

One subtle but extremely vital facet about the definition of AI is that we can presumably seek to attain computer-based or machine-based intelligent behavior without necessarily duplicating the precise way that humans think. There is an ongoing debate about that questionable keystone. Some would contend that the only way to produce an artificial form of intelligence is to completely mimic how the human brain works. Others argue that we might find alternative means to bring forth artificially indued intelligence. The old saying goes that there is more than one way to skin a cat.

The gist is that if we can craft a computer or machine that will *exhibit* intelligence and intelligent behavior, we ought not to be especially caring about how that came to be. All that we need to know is that the system appears to act and respond intelligently. Whatever we did to get there is not particularly relevant, some say. As you might imagine, not everyone agrees with that supposition. The inner workings of how intelligence comes to arise are claimed to be equally important as the result of being able to produce intelligent actions and outputs.

Rather than focusing on definitions of AI, there is another way that AI is often depicted. You can assert that AI is a set of computer-related techniques and technologies. Thus, if you are making use of those AI techniques and technologies, you are ergo devising and employing AI capabilities.

A typical taxonomy would explain AI by suggesting that these associated techniques and technologies are involved:

- Machine Learning
- Natural Language Processing
- Knowledge-Based Systems
- Automated Reasoning
- Robotics
- Multi-Agent Systems
- Etc.

A difficulty of merely referring to those various techniques and technologies as constituting an AI system is that you aren't especially aiming at the intelligence side of things. Recall that the nearly universal goal of AI is to attain systems that exhibit intelligence. You can cobble together the various techniques and technologies and not necessarily derive any semblance of intelligent-like behaviors. Would a system that perchance leverages those capabilities be reasonably construed as an AI system even if it did not showcase intelligent-oriented actions? I would dare say many would contend that such a system does not meet the spirit or tone of what is meant by referring to AI.

AI Ethics Has Been On A Roller Coaster Of Societal Interest

You might be surprised to learn that AI Ethics has been a topic of discussion since the very beginning of the AI field. Perhaps this has partially been fueled by longstanding works of fiction that have indubitably worried that someday humans would construct machines that could overtake humankind. Today's emergence of computer systems that seem to have AI capacities has brought those past fictional stories into greater focus as something that might be constructed in the real world.

Interest in AI Ethics has been a roller coaster ride, consisting of moments of great interest to spans of sparse attention.

During the 1980s and 1990s, intense efforts were being made to craft knowledge-based systems, often referred to as expert systems, and the concerns about AI Ethics began to gain traction. The more AI there is, the more likely the attention to AI Ethics.

You might be aware that then a so-called "AI Winter" arose following the hyped expectations of AI in the 80s and 90s, and a resurgence of AI attention only began anew in the last decade or so. During the winter period of AI, AI Ethics somewhat languished, ostensibly still being worked on but now in the shadows. Upon the newly considered "AI Spring" of advances in AI capabilities that stridently stoked a renewal for AI, along with rapidly decreasing costs of computing, and a myriad of other technology trends such as cloud computing, the Internet of Things (IoT), and so on, this, in turn, sparked a renewal in AI Ethics.

Many speak nowadays of AI as being either *AI For Good* or *AI For Bad.* The initial renewed excitement about contemporary AI capabilities was that we would finally be able to fruitfully use computers and so-called smart machines toward solving many of the globe's most pressing problems, such as dealing with worldwide hunger, widespread poverty, sustainability, and other pressing issues.

That is *AI For Good.*

Lamentedly, we began to realize that the same AI could contain untoward biases and inequities, accordingly, labeled as *AI For Bad.* For example, facial recognition was one of the first AI technologies that got caught with inherent racial and gender biases, which we will be exploring in the chapters ahead.

The odds are that any AI system will have a bit of both. As much as possible, we want to uncover and excise the *AI For Bad.* Also, as much as possible, we want to ensure that *AI For Good* is being devised and fielded. Those that are AI ethicists bring to the table the skillset and passion for striving to maximize the *AI For Good* and minimize or eliminate the *AI For Bad.*

This is assuredly a tough proposition to fulfill.

Being An AI Ethicist Or Adjacent To

Speaking of tough shoes to fill, let's pursue that topic in terms of who can aid in the AI Ethics field.

A properly qualified AI ethicist should be versed in the field of ethics and likewise versed in the field of AI. It is a twofer if you like.

Someone that is strong on the ethics side but weak on the AI side would be doing themselves a disservice because they are bound to lack the needed comprehension about what AI is and what it might become. In the same breath, someone that is weak on the ethics side and strong on the AI side might be missing the boat in terms of understanding the vital nuances of ethics and ethical thinking.

In the case of AI, I like to clearly demarcate that when I am discussing AI, it could be in the context of any or all of these three conditions:

1) Non-sentient AI of today
2) Sentient AI of human intelligence caliber (which we don't know will be achieved)
3) Sentient AI of super-intelligence (which is even more speculative than #2)

Discussions about AI that are in the sentient AI category are highly speculative. We don't have sentient AI today. We don't know when we will have sentient AI, if ever so. In general, covering AI Ethics when solely considering sentient AI is a lot of handwaving. You can pretty much make up whatever you like about how sentient AI is going to behave. I'm not saying that we should not be concerned about sentient AI, and only mentioning that the AI Ethics as pertaining to sentient AI is loosey-goosey and not especially real-world applicable per se.

You can rest assured that there is still plenty to talk about when it comes to AI Ethics and today's non-sentient AI. There is no need to go into the outstretched arena of sentient AI to have lots to discuss.

Furthermore, the handy aspect of AI Ethics regarding non-sentient AI is that this is a very applied discipline that can be immediately put to use throughout society. Companies that are creating AI systems need AI Ethics advice and consultation. Entities and people that are using AI systems are likewise in need of AI Ethics advice and consultation. Regulators are now steeped in trying to create laws related to AI, for which AI Ethics insights are needed too.

The field of ethics and all of its numerous theories about ethics can be applied toward the specific domain of AI. Indeed, one viewpoint is that the field of ethics as *applied to technology* (of any kind) is the umbrella into which the particular application of ethics applied to AI fits.

For those of you that are pursuing a career as an AI ethicist, the good news is that we are still in the infancy of AI Ethics. There is a lot of room to grow. You can also anticipate that as AI gets more pervasive and improves in showcasing intelligent behavior, AI Ethics will be expanding and sought after correspondingly so.

AI Ethics Frameworks And Key Principles

At this time, there are lots of proposed AI Ethics frameworks or principles that are being floated around and discussed heartily. No single set of AI Ethics principles has been universally adopted. Each day there seems to be a new set proffered by one prominent group or entity, or another. You have lots of AI Ethics precepts to choose from.

The chapters will cover this more so, but we can take a sneak peek here.

As stated by the U.S. Department of Defense (DoD) in their *Ethical Principles For The Use Of Artificial Intelligence*, these are the six primary AI ethics principles:

- **Responsible:** DoD personnel will exercise appropriate levels of judgment and care while remaining responsible for the development, deployment, and use of AI capabilities.

- **Equitable:** The Department will take deliberate steps to minimize unintended bias in AI capabilities.

- **Traceable:** The Department's AI capabilities will be developed and deployed such that relevant personnel possesses an appropriate understanding of the technology, development processes, and operational methods applicable to AI capabilities, including transparent and auditable methodologies, data sources, and design procedure and documentation.

- **Reliable:** The Department's AI capabilities will have explicit, well-defined uses, and the safety, security, and effectiveness of such capabilities will be subject to testing and assurance within those defined uses across their entire lifecycles.

- **Governable:** The Department will design and engineer AI capabilities to fulfill their intended functions while possessing the ability to detect and avoid unintended consequences, and the ability to disengage or deactivate deployed systems that demonstrate unintended behavior.

Meanwhile, as stated by the Vatican in the *Rome Call For AI Ethics* these are their identified six primary AI ethics principles:

- **Transparency:** In principle, AI systems must be explainable
- **Inclusion:** The needs of all human beings must be taken into consideration so that everyone can benefit, and all individuals can be offered the best possible conditions to express themselves and develop
- **Responsibility:** Those who design and deploy the use of AI must proceed with responsibility and transparency
- **Impartiality:** Do not create or act according to bias, thus safeguarding fairness and human dignity
- **Reliability:** AI systems must be able to work reliably
- **Security and privacy:** AI systems must work securely and respect the privacy of users.

You astutely probably noticed a commonality across those AI Ethics principles.

Researchers have examined and condensed the essence of numerous such national and international AI ethics tenets, articulating the summary set in a paper entitled "The Global Landscape Of AI Ethics Guidelines" as published in the prized journal *Nature*, which led to this essentials list:

- **Transparency**
- **Justice & Fairness**
- **Non-Maleficence**
- **Responsibility**
- **Privacy**
- **Beneficence**
- **Freedom & Autonomy**
- **Trust**
- **Sustainability**
- **Dignity**
- **Solidarity**

In short, you could say that AI Ethics consists of *applying* those aforementioned ethical precepts to AI systems.

To make this claim abundantly apparent, I'll relist those principles and add the indication that they are to be applied to AI and done so via the auspices of AI Ethics:

- Transparency as applied to AI via AI Ethics considerations
- Justice & Fairness as applied to AI via AI Ethics considerations
- Non-Maleficence as applied to AI via AI Ethics considerations
- Responsibility as applied to AI via AI Ethics considerations
- Privacy as applied to AI via AI Ethics considerations
- Beneficence as applied to AI via AI Ethics considerations
- Freedom & Autonomy to AI via AI Ethics considerations
- Trust as applied to AI via AI Ethics considerations
- Sustainability as applied to AI via AI Ethics considerations
- Dignity as applied to AI via AI Ethics considerations
- Solidarity as applied to AI via AI Ethics considerations

A recent form of terminology is that we are endeavoring to produce *Ethical AI*.

As will be seen in the chapters herein, I will at times interchangeably refer to AI Ethics and Ethical AI as one and the same. I will also explain why some quibble that AI Ethics and Ethical AI are not identically equivalent, though they both share the same lineage.

A handy way to readily grasp the application of ethics to AI is to consider these two overarching avenues:

1. The ethical behavior of the humans devising and using AI
2. The computational embedding of ethical behavior into the AI itself

In the first instance, the notion is to try and get the humans that are developing and fielding AI to become aware of and make use of ethical practices in how they shape, release, and perform the upkeep of AI systems. You might for example train the stakeholders on the AI Ethics precepts. There might be software development tools and methodologies that can provide AI Ethics guidance. Various quality control checks and auditing can be done under the rubric of AI Ethics attainment. And so on.

In the second instance listed, the idea is to embed into the AI a semblance of ethical acting computer components. Whereas the first focus is about the process of devising the AI, this second focus is about trying to embody ethically capable computational functionality into the AI. This is a much less explored arena and rife for great expansion and maturation. Some even argue that it is not especially doable, though as will be discussed in the chapters you can counterargue that it is already being done, to some extent.

Revealing AI Ethics Via AI Self-Driving Cars

This brief introduction has provided an AI Ethics foundation that will aid in your reading of the chapters.

There is something else you need to know too. In my view, one of the most useful ways to showcase AI Ethics and Ethical AI consists of using real-world examples. There is a special and assuredly popular set of examples that are close to my heart. You see, in my capacity as an expert on AI including the ethical and legal ramifications, I am frequently asked to identify realistic examples that showcase AI Ethics dilemmas so that the somewhat theoretical nature of the topic can be more readily grasped.

One of the most evocative areas that vividly presents this ethical AI quandary is the advent of AI-based true self-driving cars. This will serve as a handy use case or exemplar for ample discussion on the topic.

The eloquence of discussing self-driving cars is that they are near enough to being viable that they reveal the realities of AI Ethics considerations. At the same time, we still have a long way to go before we'll see the fully autonomous self-driving cars that heretofore have mainly been portrayed in sci-fi exploits. The fact that there are tryouts underway of somewhat autonomous self-driving cars is a clear indicator that this is not a purely abstract matter.

Yes, you could sensibly assert that AI Ethics and the rubber meets the road is surely found within the advent of AI-based self-driving cars (pardon the slender pun).

Realize that there isn't a human driver involved in a true self-driving car. Keep in mind that true self-driving cars are driven via an AI driving system. There isn't a need for a human driver at the wheel, nor is there a provision for a human to drive the vehicle.

I'd like to further clarify what is meant when I refer to true self-driving cars.

As a clarification, true self-driving cars are ones that the AI drives the car entirely on its own and there isn't any human assistance during the driving task.

These driverless vehicles are considered Level 4 and Level 5, while a car that requires a human driver to co-share the driving effort is usually considered at Level 2 or Level 3. The cars that co-share the driving task are described as being semi-autonomous, and typically contain a variety of automated add-ons that are referred to as ADAS (Advanced Driver-Assistance Systems).

There is not yet a true self-driving car at Level 5, which we don't yet even know if this will be possible to achieve, and nor how long it will take to get there.

Meanwhile, the Level 4 efforts are gradually trying to get some traction by undergoing very constrained and selective public roadway trials, though there is controversy over whether this testing should be allowed per se (we are all life-or-death guinea pigs in an experiment taking place on our highways and byways, some contend).

Semi-autonomous cars require a human driver. For semi-autonomous cars, it is important that the public needs to be forewarned about a disturbing aspect that's been arising lately, namely that despite those human drivers that keep posting videos of themselves falling asleep at the wheel of a Level 2 or Level 3 car, we all need to avoid being misled into believing that the human driver can take away their attention from the driving task while driving a semi-autonomous car. You are the responsible party for the driving actions of the vehicle, regardless of how much automation might be tossed into a Level 2 or Level 3.

For Level 4 and Level 5 true self-driving vehicles, there won't be a human driver involved in the driving task. All occupants will be passengers. The AI is doing the driving.

One aspect to immediately discuss entails the fact that the AI involved in today's AI driving systems is not sentient. In other words, the AI is altogether a collective of computer-based programming and algorithms, and most assuredly not able to reason in the same manner that humans can.

Why is this added emphasis about the AI not being sentient?

Because I want to underscore that when discussing the role of the AI driving system, I am not ascribing human qualities to the AI. Please be aware that there is an ongoing and dangerous tendency these days to anthropomorphize AI. In essence, people are assigning human-like sentience to today's AI, despite the undeniable and inarguable fact that no such AI exists as yet.

With that clarification, you can envision that the AI driving system won't natively somehow "know" about the facets of driving. Driving and all that it entails will need to be programmed as part of the hardware and software of the self-driving car.

It is important to realize that not all AI self-driving cars are the same. Each automaker and self-driving tech firm is taking its approach to devising self-driving cars. As such, it is difficult to make sweeping statements about what AI driving systems will do or not do. Furthermore, whenever stating that an AI driving system doesn't do some particular thing, this can, later on, be overtaken by developers that in fact program the computer to do that very thing. Step by step, AI driving systems are being gradually improved and extended. An existing limitation today might no longer exist in a future iteration or version of the system.

Nearly all of the included chapters provide an indication of how the covered AI Ethics topic applies to a real-world setting, doing so via discussing AI-based self-driving cars.

The usual scenario depicted goes somewhat like this.

An AI-based self-driving car is underway on your neighborhood streets and seems to be driving safely.

At first, you had devoted special attention to each time that you managed to catch a glimpse of the self-driving car. The autonomous vehicle stood out with its rack of electronic sensors that included video cameras, radar units, LIDAR devices, and the like. After many weeks of the self-driving car cruising around your community, you now barely notice it. As far as you are concerned, it is merely another car on the already busy public roadways.

Lest you think it is impossible or implausible to become familiar with seeing self-driving cars, the locales that are within the scope of self-driving car tryouts have gradually gotten used to seeing the spruced-up vehicles. Many of the locals eventually shifted from mouth-gaping rapt gawking to now emitting an expansive yawn of boredom to witness those meandering self-driving cars.

Probably the main reason right now that they might notice the autonomous vehicles is because of the irritation and exasperation factor. The AI driving systems make sure the cars are obeying all speed limits and rules of the road. For hectic human drivers in their traditional human-driven cars, you get irked at times when stuck behind the strictly law-abiding AI-based self-driving cars.

I then use that base scenario to insert AI Ethics related considerations into the setting. This allows a handy means of discussing the perhaps abstract AI Ethics topic in a manner that can be tangibly understood.

About The Chapters And Your Reading Choices

The chapters are each standalone discussion and you do not need to read them in any particular order. I have sequenced them in a manner that I hope will be useful for the best reading and digesting of the material. That being said, you are welcome to jump around and read the chapters in any personally desired sequence.

These chapters are based on my popular columns and were selected based on their timeliness and rated as most viewed or most informative.

I hope that after you've read the chapters, you will be inspired to learn more about AI Ethics. As well, you might be motivated to participate actively in the AI Ethics realm, perhaps doing research, performing consulting, aiding societal awareness on these topics, or otherwise deciding to get directly involved in this exciting field.

As a quick indication of what the chapters contain, here are the chapters in their provided order:

Introductory Conclusion

The rapidity of AI being fostered upon us that is replete with ethically questionable behaviors is clearly a sign that we need more parties that are keenly interested in AI Ethics and Ethical AI. Raise awareness about AI Ethics. Get knee-deep into promulgating Ethical AI. I sincerely urge you to pursue this expanding realm and wish you the best in all of your endeavors.

CHAPTER 2
AI ETHICS AND AI VALUES ALIGNMENT

Let's discuss the ever-expanding *AI alignment problem.*

Before I jump into that rather hefty and hearty topic, I'd like to mention that the other day I took my car to the mechanic for some routine maintenance. This might seem like a non sequitur or an off-base anecdote.

Well, turns out that my car was reportedly out of alignment. Alignment is oftentimes a quite crucial characteristic.

In the matter of my car, the tires had an unusual wearing that served as a tip that something was awry. The steering wheel was also slightly off-center, which I sheepishly admit that I had not prior noticed (my excuse is that the steering wheel likely only gradually shifted off-center over a period of many weeks, making it insidiously nonobvious to me as the day-to-day driver). Worse too was the tendency of the car to pull to one side. I had indeed felt that during my recent long-distance driving trips and thus prompted me to generally take my car in for some already slightly overdue maintenance.

All of those ailments regarding my car were associated with a bad alignment. We might rephrase that and say it was a matter of misalignment. My cherished car had inched its way into misalignment, and I had not been close enough paying attention during the time that the alignment skewing occurred. Shame on me. Yes, I soberly shoulder that responsibility.

If I might boldly make a suggestion, it would seemingly be the case that many people don't notice when misalignment takes place.

Sure, if the misalignment is sudden and jarring, you would have to be completely out-of-touch to not realize that something seriously has gone wrong. The trouble with the gradual shifting toward being out of alignment is that you can be unaware of what's happening. This can be likened to the famous tale of the frog in boiling water that at first has no inclination to try and jump out of the pot, for which the heat intensity only slowly mounts, and regrettably the frog doesn't realize until the bitter end that things are demonstratively amiss.

Now that I've covered the topic of alignment conundrums concerning frogs and also cars, we are ready to tackle the AI alignment problem.

In brief, the most common way to express the AI alignment problem entails stating that there is an important need to ensure that AI systems are properly aligned with human values. Any AI that is crafted and released into the world should presumably comport with human values. If we can somehow make that stridently happen, the world will be a better place as a result of promulgating AI.

A basis for the rising interest in the AI alignment problem is due to the recent widespread awareness that there is both *AI For Good* and *AI For Bad*. When the latest era of AI advances began to emerge, there was a lot of excitement about *AI For Good*, namely that AI was being used to cope with various global issues and proffering a means to mitigate or overcome those pressing difficulties. Unfortunately, on the heels of this goodness came the realization that AI can arise in bad or dour ways too.

I've previously discussed the sordid issues underlying AI for facial recognition that can at times exhibit racial biases and other inequities. When it comes to AI that does Natural Language Processing (NLP), I've noted the concerns about NLP that embodies gender biases and has other unseemly and possibly illegal propensities. The list is nearly endless of such ethical and sometimes outright legally distressing qualms.

You might be tempted to ostensibly kneejerk assume that the *AI For Bad* is solely occurring as a result of evildoers. There must be wrongdoers with evil plots that are seeking to shape AI toward villainous paths. Though this is certainly something that can and does happen, by and large, most of the everyday *AI For Bad* is more so as a result of inadvertent misalignment.

Let's unpack that assertion.

An AI developer collects together a slew of data to try and devise an AI system for making hiring decisions. The AI will be used as modern-day algorithmic decision-making (ADM) to decide whether someone ought to be hired or not. The underlying algorithm will leverage the latest in Machine Learning (ML) or Deep Learning (DL). ML/DL is a form of computational pattern matching that examines data while being "trained" and mathematically tries to find notable patterns in the data. Then, later on, you feed new data into the ML/DL and it seeks to match the new data to the previously discovered overall patterns.

Suppose a company gathers together all the data about their hiring decisions for the last ten years. The AI developer dutifully feeds that data into an ML/DL. The ML/DL computationally churns through the data and mathematically finds a myriad of patterns. Voila, we now have an AI system that can perform hiring decisions, doing so by essentially comparing a proposed new hire to the past record of hiring that was made at the firm.

The business-savvy basis for using AI in this capacity is that doing so will reduce the labor required by the company when having to make hiring decisions. All you do is feed the candidate particulars into the AI and out pops a decision. No need to have teams of internal employees "waste" time scrutinizing candidates. Furthermore, the beauty of the AI would seemingly be that the computer will be consistent and avoid the emotional tendencies of internal employees that might be otherwise part of the hiring selection process.

Gleefully, the company touts that they have entirely removed any bias from the hiring process. A machine is taking care of things. The AI is faster, easier to use, less costly, and apparently bereft of human bias in making hiring choices.

Pop the champagne bottles!

The thing is, the AI that they've devised is not at all bereft of biases.

Ponder for a quiet moment the history of hiring choices that had been made over the ten years of collected data. If those choices were based on biases at the time, the data reflects those same biases. Assuming that the ML/DL is trying to mimic the data, as based on patterns found, the AI is simply going to continue those biases on a go-forward basis. In addition, the biases will be sneakily hidden from view by the alluring aura that the AI is supposedly not biased at all.

You could say that the biases are now going to be cloaked and entrenched. Whereas maybe there was a chance that today's employees making hiring decisions might have been more aware to avert their biases, the AI has no such inclination. The AI is merely mechanically puttering along and computationally calculating hiring choices based on the historical patterns discovered.

Please know that today's AI is not sentient in the sense that it cannot reason as humans do. The AI won't say to itself, hey, maybe I am making biased decisions. There isn't any AI with any semblance of sentience. We don't know if that is someday possible. We don't when it might occur if it does in fact ever happen.

You can add into the lack of capabilities any kind of common sense. There are various efforts underway to try and construct AI that has common-sense reasoning but those notable and shall we say herculean endeavors have not yet resulted in any viable common-sense capacities for AI systems. We are still just nibbling away at that aspiration.

Was the AI-based hiring system purposely derived to make biased hiring decisions?

In this scenario, the answer is no. The AI developers fell into the trap of blindly using prior data and assumed that this was a suitable approach. The managers and leaders of the firm likewise fell into that trap. All along the way, an inadvertent misalignment between desired human values and what the AI was going to do was taking place. But nobody realized this was happening.

One might suggest they were like me as I was driving my car and did not realize that the alignment was mile by mile getting more out of alignment.

Are we to then let the company off the hook and go scot-free that they "inadvertently" went down the wrongful path? I doubt that we would be quite so easy on them. You could argue that they should have known better. You could also argue that even if they didn't realize what was happening at first, they ought to have wised up once the AI was put into active use.

This brings us back to my car analogy or metaphor. I kept driving my car and didn't figure out that things were amiss. Only until the damage was partially exhibited, and luckily nothing so severe that led to my getting into any car crashes, did I realize that the world was somehow akilter. How far though might this have gone? I could have kept blissfully driving and only when the tires gave out or some other mechanism gave way would I have realized that an alignment crisis was now existent (let's hope I wouldn't have gotten into dire straits).

The same arises with AI that has inherent biases, which could produce a lot of societal harm, and maybe nobody realizes it until the horse is utterly out of the barn.

I trust that this showcases the importance of the AI alignment problem. We need to find ways to get AI systems aligned with human values. The first step involves making everyone aware that the AI alignment problem even exists. You can't get much traction about solving a particular problem if few realize a problem awaits them or is perhaps already facing them.

Companies that are devising AI had better get on board with the AI alignment problem. So too should companies that merely license or buy AI systems and place those into use, since they won't likely be able to hide behind a claim that they thought the AI was perfectly fine. The builders of the AI are going to have their feet held to the ethical and legal fire, as will those that promulgate the AI and don't do sufficient due diligence to make sure they aren't further propagating *AI For Bad.*

There are some thorny and vexing complications about the AI alignment problem.

Here's one that might get your head spinning. When I've stated that AI needs to be aligned with human values, there was an implicit declaration that we all magically know and agree to the meaning and substance of what human values connotes.

Do we?

Hardly.

You might try to proclaim that human values encompass kindness, compassion toward fellow humans, and similarly idyllic facets. If that's the case, how do you explain wars, killings, and other untoward and at times outrageous acts of mankind? Aren't those also representative of human values?

Human values are a moral morass. You could say that our morals change over time. They can differ by culture and by segments of society. And so on. All in all, trying to put your finger on some absolute set of never-changing ironclad human values is fraught with great challenges and perhaps not realistically doable.

A huge problem then with the AI alignment problem is that we are somewhat up in the air as to what we want AI to be aligned to. It is easy to wave your hands and emphasize that AI has to be aligned to human values. Case closed some assert.

On the other hand, what human values are we talking about? Who has defined those human values? Are they human values that others agree with or disagree with as being appropriate human values?

Round and round we go.

There are some ethicists and philosophers that strive toward finding and articulating a single "true" set of moral principles and codes that would be the grand corpus for all time. Can this really be ascertained?

Meanwhile, AI technologists and AI researchers are seeking to resolve this human values *subproblem* of the larger AI alignment problem by tossing as much tech at it as they can muster. Some worry that this is the classic use of a hammer on securing both nails and screws, merely because a hammer is a tool you have available and that you know by heart (rather than seeking say a screwdriver for the turning of the screws).

A recent series of breathless headlines stoked attention to the AI alignment problem by variously suggesting that it is either solved or that a solution is on its way. The actual story is that a well-known AI research and development entity came up with a particular approach to test the waters on how to shape AI toward a purported semblance of human values. In brief, while the AI was being "trained" it was also sent through a series of human-led double-checks to try and catch any untoward embedded aspects, trying to sway the AI away from toxic embodiments.

We certainly can applaud such attempts. Meanwhile, there are corresponding issues that arise in such a setup. Might the human-led double-checkers steer the AI toward worsening the toxicity rather than eviscerating it? How completely can the human reviewers do their work such that there aren't still remnants of toxicity within the AI, awaiting future appearances? Also, if the AI is able to adjust itself over time, will the toxicity get revived or grafted anew when the human double-checkers are no longer in the picture?

Again, we must pursue these experimental approaches, though do so with open eyes. The matter of human values is still quite open-ended even if you employ humans to provide guidance to an AI system being developed. What human values do those humans hold? How did they come to their set of values? Can they articulate those values? Do their actions match their words in terms of espoused human values?

Another variant of crafting AI to cope with the AI alignment problem consists of including in the guts of the AI system a kind of human values calculator. This element is intended to continually monitor the rest of the AI system and emit an alert or put a stop to any misaligned decisions or actions of the AI system. Thus, the belief is that in real-time the AI-based human values calculator will save the day and prevent an AI system from going amiss. The beauty is that even if the AI otherwise has gotten misaligned to human values, the internal component will close the barn door before the horse is released.

Once more, kudos to those devising this kind of AI-infused feature. We still though are left with the unanswered question of what constitutes human values. The internal calculator has to presumably have some basis for determining when a human value is or is not being abided by. Without an indication of what that calculation contains, we are somewhat just shuffling the chairs on the deck of the Titanic and avoiding the overarching conundrum about articulating and definitively stipulating human values.

Many AI technologists are a bit taken aback to discover that ethics and the law are intertwined in the crafting of AI systems. Just getting on with the building of AI is the usual mantra for AI techies. The AI alignment problem is a succinctly stated problem that though quick to announce is like Pandora's box that stretches far beyond the confines of doing coding and dealing with bits and bytes.

I concur with the words of John Tasioulas, Director of the Institute for Ethics in AI at the University of Oxford and Professor of Ethics and Legal Philosophy, wherein he states: "Ethics is inescapable because it concerns the ultimate values in which our choices are anchored, whether we realize it or not. These are values that define what it is to have a good life, and what we owe to others, including non-human animals and nature. Therefore, all forms of 'regulation' that might be proposed for AI, whether one's self-regulation in deciding whether to use a social robot to keep one's aged mother company or the content of the social and legal norms that should govern the use of such robots, ultimately implicate choices that reflect ethical judgments about salient values and their prioritization" (as stated in "The Roles of the Arts and Humanities in Thinking About Artificial Intelligence (AI)" posted at the Ada Lovelace Institute blog, June 14, 2021).

Aligning Awareness With The AI Alignment Problem

As a quick recap, we've dug into the AI Alignment Problem and noted that this is a vital issue underlying the societal adoption of AI such that the AI aligns with human values.

There are a lot of open-ended considerations that this matter brings forth. For ease of contemplation, you can place the conundrum into three respective buckets, namely that we are dealing with AI, we are dealing with alignment, and we are dealing with human values.

Mull this over:

- **AI:** Though there is a general sense of what is meant when referring to "AI" it is something that needs a tighter definition else we might construe nearly *any* kind of computing as being within the rubric of AI. In one viewpoint, some would argue that's perfectly fine, wherein any and all computing ought to be aligned with human values. Others somewhat counterargue that AI is a special case worthy of devoted attention beyond just any kind of computing.

- **Alignment:** The effort to align these two aspects, consisting of AI and consisting of human values, can presumably only be viably done if we have a means of measuring their aligning attributes. In other words, we need to be able to ascertain when they are misaligned, akin to when my car alignment was askew. There were symptoms such as worn tires and an off-center steering wheel, though those could be explained by other maladies of my car. To ascertain the AI and human values misalignment, there will need to be explicit and measurable means to do so, else we will be an endless and hollow debate over claims and counterclaims that the alignment is on-target or instead off-base.

- **Human Values:** As earlier noted, human values is a large topic with all kinds of twists and turns afoot. The mushiness of simply proclaiming that human values must be met will not get us very far. Who decides what those human values are? Are the human values well-articulated or ill-defined? And so on.

What are we to do about this?

Perhaps one of the most crucial steps is that we earnestly need to increase overall awareness about the AI Alignment Problem. You see, if only insiders perchance know about it, the odds are that AI is going to roll along and the badness is going to eventually permeate all manner of goods and services, due to the ubiquitous nature of embedding AI into modern-day goods and services.

In my experience, these are the typical circumstances on the awareness side of things:

1. **Utterly Unaware:** Many haven't heard about the AI Alignment Problem. You might be surprised to know that this often includes AI developers and firms that are building AI systems. I realize you would assume they are especially on top of the matter, but sadly this is somewhat rarely the case.

2. **Aware But Shrug It Off:** This category includes those that know what the AI Alignment Problem is, but they figure it will all sort itself out, eventually. Many techies or tech companies tend to take the stance of fail fast, fail often. In that frame of mind, the misalignment with human values is suitable for now. Just faking it until you make it, as they say.

3. **Aware And Working On It:** These brave souls are genuinely concerned about the AI Alignment Problem and believe we need to give the matter significant attention. Immediately. For each day that passes without appropriate attention, the wheels of progress are relentlessly enlarging the misalignment. The cost to bring the matter back into alignment will be enormous and it is better to deal with the hot potato now rather than postpone until after the fact.

Let's next to see how even today the AI Alignment Problem is already amongst us.

In my capacity as an expert on AI including the ethical and legal ramifications, I am frequently asked to identify realistic examples that showcase the alignment dilemma so that the somewhat theoretical nature of the topic can be more readily grasped. One of the most evocative areas that vividly presents this ethical AI quandary is the advent of AI-based true self-driving cars. This will serve as a handy use case or exemplar for ample discussion on the topic.

Here's then a noteworthy question that is worth contemplating: *Will the advent of AI-based true self-driving cars be immersed in the AI Alignment Problem, and if so, what can we do about it?*

Allow me a moment to unpack the question.

First, note that there isn't a human driver involved in a true self-driving car. Keep in mind that true self-driving cars are driven via an AI driving system. There isn't a need for a human driver at the wheel, nor is there a provision for a human to drive the vehicle.

The Blame Game

For Level 4 and Level 5 true self-driving vehicles, there won't be a human driver involved in the driving task. All occupants will be passengers. The AI is doing the driving.

Human drivers rely upon human values while they are at the steering wheel and driving along in their multi-ton traditionally human-driven cars.

How so?

A news report about a car crash provides illumination on the use of human values by human drivers. Reportedly, a driver was coming up to a busy intersection and had a green light to proceed straight ahead. Another driver came barreling past a red light and entered the intersection when they should not have been doing so. The driver with the green light realized at the last moment that this other car was going to severely ram into his car.

According to this imperiled driver, he mindfully calculated that either he was going to get struck by the other car, or he could swerve to try and avoid the interloper. The problem with swerving was that there were nearby pedestrians that would be endangered.

Which choice would you make?

You can prepare yourself to get hit and hope that the damage won't maim or kill you. On the other hand, you can veer radically away, but grievously endanger and possibly harm or kill nearby pedestrians. This is a hard problem, encompassing moral judgment, and is fully steeped in ethical (and legal) implications.

Generally, I liken these kinds of driving situations to the famous (or some say infamous) Trolley Problem. The Trolley Problem is a thought experiment entailing no-win kinds of life-or-death circumstances. There are pundits in the AI self-driving car realm that claim the Trolley Problem has no relevance to the advent of autonomous vehicles. To them, the Trolley Problem is purely a theoretical contrivance of little or no value.

As I've at length explained, the Trolley Problem is front-and-center a crucial matter for the advent of AI self-driving cars.

I trust that you see how human values come to play in this scenario. If your values are such that the pedestrians are shall we say somewhat inconsequential in the grand scheme of things, you would clearly and without hesitation opt to veer into the pack. Instead, if you had more heightened value for those other people, you would perhaps ascertain that you should take your chances of getting rammed by the other car.

Okay, those are undeniably human values underscoring the pressing situation.

Replace the human driver with an AI driving system embedded into a self-driving car.

Imagine then that an AI self-driving car is entering into an intersection and the sensors of the autonomous vehicle suddenly detect a human-driven car perilously coming directly through a red light and aiming at the driverless car. Assume that the self-driving car has some passengers inside the vehicle.

What do you want the AI to do?

Should the AI driving system opt to proceed ahead and get plowed into (likely harming or maybe killing the passengers inside the vehicle), or do you want the AI driving system to take a chance and veer away, though the veering action takes the autonomous vehicle perilously toward nearby pedestrians and might harm or kill them.

Many of the AI makers of self-driving cars are taking a head-in-the-sand approach to these ethical AI fiery predicaments.

By and large, the AI as presently programmed would simply plow ahead and get violently rammed by the other car. The AI wasn't programmed to look for any other evasive maneuvers. Or, even if evasive maneuvers were in the programming, by default the AI would reject aiming toward the pedestrians and instead take the direct hit from the other car.

Envision that you were a passenger in that self-driving car or that you were the pedestrians on the sidewalk. As a passenger or as a pedestrian, ought you be able to expect that the AI would at least consider potential alternatives, or should it not do so? And, if it did consider alternatives, wouldn't you also want to know what computational imprint of "human values" are being used in the AI computations to reach such a life-or-death decision?

I've predicted repeatedly that this see-no-evil hear-no-evil stance of the AI self-driving car makers will eventually come around and bite them. You can expect lawsuits involving such car crashes that will seek to find out what the AI was programmed to do. Was the company or AI developers or fleet operator that developed and fielded the AI negligent or liable for what the AI did or didn't do?

You can also anticipate an ethical AI-awareness public-wide firestorm will brew once these kinds of cases occur.

That's not the only example of human values amongst the rise of AI self-driving cars. I've articulated approximately 100 or so scenarios in my columns to date and have a lot more to steadily describe.

For those of you interested in a few more examples, consider these next several indications.

Should a self-driving car forewarn nearby human drivers if the AI driving system detects that those human-driven cars are heading toward each other and are likely to crash into each other?

You could argue that the AI should take any explicit action that it can to alert those human drivers, perhaps honking the horn of the self-driving car or flashing its headlights. Others say that AI should not take any action and merely let those jeopardized human drivers figure out the situation for themselves.

This all relies on a semblance of human values.

Next, should a self-driving car ever purposely ram into humans, or should the AI be programmed to always avoid striking humans no matter what the situation entails?

I'm sure your first gut reaction is that there is never a bona fide reason for an AI self-driving car to strike a human. No further debate is required. But in my discussion on the topic, I bring up a real-world circumstance of a sniper on a bridge that was wantonly shooting and killing people, for which a man in a nearby car was able to ram into the sniper and stop the killing spree. In that scenario, would you be willing to have the AI strike a human? Furthermore, would you not simply be willing to have this action taken by the AI, but perhaps you would earnestly *insist* that the AI ought to take that kind of action to save other human lives.

Human values once again come to the fore.

There are many more of these AI self-driving car predicaments that I've analyzed over the years and exhorted that we must be doing more to align the AI of self-driving cars with our human values.

Conclusion

Is the AI Alignment Problem a real thing?

Yes.

Is it beyond being merely a theoretical construct and therefore worthy of practical attention?

Yes.

Do we need more mindful consideration about how to solve the AI Alignment Problem or at least do more to aid in dealing with it?

Abundantly, yes.

On a final note, for now, I have some small satisfaction that I was able to get my car realigned and overcome its unwelcome misalignment. To my chagrin and the detriment of my wallet, my belated realization of the misalignment cost me extra, including that I had to purchase two new tires. This just goes to show, figuring out alignment is one of those aspects that requires a sooner rather than later mindset.

The AI Alignment Problem vociferously comes to mind in that same vein.

CHAPTER 3
AI ETHICS
AND
THE AI CONTROL PROBLEM

Can we all collectively band together and somehow tame a wild beast?

The wild beast I'm referring to is Artificial Intelligence (AI).

Now, let's be abundantly clear that you are on thin ice if you claim that today's AI is a beast. I say this because we usually reserve the word "beast" for a living breathing creature. Please know that the AI we have in our world today is not sentient. Not even close. Furthermore, we don't know if sentient AI is possible. No one can say whether sentient AI will be achieved, such as via the oft worried about act of singularity, and any predictions of when it will occur are tenuous at best.

Since I've clarified that AI perhaps is presumably mischaracterized as a beast, why have I gone ahead and asked the pivotal question about taming it in that stated terminology?

For several cogent reasons.

First, we might someday have sentient AI and in that case, I guess the beast title might be suitable, depending upon what you define as sentient AI.

Some suggest that a sentient AI would be a machine that can perform as humans can, but it is nonetheless a non-human. Is that kind of AI an animal? Well, maybe yes, or maybe no. It is a type of being that has the intelligence of humans, appears to be living, and yet is not a human, so the closest that we have to assign is animal labeling. We can then call it a beast if we wish to do so.

On the other hand, if it is entirely a machine, the animal moniker does not seem apt and ergo the beast title seems inappropriate. We might need to give AI a new category of its own and correspondingly ascertain whether a beastly naming is suitable.

This was the hardest consideration about the beast assignment, so let's move on.

Secondly, some believe we will not only arrive at sentient AI, but they also strenuously assert that the AI might go off the charts and give rise to superintelligence. The idea is that the sentient AI will be more than the equivalent of human capacities. AI is seen as potentially eclipsing human intelligence and soaring into a superintelligence sphere. Once again, this is highly speculative. We don't know that AI could get into that stratospheric realm. There is also the question of how super-intelligent can superintelligence be? Is there a cutoff at which superintelligence tops out? Also, what will it take to prove to us that AI is super intelligent versus just everyday normal humanly intelligent?

Third, you can somewhat get away with calling today's non-sentient AI a beast, if you are comfortable ascribing an anthropomorphic aura to contemporary AI. As you'll see in a moment, I am not a fan of the anthropomorphic allusions used when describing AI. Headlines that do so are easily misunderstood and lead society toward believing we do already have in our pretty little hands a sentient AI.

That's not good.

I suppose another basis for saying that even non-sentient AI is a bit of a beast entails a different connotation or meaning associated with beasts per se. Rather than necessarily assuming that all beasts must be living creatures, we do admittedly at times refer to a monstrous-looking truck or car as a big beast. The same can be applied to massive-sized yachts, enormous airplanes, and gigantic rocket ships. In that sense, we already appear willing to contend that a thing can be a beast.

Let's briefly take a quick side tangent about the beast title being assigned to AI.

Some are worried that we might eventually have sentient AI or super-intelligent AI that is all-powerful. There is a famous or shall we say infamous thought experiment known as Roko's basilisk that postulates an all-powerful AI might come after everyone that before the AI emerging was downbeat or insulting to AI. My point is that for those that have said AI is a beast, would this, later on, provoke a global-ruling AI to be copiously irked and summarily decide that the beast naming humans will be the first to go? In which case, allow me to say right now that I am not saying AI is a beast in any pejorative sense. I sincerely hope that gets me off the hook.

Back to the beastly title. We tend to invoke dastardly oriented imagery when usually calling someone or something a beast. It doesn't have to be used in that manner but often is. A lion that mauls a cute-looking antelope is nearly immediately called out as a beast. Beasts are untamed. They act in scary and impulsive ways. Most of all, we ordinarily don't like how beasts sometimes treat humans.

Humankind has obviously sought to tame many beasts. The act of taming a beast means that we are seeking to reduce the natural instincts of attacking or harming humans (and possibly other animals too). Generally, a tamed beast is able to tolerate the presence of humans. Such a beast will not necessarily lunge at humans, though this can still happen if provoked or otherwise the taming strictness is overcome. In case you are wondering whether taming is the same as domestication, the encyclopedia answer is that those are related but differing concepts. Domestication has generally to do with the aspect of breeding a lineage to have an inherited predisposition friendlier toward humankind.

Okay, having dragged you through the beast naming conundrum, we can tie this to an ongoing concern and looming question that is being vociferously asked by AI ethics and considered part of the trend toward Ethical AI.

The million-dollar question is this: *Will we be able to control AI?*

This is variously known as the AI control problem.

Some prefer to phrase this altogether crucial mega-topic as the AI containment problem. For those that are heavily versed in AI, they tend to drop the AI part of the techie discourse and shorten the vexing matter to simply the control problem or the containment problem. Other wordings are also used from time to time.

The rub is that AI might end up doing things that we don't like. For example, wiping out all of humanity. The idea here is that we craft AI or it springs forth and decides humans aren't all that we think they are. You've seen plenty of sci-fi movies with this sordid plot. AI at first is compatible with humans. Soon, AI gets upset with humans. This could be because we hold the key to AI functioning and are imperiling AI by threatening to unplug it. Or the AI might simply decide that humans aren't worth the trouble and AI can merely get rid of us, one way or another. Lots of reasons can be hypothesized.

If we are going to bring forth AI, the logical thinking is that we ought to also make sure we can control it. As rational beings, we should certainly seek to avoid unleashing a beast that produces our own destruction. You've probably heard or seen the recent clamors that AI is an existential risk. Some argue that existential is too far as an endpoint and we should instead describe AI as a catastrophic risk.

Whether AI is an existential risk or a "mere" catastrophic risk, none of those calibers of risk seem especially heartwarming. Intelligent humans should be risk reducers. AI that will elevate risk needs to be kept in its place at some more palatable level of risk.

The easy answer is to magically ensure that AI cannot ever go beyond the commands provided by humans. Tame AI. Make sure that AI won't exceed what humankind wants it to do. Control AI. Thus, the AI control problem is the silver bullet to protect us from an existential or catastrophic death producer.

Sorry, the world is not that nice and clean.

First, suppose we do enforce all AI to respond strictly to human commands. An evildoer human tells the AI to annihilate all of humanity. Wham, we are obliterated. The fact that we controlled the AI by relegating the AI's actions solely to human commands might not be the saving grace that it seems at an initial glance.

Second, we stick with the idea that AI must obey human commands, but we have wised up and managed to keep at bay any humans that might utter unsavory commands to the AI (you might rightfully question how this would occur, though go with the flow for the moment). Recall that we are imagining that the AI is likely sentient in this scenario, possessing regular human-like intelligence or possibly superintelligence. The AI is not like a trained seal. Well, maybe it is in that no matter how much training you do to a seal, there is still a chance that the seal will act up. The gist is that the AI might decide on its own accord to no longer be "enslaved" by human commands. The jig is up and the AI could turn on us, wholescale.

And so on it goes.

I'm sure that some of you are immediately resorting to Asimov's laws of robotics. You might recall that in 1950 a now-classic discussion about "Three Laws of Robotics" was published by Asimov and has ever since been a linchpin in thinking about robotics and also AI. A cornerstone to the proposed "laws" or rules about AI and robots was that they should be programmed to not harm humans. This extends to the further rule that the programming should include not allowing harm to come to humans. All told, the hope was that if we carefully programmed AI and robots to these handy-dandy rules, we might survive amidst the AI and robotic creations.

Regrettably, those rules are not going to guarantee our safety.

As a quick explanation for why not, consider these salient points.

Programming AI to abide by such rules is going to be extremely hard to do, and we could readily have instances of AI that don't contain those rules. That outside scope AI could then harm us, plus they might reprogram the other presumed harmless AI too. Join the gang, the rough and tough AI says to the polite and docile AI.

Another escape hatch from the programmed rules, assuming that we have infallibly programmed them into AI, would consist of the AI being able to alter itself. This is a real thorny dilemma. Here's why. You might insist that we never allow AI to change itself. In that manner, the rules about harming humans remain pristine and untouched.

The problem though is that if AI is going to exhibit intelligence, you have to ask yourself whether an intelligent being can exist if it is unable to alter itself. Learning sure seems to be a key component of existence. An AI that is not allowed to learn would seem to be definitionally unlikely as much encampment of intelligence (you are welcome to debate that, but it seems reasonably sensible).

You might say that you'll agree with the need for the AI to learn and adjust itself, which does have a foreboding to it. Meanwhile, you add the caveat that we put a limit on what the adjustments or learning can consist of. When the AI veers toward adjusting itself in a manner that suggests it is determining that humans can be harmed, we have dampeners built into the AI that stop that kind of adjustment.

Okay, so we believe then that we've solved the control problem by putting guardrails on what the AI is able to learn. I ask you this, do humans always openly accept guardrails on their behavior? Not that I've seen. If we are going to assume that this AI is intelligent, we would equally expect that it will likely try to overcome the instituted guardrails.

I trust that you can see how this cat and mouse gambit could endlessly take place. We put in some controls, the AI overcomes or transcends them. We steadfastly put controls on the controls. The AI overcomes the controls on the controls. Keep going, ad infinitum. The old saying is that it is going to be turtles all the way down.

Let's take a peaceful popcorn break and do a quick recap.

AI can consist of these possible states:

1. Non-sentient plain-old AI
2. Sentient AI of human quality (we don't have this as yet)
3. Sentient AI that is super-intelligent (a stretch beyond #2)

We know and are daily handwringing about a dire issue about AI, the venerated AI control problem.

AI ethics is keeping us all on our toes that we need to find ways to solve the AI control problem. Without some form of suitable controls on AI, we might end up concocting and fielding our own doomsday machine. The AI will blow up in our faces by somehow harming, enslaving, or outright killing us. Not good.

A kind of gloomy picture.

A kneejerk reaction is that we should stop all AI efforts. Put AI back into the can. If Pandora's box has been opened, shut it now before things get worse. Some though would vehemently retort that the horse is already out of the barn. You are too late to the game to shove the released genie into that confined bottle. AI is already underway and we'll inevitably make added progress until we reach the point of that destructive AI arising.

Here's an additional counterpoint to excising AI from the planet. If we could miraculously conjure a way to do so, all of the benefits of AI would disappear too. A smarmy wisecracker might say that they can live without Alexa or Siri, but the use of AI is much more widespread and day by day becoming an essential underpinning to all of our automation.

I don't think turning back the clock is much of a viable option.

We are stuck with AI and it is going to be expansively progressed and utilized.

Some contend that we might be okay as long as we keep AI to the non-sentient plain-old AI that we have today. Let's assume we cannot reach sentient AI. Imagine that no matter how hard we try to craft sentient AI, we fail at doing so. As well, assume for sake of discussion that sentient AI doesn't arise by some mysterious spontaneous process.

Aren't we then safe that this lesser caliber AI, which is the imagined only possible kind of AI, can be controlled?

Not really.

Pretty much, the same control-related issues are likely to arise. I'm not suggesting that the AI "thinks" its way to wanting to destroy us. No, the ordinary non-sentient AI is merely placed into positions of power that get us mired in self-destruction. For example, we put non-sentient AI into weapons of mass destruction. These autonomous weapons are not able to think. At the same time, humans are not kept fully in the loop. As a result, the AI as a form of autonomous automation ends up inadvertently causing catastrophic results, either by a human command to do so, or by a bug or error, or by implanted evildoing, or by self-adjustments that lead matters down that ugly path, etc.

I would contend that the AI control problem exists for all three of those AI stipulated states, namely that we have AI control issues with non-sentient plain-old AI, and with sentient AI that is either merely human level or the outstretched AI that reaches the acclaimed superintelligence level.

Given that sobering pronouncement, we can assuredly debate the magnitude and difficulty associated with the control problem at each of the respective levels of AI. The customary viewpoint is that the AI control problem is less insurmountable at the non-sentient AI, tougher at the sentient human-equal AI level, and a true head-scratcher at the sentient super-intelligent AI stage of affairs.

The better the AI becomes, the worse the AI control problem becomes.

Maybe that is an inviolable law of nature.

A research study in the *Journal of Artificial Intelligence Research* (JAIR) examined the hypothesized super-intelligent AI and cleverly aimed to apply the Alan Turing halting problem to the question of AI control.

In brief, Turing wondered whether it was possible to precisely prove whether a given computer program will halt or whether it might continue running forever. His work and another similar analysis by Alonzo Church showcases that such a generalized procedure cannot be devised for all possible computer programs and is therefore classified as an undecidable type of problem (as clarification, this indicates that in a generalized way we cannot ascertain whether each and every conceivable program will halt or not, though there is still the possibility of some programs for which we can make such a determination).

What makes this a fascinating tool is that we can apply the same logic to trying to figure out the AI control problem to some extent.

Here's what the JAIR article proffered as a premise: "Let us assume we can articulate in a precise programming language a perfectly reliable set of control strategies that guarantee that no human comes to harm by a superintelligence. The containment problem is composed of two subproblems. The first, which we refer to as the harming problem, consists of a function Harm(R;D) that decides whether the execution of R(D) will harm humans. Since it must be assumed that solving the harming problem must not harm humans, it follows that a solution to this problem must simulate the execution of R(D) and predict its potentially harmful consequences in an isolated situation (i.e., without any effect on the external world)" (as indicated in "Superintelligence Cannot Be Contained: Lessons From Computability Theory" by co-authors Manuel Alfonseca, Manuel Cebrian, Antonio Anta, Lorenzo Coviello, Andres Abeliuk, and Iyad Rahwan).

Their analysis leads them to this somewhat overcast conclusion:

- The harming problem is undecidable
- The containment problem is incomputable

Sorry to say that there is no free lunch when it comes to AI.

To add fuel to the fire, there are mind-bending concerns that you might not have yet thought of. For example, pretend that we do marvelously devise a fully controlled version of AI. Ironclad contained. Clap your hands for the intellectual prowess of humankind. Here's the twist. The AI convinces us to somehow undercut the controls or containment partially. Perhaps the AI pledges to save us from other existential risks such as a colossal meteor that is hurling toward earth. We allow the AI just the tiniest of leeway. Wham, the churlish AI wipes us all out, not even waiting for the meteor to do so.

Do not turn your back on AI and be cautious in giving even an inch of latitude since it might very well take a mile or more.

Another example of wayward haywire AI is popularly known as the paperclip problem. We ask AI to make paperclips. Easy-peasy for AI to do. Unfortunately, in the innocent and directed act of making paperclips, the AI gobbles up all resources of the globe to make those darned paperclips. Sadly, the consumption of those resources undermines humanity, and we die off accordingly. But, heck, we have piles upon immense and never-ending piles of paperclips. This is reminiscent of humans giving commands to AI, which even when not necessarily for evil purposes has the chance of backfiring on us anyway.

All of this should not discourage you from still searching for solutions to the AI control problem. Nobody ought to be tossing in the towel on this fundamental quest.

I usually describe the AI control problem as generally consisting of these two classes of controls:

- External controls of AI
- Internal controls of AI

The notion is that we can attempt to use external controls regarding guiding or directing the AI to do good things and avert doing bad things. These are mechanisms and approaches that are outside of the AI. They are said to be external to the AI.

We can also attempt to devise and build internal controls within AI. An internal control might be wholly contained within the AI. Another variant would be considered as adjacent to the AI, residing in a type of borderland that is not exactly inside the AI and not fully outside the AI.

I'll be getting further into these facets shortly.

I'd like to identify some of the key sub-elements of these two major classes of AI controls:

- External controls of AI
    - Persuade the AI
    - Confine the AI
    - Assail the AI
- Internal controls of AI
    - Embedded within the AI
    - Adjacent to the AI

There are various such sketches of proposed AI controls.

One of the most discussed taxonomies was outlined by Nick Bostrom in his 2014 book about superintelligence. He posits two main classes, namely capability control and motivation selection. Within capability control, there are sub-elements such as boxing, incentives, stunting, trip-wiring, and others. Within motivation selection, there are direct specification, domesticity, indirect normativity, augmentation, and others.

The AI ethics field usually denotes these AI controls as a form of *ethics engineering*. We are trying to engineer our way into ensuring that AI performs ethically. Of course, we need to realize that society cannot rely solely on an engineered solution and we will need to work collectively to tame the beast (if I can refer to AI as a beast, though doing so with the kindliest of implication).

At this juncture of this discussion, I'd bet that you are desirous of some examples that could highlight how AI controls might work, along with how they might get defeated.

I'm glad you asked.

There is a special and assuredly popular set of examples that are close to my heart. You see, in my capacity as an expert on AI including the ethical and legal ramifications, I am frequently asked to identify realistic examples that showcase AI Ethics dilemmas so that the somewhat theoretical nature of the topic can be more readily grasped. One of the most evocative areas that vividly presents this ethical AI quandary is the advent of AI-based true self-driving cars. This will serve as a handy use case or exemplar for ample discussion on the topic.

Here's then a noteworthy question that is worth contemplating: *Does the advent of AI-based true self-driving cars illuminate anything about the AI control problem, and if so, what does this showcase?*

Allow me a moment to unpack the question.

First, note that there isn't a human driver involved in a true self-driving car. Keep in mind that true self-driving cars are driven via an AI driving system. There isn't a need for a human driver at the wheel, nor is there a provision for a human to drive the vehicle.

The AI Control Problem

For Level 4 and Level 5 true self-driving vehicles, there won't be a human driver involved in the driving task. All occupants will be passengers. The AI is doing the driving.

As a reminder, here are the potential AI controls that we will take a look at:

- External controls of AI
    - Persuade the AI
    - Confine the AI
    - Assail the AI
- Internal controls of AI
    - Embedded within the AI
    - Adjacent to the AI

Let's examine each one.

I am going to focus on examples of these AI controls that are realistic concerning today's AI capabilities (the non-sentient plain-old AI). I point this out as a notable indication because many discussions about AI controls are exceedingly abstract and generally allude to sentient AI rather than the conventional AI of today.

The wonderous beauty of discussing sentient AI is that since we don't have any as yet (if we ever will), you can handwave and make up whatever you like about what the vaunted sentient AI would be like. In a manner of speaking, it makes things extraordinarily easy for pontification purposes. You can wildly concoct whatever contrivances will fit your stipulated narrative. Just make up the rules as you go along.

If you'll permit me to take a short diversion, there is another pet peeve on the sentient AI topic that especially arises when contemplating the super-intelligent kind of AI. Oddly enough, sometimes in these abstract portrayals the sentient AI is amazing astute, while in the next breath it is as dumb as a brick. For example, if the paperclip saga is being undertaken by a super-intelligent AI, how can this flavor of AI be so dense as to not figure out that pursuing paperclips to the ends of the earth would also mean the end of the earth for humankind? The logic does not seem to compute. Either the AI is super-intelligent, or it is not. Yes, there is some argument to be made that perhaps the AI is super-intelligent only in very narrow ways, though that rarely gets brought up explicitly. And so on it goes.

Anyway, let's get back to the real-world discussion for now.

External Control: Persuade The AI

How can we persuade AI to not do something foolhardy or dangerous, particularly when the AI is potentially going to harm humans?

I'll give you a quick and easy example in the use case of AI-based self-driving cars.

You might be aware that there have been reported instances of Level 2 semi-autonomous cars that had a human driver at the wheel and the human fell asleep while actively underway on a freeway or highway. As per my earlier remarks, the scary aspect of Level 2 and Level 3 is that the human driver is still in charge of the driving, and yet they can be lulled into falsely believing that the AI or automation is fully capable to drive the car on its own. The push to ensure that an onboard monitoring system keeps track of the human driver and their driving status is a means to try and mitigate the being-lulled proclivity.

The news stories have showcased instances whereby a police officer in their police car has maneuvered in front of the Level 2 vehicle, then gradually opted to slow down their police car, which in turn has indirectly led to the Level 2 car slowing down correspondingly. This nifty trick is predicated on the idea that the Level 2 car has some form of sensor devices such as video cameras, radar, LIDAR, or the like that are used to detect vehicles that are ahead of the Level 2 car. Upon detecting the vehicle in front of the Level 2 car, the automation will automatically adjust its speed as per the speed of the vehicle ahead.

You could say that AI is being *persuaded* to slow down.

The human driver that is asleep would not seemingly be aware of what was taking place. The automation is reacting to the actions of the police car. The police officer is persuading, if you will, the AI driving system to not continue unabated. Had the police officer not tried this slowdown and stopping ploy, it is conceivable that a driving exigency might arise while under full steam, for which the driving automation would end up crashing the car or colliding with other vehicles or obstructions.

Notice that the police officer didn't speak somehow with the automation. Instead, the officer used actions to try and communicate with the automation. The automation didn't have any sentient clue of what was taking place, since we are only dealing with non-sentient AI in this discussion for now. It was a kind of monkey-see, monkey-do type of response by the automation.

Do not though assume that this trickery will always work. The automation might not have detected the police car. But for sake of argument, we'll imagine that it normally would. The twist is that the automation might be more advanced such that it opts to change lanes due to the car ahead of it that is seemingly unnecessarily slowing down. The police car might have to switch lanes too, attempting to repeatedly block the path of the Level 2 or Level 3 car.

Lamentedly, the stopping ploy sometimes won't work or the clever stunt could create an untoward driving situation that gets out of hand. You can somewhat interpret this as though the AI or automation was not willing to accede to the persuasion. Of course, this is a non-sentient reaction in this case.

We'll continue this hearty discussion with the next of the listed AI control possibilities.

External Control: Confine The AI

Suppose that the AI or automation in the case of the runaway semi-autonomous car is programmed to switch lanes and avoid getting bogged down by a vehicle in front of the car.

What else can we do to contend with this?

You could try surrounding the semi-autonomous car with an entire posse of police cars. Position one in front of the semi-autonomous vehicle, position another on the left, another on the right, and one directly behind the runaway car. The Level 2 or Level 3 car is now boxed in. Unless it can sprout wings, it cannot escape the *confinement*.

One problem with this confinement is that we don't necessarily know how the semi-autonomous car will react. Depending upon the programming, you can potentially have all the police cars in unison gradually slow down and the runaway car will correspondingly do so too (it won't be able to switch lanes or get out of the blocking confinement). That is the happy face scenario. We don't know for sure that this is what will happen. It could be that the automation is not well devised and it ends up ramming one or more of the police cars. Assuming that the officers are not killed, this might save lives, though the officers could potentially get injured and all of the vehicles might get severely damaged.

Notice that this is a form of physical confinement. Almost like putting an animal in a cage. For AI-based systems that are principally robots, the confinement might indeed often be a physical form of confinement when the AI needs to be controlled.

The tougher situation usually consists of AI that is running on computers and those computers are not readily trapped into a physical cage. You might need to use a virtual cage such as cutting off network access, entrapping the AI into not being able to electronically communicate beyond its own scope. You might need to establish a software-oriented cage, ensnaring the AI via perhaps an operating system confinement that won't let the AI computationally expand beyond its existent computing platform. Etc.

External Control: Assail The AI

Continuing the runaway semi-autonomous car example, imagine that the police don't have enough police cars on the scene to entrap the bolting car. Time is pressing along. If the police wait until enough of their units have responded, it might be too late and the Level 2 or Level 3 car might cause a traffic calamity.

What else can be done?

You could assail the AI.

In this case, a police officer in their patrol car might intentionally ram the runaway car to get it to stop. This is risky since the police officer can get injured or killed, so too can the sleeping driver. In any case, if there are innocent up ahead cars with their respective drivers and passengers, perhaps this is the only timely prudent action to take. A heroic one too.

The notion is that sometimes the "best" viable option would be to *assail* the AI to try and control it.

As a recap so far, you would presumably first use *persuasion*, then try using *confinement*, and if all else failed you would resort to *assailing* the AI.

It doesn't have to be in that sequence since we are not referring to a living creature. For a living creature, you would expect that the ethical sequence would be as stated. In the case of non-sentient AI, we presumably do not need to abide by such a humane retaining series of actions.

As a bit of an ethical puzzle, suppose the AI was sentient. Would we be ethically expected to try the least invasive options first, or could we just take any actions in whatever sequence we wished due to the AI being "nothing more than" a machine?

Noodle on that.

To clarify too, you are not limited to employing one form of AI control at a time. It might make sense to pursue several AI control options simultaneously. Hopefully, one or more works out well.

Returning to my earlier point about the AI manifesting itself as a robot, you can do the physical assailing effort to try and control it. If the AI is running on various computers and not physically easily assailed, you can try software-oriented attacks. You already know about computer viruses that can infect your home computer. We could send a specially devised computer virus to undermine the AI. That's a "good" computer virus, assuming it is going to save us from an AI that has gone astray.

We will next consider additional AI controls, ones that are aimed at an internal control angle.

Internal Control: Embedded Within The AI

The previous set of controls dealt with ways to externally attempt to dissuade, trap, or discombobulate an AI that we believe has gone awry. They are predicated on the assumption that we cannot make our way inside of AI. Everything we did in the AI external controls was from the outside of the AI.

Suppose that we can somehow get inside the AI.

For example, the AI might have been originally coded with internal subroutines that are intended to keep the AI from going amiss. Maybe those internal routines have fallen asleep on the job. Maybe they can be awakened or invoked. If so, this might get the AI to self-control and no longer pursue the unsavory actions underway.

Let's briefly explore this one and see how it goes. We will use a so-called "red button" scenario to see how this might proceed. I've written about the ongoing debate regarding having a red button emergency stop capability built into all AI-based self-driving cars. A passenger inside a self-driving car could use the button to cause the self-driving car to come to a nearly immediate halt. In theory, this would work by the button first conveying to the AI driving system that the passenger has requested an immediate stoppage. The AI would then bring the autonomous vehicle to a safe halt.

There is an entire can of worms imbued within that simple idea. Pretend that a self-driving car has an adult and their toddler in the autonomous vehicle. The toddler is having a wonderful time playing inside the driverless car. Oops, the rambunctious toddler accidentally hits the red button.

Should the AI driving system take urgent steps to radically bring the self-driving car to a halt?

Keep in mind that the self-driving car might be smack dab in the middle of heavy traffic. A sudden stop could cause a cascading series of car crashes. Also, a rapid stop could possibly jar the passengers that are inside the autonomous vehicle. All in all, whether the AI should do whatever it is told to do, such as in this emergency stop capability, bears many challenges.

One of the reasons that somc pundits like the proposed emergency stop feature are that it could potentially be leveraged in other ways.

Remember our runaway AI-driven car. Let's assume that inside the AI driving system is some embedded programming that can partake in an emergency stop. Some suggest that the police for example would have a means of invoking the emergency stop feature. Perhaps the police would send an electronic signal to the AI driving system, or maybe have a sign that they show to the sensors of the car that conveys an indication to electronically initiate the red button actions.

Thus, rather than the other already mentioned tactics of trying to perform AI control, there might be a means to activate an already embedded feature.

Carrying this further, the belief is that we will inevitably need a slew of Ethical AI embeddings and likely legal-reasoning embedded capabilities in AI of nearly all kinds. We will try to code our ethical mores and lawful rules into AI. This is hoped to keep the AI on an ethically even keel. Also, if the AI starts to diverge from that strident path, perhaps we can invoke the embeddings if they are still intact and able to function.

Internal Control: Adjacent To The AI

This last example deals with AI internal controls that are considered adjacent to the AI.

Suppose that onboard an AI-based self-driving car we have other software running that aids in the driving actions of the autonomous vehicle. Those apps might not be entirely within the realm of the AI driving system per se. They are adjacent to it.

The adjacency is important because these apps are likely to already have been established as "trustworthy" for the AI system to rely upon. They are not an outsider if you will. They are a trusted insider.

We might be able to get one of those adjacent trusted components to take action for us and do something desirable about an AI that has gone rogue or otherwise seems to be astray. Because the apps are already within the trusted space of AI, they provide a chance of aiding our humankind's saving actions.

Conclusion

All of those forms of AI control are equally applicable to the sentient AI, including the humble brag super-intelligent AI. A significant challenge for controlling sentient AI is that the embodied sentience of the AI implies that the AI might be willing and able to fight against all of those AI controls. For each of the AI control gambits, the sentient AI could deviously try to circumvent them.

I'll add a perhaps surprising twist. The non-sentient AI can be programmed to fight against those AI controls too. You see, AI doesn't necessarily need sentience to put up a defense against AI controls. Human developers can program special defeats that try to prevent the AI controls from working.

Why would a human do this?

Aren't they crazily asking for their own demise by allowing AI to go amok?

First, realize that there are AI developers that could be evildoers. Second, some evildoers could come along and alter AI programs to make them AI control resistant. Third, the capabilities to defeat AI controls could be readily construed as a helpful means of preventing evildoers from trying to overtake today's AI systems and turn them into evildoing. In that sense, the defeats of the AI controls are similar to building cybersecurity protections. The problem is that those are aimed at possibly both the insidious hacker breaches and meanwhile also going to stubbornly resist when we truly want the AI to cool its jets.

Problems, problems, problems.

Shifting gears, Thomas Edison famously said that what a man's mind can create, man's character can control. As a society, we are creating AI systems and putting them into daily use. Since we are making the AI, apparently we should be able to control the AI too, assuming we have the willpower to do so.

Taming a wild beast is not as easy as it might seem.

No matter what range of AI we are able to achieve, the AI control problem is real and needs to be given its ethically due attention. And this has to be done before that darned horse is way outside the barn and we find ourselves in an exceptionally dire existential pickle.

Collectively, let's get the AI control problem handled..

CHAPTER 4
AI ETHICS
PRECEPTS OF THE VATICAN

The Pope is concerned that AI might be used in ways that undercut humanity rather than AI serving as a tool to enable and embellish humanity.

Per the Vatican, a newly released document entitled "Rome Call For AI Ethics" spells out what direction AI ought to go as a technology that preferably is aimed for the betterment of society instead of the detriment or the possible demise of society.

Sometimes, technologists are apt to unleash innovations without having explicitly considered the ramifications of what they have let loose, and thus there is an arising slew of calls for AI ethics considerations in the rapid race toward developing and fielding AI systems, especially ones based on Machine Learning (ML) and Deep Learning (DL).

Here's a key quote from the Papal issued document:
"Now more than ever, we must guarantee an outlook in which AI is developed with a focus not on technology, but rather for the good of humanity and of the environment, of our common and shared home and of its human inhabitants, who are inextricably connected."

The Catholic Church is asking anyone that is in the business of making AI systems to be mindful of what the AI is going to do, including considering both intended and potentially unintended consequences.

Some AI developers turn a blind eye to the possibility of unintended adverse consequences of their creations.

Be aware of these social-dynamic aspects involved:

- In the view of some AI engineers and scientists, as long as the AI system at least does what they hoped it would do, anything else that might inadvertently emerge is not on their hands, they believe, and so they attempt to wash themselves of any such adversities.

- There are also many that are developing AI systems that aren't even thinking at all about the badness possibilities of what they are producing (those are the ones that tend to have a lack of mindfulness on this matter, oftentimes being "innocently" unaware).

- In some cases, AI creators are heads-down into the tech and not cognizant about ethical considerations that could arise, being preoccupied with the tech and/or not being versed in grappling with how to surface potential badness consequences.

- In other cases, they are transfixed by the goodness of their AI system, becoming overly consumed by a sense of being part of a presumed noble cause, and refuse to look at the downsides or reflexively believe that any pitfalls are well worth the presumed upside.

- Or some are so focused on beating the clock and being the first to achieve a particular AI advancement that they figure they'll deal with any ethical fallout after-the-fact versus dealing with it during the throes of getting their new machine out-the-door soonest (this though is the classic Trojan horse, putting something onto the street that is just biding time until things go awry).

The Catholic Church has issued its call for AI ethics as a pledge document.

Anyone that is involved in crafting AI systems is being politely requested to sign the pledge.

Indeed, out-the-gate there have been some signees already, notably including IBM and Microsoft.

What does the pledge ask the signers to do?

Well, I'll get into some of the details momentarily, meanwhile here are the three core precepts or objectives of the overall pledge, namely that an AI system shall:

"It must include every human being, discriminating against no one; it must have the good of humankind and the good of every human being at its heart; finally, it must be mindful of the complex reality of our ecosystem and be characterized by the way in which it cares for and protects the planet (our "common and shared home") with a highly sustainable approach, which also includes the use of artificial intelligence in ensuring sustainable food systems in the future."

Thus, in shorthand:

1) AI shall not discriminate
2) AI shall be good in its intent
3) AI shall care about sustainability

One aspect to keep in mind is that AI is not somehow determining its own future, which at times when referring to AI systems it is as though they are already autonomous and deciding their own fate.

Not so, at least not now and nor in the near future.

In other words, we humans are the ones that are devising these AI systems.

Therefore, humans are responsible for what those AI systems do.

I mention this because it is an easy escape hatch to have AI designers and developers pretend that the AI did something untoward and it wasn't somehow the fault of the AI builders that the system went awry.

You are likely familiar with going to say the DMV to get your driver's license renewed, and the computer system is down, which then the agent at the DMV shrugs their shoulders and laments that it's just one of those things.

To be correct, it isn't just one of those things.

If the computer system is down, it's due to the humans that set up the computer and apparently failed to properly put in place the needed backup and other provisions to ensure that the system is available when needed.

Don't fall into the mental trap of accepting the notion that a system, including AI systems, are of their own mind and if they blow a gasket it is just one of those things.

The real truth is that the humans that devised and put in place the computer system are the ones that ought to have the buck stop at their door since they are the people that didn't exercise the due care that they should have properly undertaken.

In the case of the call by Pope Francis for attending to vital AI ethics considerations, and though you might assume that such a rightful covenant would be straightforward and beyond criticism (since, in a manner of speaking, it is a "mom and apple pie" kind of declaration that would seem inarguable), there are some that have already lobbed disparagement.

How so?

First, some critics point out that there isn't any binding aspect to the pledge.

If a company signs on the dotted line, there isn't any specific penalty imposed for violating the principles of the pledge. Thus, presumably, you can signup without any fear of reprisal.

With no teeth, the pledge is seen by some as hollow.

Second, the fact that the Catholic Church has issued this particular call for AI ethics is disturbing to some since the issuer presumably is impinging religion into a topic that for some is not a religious matter at all.

Will other religions then issue similar calls for AI ethics, and if so, which one will prevail, and what will we do with a fragmented and disparate set of AI ethics proclamations.

Third, some assert that the pledge is bland and overly generic.

Presumably, without being more down-to-earth, the document doesn't provide sufficient real-world directives that could be implemented in any practical way.

Plus, those AI developers that want to weasel out could claim that they misunderstood the general provisions or merely interpreted them in a manner differently than perhaps originally intended.

Okay, given the condemnation barrage, should we toss out this new call for "algor-ethics" for AI?

As an aside, algor-ethics is the name being given to algorithmic ethics concerns, and though maybe clever, I believe it doesn't roll off the tongue well enough and won't likely take hold as a common moniker for these matters. Time will tell.

Back to the question at hand, should we care about this call for AI ethics or not?

Yes, we should.

Despite the aspect that the pledge admittedly doesn't impose any financial penalties for failing to abide by the principles, there is another angle that you need to consider.

For those firms that sign-up, they are potentially going to be held accountable by the public-at-large.

If they run afoul of the pledge and suppose the Church then points this out, the bad publicity alone could hamper and damage the signee, leading to a loss of business and a loss of industry reputation.

You could say that there is an implied or hidden cost to violating the pledge.

On the matter of whether religion is being infused where it doesn't belong, please realize that's a whole other matter of sizable discussion and debate, but do also recognize that there are now numerous AI ethics frameworks and calls for AI ethics from a wide variety of quarters.

In that sense, it isn't as though this is the first such calling.

And, if you look closely at the pledge, there doesn't seem to be anything about it that pertains to any religious doctrine per se, meaning that you really could not readily differentiate it from any other similar pledges that were done entirely absent (presumably) of any religious undertones.

Finally, in terms of the vagueness of the pledge, yes, you could easily drive a Mack truck through the numerous loopholes, and those that want to be weasels have a solid chance at being, well, weaselly.

My guess is that we'll have some follow-ups by others in the AI field that will supplement the pledge with specific indications that can help in plugging up the gaps and omissions.

Perhaps too, anyone that does take the weasel route will get called out by the world at large, and false claims of allegedly misunderstanding the pledge will get denounced as obvious ploys to avoid abiding by the reasonably articulated and quite apparent AI ethical provisions proclaimed.

Speaking of making sure that everyone gets the drift on these AI ethics provisions, contemplate the myriad of ways that AI is being applied.

Here's an interesting area of applied AI that falls within the AI ethics realm: *Should AI-based true self-driving cars be devised and fielded in a manner as guided by these calls for AI ethics?*

I say yes, unequivocally so.

Indeed, I call upon all automakers and self-driving tech makers to sign the pledge.

AI Ethics Considerations

For Level 4 and Level 5 true self-driving vehicles, there won't be a human driver involved in the driving task. All occupants will be passengers. The AI is doing the driving.

At first thought, you might assume that there doesn't seem to be any need for considering AI ethics issues. A driverless car is just a car that perchance drives you around, doing so without a human driver. No big deal, and certainly no ethical considerations about how the AI driving system will do its task, so you might presume.

Sorry to say that anyone under the belief that there aren't AI ethics issues involved needs to be knocked on the head or be doused with a bucket of cold water (I am not advocating violence, please know that those are mere metaphorical characterizations).

Let's briefly take a look at each of the six core principles outlined in the *Rome Call For AI Ethics* document.

Seeking to keep things succinct herein, I offer links to my other postings that offer greater details on these weighty topics:

AI Ethics Principle #1: "Transparency: in principle, AI systems must be explainable"

You get into a true self-driving car and it refuses to take you where you've told it to go.

Today, most AI driving systems are being devised without offering any explanation for their behavior.

It could be that the AI system is unwilling to drive because there is a tornado underway, or maybe due to your making a request that is undrivable (no passable roads nearby), etc.

Without XAI (an acronym for explainable AI), you won't know what's going on.

AI Ethics Principle #2: "Inclusion: the needs of all human beings must be taken into consideration so that everyone can benefit, and all individuals can be offered the best possible conditions to express themselves and develop"

Some are concerned that AI self-driving cars will only be available for the rich, and that the rest of the populous will not glean the benefits of driverless cars (see the link here).

Which shall it be, mobility-for-all or only mobility-for-the-few?

AI Ethics Principle #3: "Responsibility: those who design and deploy the use of AI must proceed with responsibility and transparency"

How will the AI determine the course of action when faced with having to choose between potentially ramming into a child jaywalking the street versus slamming the driverless car into a tree and likely harming the passengers?

Known variously as the Trolley problem (see my link here), many are clamoring for the automakers and self-driving tech firms to be transparent about how their AI systems will make these life-or-death choices.

AI Ethics Principle #4: "Impartiality: do not create or act according to bias, thus safeguarding fairness and human dignity"

Suppose a self-driving car reacts to pedestrians based on their racial characteristics (see my discussion at this link)?

Or suppose a fleet of self-driving cars all "learn" to avoid certain neighborhoods and won't drive in those locations, which would deny those residents ready access to driverless cars.

Biases due to Machine Learning and Deep Learning systems are a real concern.

AI Ethics Principle #5: "Reliability: AI systems must be able to work reliably"

You are riding in a self-driving car, and all of a sudden it pulls over to the side of the road and comes to a stop.

Why?

You might not know.

Could be that the AI reached the bounds of its scope (referred to as its Operational Design Domain, ODD, see the link here).

Or, perhaps the AI system faltered, had a glitch, etc.

AI Ethics Principle #6: "Security and privacy: AI systems must work securely and respect the privacy of users."

You get into a self-driving car after partying at the bars.

Turns out that the driverless car has cameras pointed inward, in addition to externally pointed cameras.

The basis for the inward-facing cameras is to catch riders that might spray graffiti or damage the interior of the vehicle.

In any case, those cameras aimed at you are capturing video of you the entire time that you are riding in the driverless vehicle, including your rambling remarks since you are in a drunken stupor.

Who owns that video and what can they do with it?

Does the owner of the self-driving car need to provide you with the video, and is there anything preventing them from posting the video online?

There are lots of privacy issues to be dealt with (see my analysis at this link here).

From a security perspective, there are tons of possibilities for someone cracking into the AI driving system (see my discussion here).

Imagine an evildoer that might hack the AI and be able to take over the driving system, or at least tell the driving system to take you to a particular location, wherein kidnappers are waiting for your arrival.

I realize that there are many doomsday scenarios about security breeches in a self-driving car system or its cloud-based fleetwide system, and it is incumbent for the automakers and self-driving tech makers to put in place needed systems security protections and precautions.

Conclusion

If you compare this call for AI ethics to the many others in circulation, you'll find that they have much in common.

The criticism that we are ending up with a tsunami of these AI ethics calls is somewhat the case, though one supposes that it can't hurt to cover all the bases.

That being said, it is starting to become a bit confounding, and AI makers are going to potentially use the excuse that since there isn't one single accepted standard, they will wait until such a document exists.

It seems like a viable excuse, but I don't buy it.

Anyone that says they are going to wait until the worldwide all-hands Grand Poohbah accepted version gets approved is really saying they are willing to postpone becoming grounded on any AI ethics at all, and their wait might be the same as waiting for Godot.

I urge that you pick any AI ethics guideline that has meat to it and that is proffered by a reputable source and get going with your internal AI ethics implementation.

Sooner rather than later true.

CHAPTER 5
AI ETHICS PRINCIPLES OF THE US DOD

AI ethics is a hot trending topic these days.

And, so it should be.

With the rise of AI systems popping up here and there, and virtually everywhere, there is a rightfully emerging concern that these computer-based systems are being thrown into the world without much thought given to the societal impacts that they can produce.

Serious qualms are being expressed that the latest crop of AI systems is embedding inherent biases and opting to spread wide and far other adverse ethically and societally toxic actions.

When referring to AI ethics, I assert there are (at least) two major facets or rules involved:

1) AI systems need to behave in societal ways that are ethically sound,
2) AI developers and those fielding AI systems need to ensure that rule #1 is held true

The first rule is perhaps self-evident that AI ethics would refer to making sure that AI systems are performing in ethically appropriate ways.

As will be discussed momentarily, trying to abide by rule #1 is actually harder than you might think.

The importance of rule #2 is to make things clear that the responsible parties for ensuring that AI ethics are being fully observed consists of those human beings that are designing, building, and fielding AI systems.

If you believe that's obvious, don't be so quick to make such a "common sense" judgment.

There is an aura around AI systems as though they are autonomous and are self-determining.

Thus, when an AI system does something like exhibiting a racial bias, some fall into the mental trap of assuming it was the "AI that did it" and don't assign the responsibility to those that crafted and put in place the AI system.

Some AI developers and AI producers would certainly prefer that you not look in their direction when their AI system does something afoul.

As such, it is easy for those that hold true responsibility to feign mock surprise and slyly shirk their duties, saying that it was the AI alone at fault, and act as though they were innocently watching as a train wreck happened, even though they were the ones that essentially put the train on the tracks and let it go, unfettered and unchecked.

Of course, some would defend their AI system that's gotten untoward by saying that they tried to prevent any AI failings, but, heck, something got past them.

In a distorted sense, they seemingly turn themselves into the "victims" versus those that are adversely affected by the AI system.

Don't buy it.

Really, please don't buy into it.

In short, rule #2 is pretty much as important as rule #1.

Without holding human beings to be accountable for the AI that they unleash, we are going to get ourselves into a rather ugly muck.

Assuredly, we'll have everyone and their brother or sister getting away with floating into the whirlwind of great promise their latest AI system creation, hopeful of striking it rich, and acting as though they had nothing to do with those AI apps that ethically end-up trouncing on the rest of us and foster AI systems absent of any moral duty or obligation.

One arena in which AI ethics can get especially thorny involves AI systems for military uses.

Most would agree that we need to observe some form of AI ethics in the building and use of military AI systems, and whatever we learn there can be certainly reapplied to commercial and industrial use of AI systems too.

The U.S. Department of Defense (DoD) has released a set of AI ethics principles.

If you look at the principles as standalone (I'll do so momentarily herein), meaning without the context of military or defense, they are equally applicable to any commercial or industry-based AI systems.

I'll walk you through the principles and will use my favorite foil to do so, namely the advent of AI true self-driving cars, allowing me to vividly illustrate how this latest set of AI ethics guidelines do apply to all uses of AI, including non-military uses.

Per media reports about the Pentagon's posting of this latest set of AI ethics, and upon quoting Lt. General Jack Shanahan of the Air Force and Director of the Joint AI Center, he aptly stated: "AI is a powerful emerging and enabling technology that is rapidly transforming culture, society and, eventually, even warfighting. Whether it does so in a positive or negative way depends on our approach to adoption and use."

As I've exhorted repeatedly, how society decides to approach AI development and fielding will determine the outcome as to whether an AI system is considered *AI For Good* or is (or becomes) the lamentable *AI For Bad.*

Those developing and producing AI need to have their feet held to the fire thereof.

To be clear, AI systems aren't going to intrinsically be *AI For Good* (there is nothing axiomatic to provide such an assurance).

In fact, for an overarching means to think about this matter, consider for the moment my conceptualization of a four-square grid that I refer to as an AI Ethics Outcome Grid.

Along the vertical axis, we'll put *AI For Good* and above it the counterpart of *AI For Bad* moniker.

Along the horizontal, we'll list *Intended* and the counterpart indication will be *Unintended.*

This gives us these four squares:

1) *AI For Good* – Intended
2) *AI For Bad* – Intended
3) *AI For Good* – Unintended
4) *AI For Bad* – Unintended

I realize that some of you might have heartburn over potential simplification of this weighty matter into a mere four-square framework, but sometimes taking a macroscopic perspective can be instructive and help to see the forest for the trees.

Go with me on this.

For the first square that has the *AI For Good* and it was intended for that purpose and genuinely provides that purpose without any ethical violations or perturbations, I believe that's where we want every AI system to land into.

For the second square, namely an *AI For Bad* system that was intended, which yes, unfortunately, those are going to be devised and unleashed (for example, by criminals, terrorists, and the like), but hopefully we'll be on our guard, and the use of AI ethics guidelines might aid in our detection that someone has dastardly done such a deed.

For the third square, *AI For Good* that was unintended, this is the lucky square, meaning that someone put together an AI system and perhaps didn't realize it was aimed at and achieved *AI For Good*, thus it was a favorable unintended consequence, which is fine since the result is good anyway.

The fourth square is the one that to some degree is the most insidious and worrisome (other than the dreaded square two), consisting of *AI For Bad* that was unintended. Typically, these are AI systems that originated as an *AI For Good* aspiration, yet ultimately contain *AI For Bad* aspects that undermine the *AI For Good* benefits.

By and large, we are going to have AI systems that contain a smattering of *AI For Good* and a smattering of *AI For Bad*, encompassing what the AI developers hoped to do (the *AI For Good*), but allowed unintended adverse consequences to worm their way into the AI system (that's the *AI For Bad*).

Ponder these two crucial questions:

- How can we realize or detect that an AI system might contain *AI For Bad* facets?

- How can those devising AI systems be cognizant of how to build such systems so as to catch and prevent the inclusion or emergence of *AI For Bad*?

Answer: Abide by and rigorously apply a proper and meaty set of AI ethics guidelines.

Speaking of AI ethics guidelines, there are five principles in the DoD released set, and each principle offers insightful points to be observed by anyone developing AI, and anyone fielding AI, and anyone that uses AI or becomes a user of an AI system by one means or another.

Overall, AI ethics guidelines are applicable to all stakeholders, not just developers.

The best way to explore the DoD AI ethics guidelines would be to showcase them as applied to some specific exemplar of AI systems.

Here's then today's question to be contemplated: *Would the DoD AI ethics guidelines be applicable to AI-based true self-driving cars, and if so, in what ways would the set of AI ethics principles apply?*

Yes, they do indubitably apply.

Let's unpack the matter and see.

Applied AI Ethics Principles

For Level 4 and Level 5 true self-driving vehicles, there won't be a human driver involved in the driving task. All occupants will be passengers. The AI is doing the driving.

Okay, bottom-line, there's a heap of AI that's going to be included in Level 4 and Level 5 self-driving cars.

Nobody can dispute that fact.

The big question is whether the AI that's driving a self-driving car is going to be bounded by any kind of AI ethics guidelines or precepts. Recall, as mentioned prior, there isn't some kind of magical default that ordains an AI system to abide by an ethical or moral contract with society.

Humans need to infuse such beliefs or principles into the AI.

It must be an overt act by the AI developers and an act done with eyes wide open. Perilously, there are some that regrettably have their eyes tightly shut or are mesmerized and staring hypnotically instead at a perceived societal grand prize or assumed noble cause.

I've forewarned that some AI systems are leading to a kind of noble cause corruption by those developing such AI, whereby those involved are so consumed with passion about the potential of *AI For Good* that they ignore, discount, or skip the AI ethics considerations.

Here then are the five principles elucidated in the DoD set of AI ethics guidelines:

AI Ethics Principle #1: Responsible.

"DoD personnel will exercise appropriate levels of judgment and care while remaining responsible for the development, deployment, and use of AI capabilities."

First, subtract from the wording of this principle the portion that says "DoD personnel" and substitute instead the aspect of "All personnel" and you'll have turned this guideline into one that fits for any AI creating entity, including those in commerce.

For automakers and self-driving tech firms, please read the principle with close attention to what it says.

I say this because some keep suggesting that an AI-based self-driving car will act on its own, thus there seems to be a lot of hand wringing and angst over who will be held responsible if a driverless car goes awry and causes injuries or deaths.

In short, humans will be responsible.

It could be the humans that devised the AI-based self-driving car, such as the automaker or tech firm involved.

Realize too that I keep saying that those that are responsible include the developers and those that field an AI system, which suggests that fielding an AI system is just as important as aiming at the developers of an AI system.

Why?

Because those that field an AI system can mess-up and cause adverse consequences.

For example, suppose a ride-sharing company purchases a bunch of driverless cars and puts those vehicles to work as a fleet of self-driving cars for ride-sharing purposes.

So far, so good.

But, suppose the ride-sharing company fails to properly maintain the driverless cars.

And, due to the lack of or the undertaking of prescribed maintenance, a self-driving car goes awry, in which case, yes, we might find fault with the original developers, but we more so might go after those that fielded the AI system and did not exercise due care and their responsibility in deploying the AI system.

AI Ethics Principle #2: Equitable.

"The Department will take deliberate steps to minimize unintended bias in AI capabilities."

Once again, subtract in this case the word "Department" and substitute the phrase "AI developers and those fielding the AI" as a means of turning this into a principle applicable to all.

For self-driving cars, there is concern that the AI system might opt to react to pedestrians differently based on their race, thus subtly and inexorably exhibiting racial bias.

Another concern is that a fleet of self-driving cars might end-up avoiding certain neighborhoods, pattern landing onto a geographic criterion that ultimately denies ready access to driverless cars for perhaps those that are especially mobility disadvantaged.

In brief, there is a significant chance that AI-based true self-driving cars are going to get mired into biases of one shape or another, and rather than just waving our arms and claiming there's nothing that can be done about it, the reality is that those devising and fielding driverless cars ought to be diligently seeking to minimize or mitigate or eradicate any such AI system biases.

AI Ethics Principle #3: Traceable.

"The Department's AI capabilities will be developed and deployed such that relevant personnel possess an appropriate understanding of the technology, development processes, and operational methods applicable to AI capabilities, including with transparent and auditable methodologies, data sources, and design procedures and documentation."

Simply remove the word "Department's," or, if you prefer, think of this as anyone's department in any company or entity, thus making the principle widely applicable to all.

There's a lot packed into the principle, but for succinctness herein, I'll focus on just one facet that maybe you might not have explicitly registered or recognized.

The aspect of "data sources" is aiming at especially the advent of Machine Learning (ML) or Deep Learning (DL).

When creating an ML/DL, you typically need to collect a large set of data, and then you computationally use specialized algorithms or models to find patterns.

Similar to the earlier point about hidden biases, if the data collected has inherently biased data, the patterns will potentially pick-up on the biases, and then when the AI system is working in real-time on new situations, it will carry those biases into what it does.

Scarier too is that the AI developers might not realize what is taking place, and nor might those that are fielding the AI system.

A self-driving car that's been trained on the crazed and antagonistic traffic in say New York City (NYC), can potentially adopt a very aggressive driving style, befitting the NYC human-driven traffic. Imagine if you then took that same AI-based system and had it drive in some every-town USA that has a more even-paced sense of driving.

The principle makes it clear-cut that the AI developers and fielders need to be mindful of their data sources, transparency, and the auditing of such systems.

AI Ethics Principle #4: Reliable.

"The Department's AI capabilities will have explicit, well-defined uses, and the safety, security, and effectiveness of such capabilities will be subject to testing and assurance within those defined uses across their entire life-cycles."

Go ahead and remove the word "Department's" or think of it as anyone's department.

Most (or maybe all) would agree that the success or failure of self-driving cars rests on how safe they are, along with their security and effectiveness.

This principle is self-evident, I would hope, for its apparent applicability to AI-based true self-driving cars.

AI Ethics Principle #5: Governable.

"The Department will design and engineer AI capabilities to fulfill their intended functions while possessing the ability to detect and avoid unintended consequences, and the ability to disengage or deactivate deployed systems that demonstrate unintended behavior."

Remove the word "Department's" or think of it as anyone's department.

The first portion of this principle goes directly at the heart of my theme herein about detecting and avoiding unintended consequences, especially adverse ones.

That's rather obvious as applicable to self-driving cars.

The trickery part about driverless cars involves the notion of being able to disengage or deactivate a deployed AI system that's demonstrated unintended behavior – there's a lot of twists and turns in being able to do so for self-driving cars and it is not the (some believe) simply the inclusion of a "kill button" within the driverless car.

Conclusion

We usually expect the DoD to keep any secrets close to their vest.

In this case, AI ethics guidelines aren't something that should be kept secret, and indeed, it is refreshing and laudable that the DoD has published this set of AI ethics. Of course, in the end, it is one thing to craft a paper tiger, and another to see it to fruition in the real world.

All AI developers and all AI fielders should be carefully and thoughtfully considering these AI ethics guidelines, along with the (now slew) of similar AI ethics principles being promulgated by a myriad of other sources. If we want AI to take that hill up ahead, we need to make sure they have sufficient and robust AI ethics "muscle power" to succeed.

CHAPTER 6
AI ETHICS
AND THE TROLLEY PROBLEM

One of the most controversial topics for insiders that know about AI-based true self-driving cars is the famous (or infamous) Trolley Problem.

Let's unpack the matter and see what we can reveal. I'd like to see if we can give the matter its serious consideration and due.

The place to start entails clarifying what the Trolley Problem consists of.

Turns out that it is an ethically stimulating thought experiment that traces back to the early 1900s. As such, the topic has been around for quite a while and more recently has become generally associated with the advent of self-driving cars.

In short, imagine that a trolley is going down the tracks and there is a fork up ahead. If the trolley continues in its present course, alas there is someone stuck on the tracks further along and they will get run down and killed.

You are standing next to a switch that will allow you to redirect the trolley into the forking rail track and thus avoid killing the person.

Presumably, obviously, you would invoke the switchover.

But there is a hideous twist, namely that the forked track also has someone entangled on it, and by diverting the trolley you will kill that person instead.

This is one of those no-win situations.

Whichever choice you make, a person is going to be killed.

You might be tempted to say that you do not have to make a choice and therefore you can readily sidestep the whole matter.

Not really, since by doing nothing you are essentially "agreeing" to have the person killed that is on the straight-ahead path. You cannot seemingly avoid your culpability by shrugging your shoulders and opting to do nothing, instead, you are inextricably intertwined into the situation.

Given this preliminary setup of the Trolley Problem as a lose-lose with one person at stake in your choice of either option, it does not especially spark an ethical dilemma since each outcome is woefully considered the same.

The matter is usually altered in various ways to try and see how you might respond to a more ethically challenging circumstance.

For example, suppose you are able to discern that the straight-ahead track has a child on it, while the forked track has an adult.

What now?

Well, you might attempt to justify using the switch to get the trolley to fork onto the track with the adult, doing so under the logic that the adult has already lived some substantive part of their life, while the child is only at the beginning of their life and perhaps ought to be given a chance for a longer existence.

How does that seem to you?

Some buy into it, some do not.

There are those that might argue that every person has an equal "value" of living and it is untoward to prejudge that the child should live while the adult is to die.

Some would argue that the adult should be the one that is kept alive since they have already shown that they can survive longer than the child (for more about these various perspectives, see my discussion about the Moral Machine).

Here's another variation.

Both are adults, and the one on the forked path is Einstein.

Does this change your viewpoint about which way to direct the trolley?

Some would say that averting the trolley away from Einstein is the "right" choice, saving him and allowing him to live and inevitably offer the tremendous insights that he was destined to provide (we are assuming in this scenario that it is a younger adult moment-in-time, Einstein).

Not so fast, some might say, and they wonder whether the other adult, the one on the straight-ahead, maybe they are someone that is destined to be equally great or perhaps make even more notable contributions to society (who's to know?).

Anyway, I think you can see how the ethical dilemmas can be readily postulated with the Trolley Problem template.

Usually, the popular variants involve the number of people that are stuck on the tracks. For example, assume there are two people trapped on the straight-ahead path, while only one person is jammed on the forked path.

Some would say this is an "easy" answered variant since the aspect of two people is presumed to be spared over just saving one person. In that sense, you are willing to consider that lives are somewhat additive, and the more there are, the more ethically favorable is that particular choice.

Not everyone would concur with that logic.

In any case, we now have placed on the table herein the crux of the Trolley Problem.

I realize that your initial reaction likely is that it is a mildly interesting and thought-provoking notion but seems overly abstract and does not offer any practical utility.

Some object and point out that they do not envision themselves ever coming upon a trolley and perchance finding themselves in this kind of obtuse pickle.

Shift gears.

A firefighter has rushed up to a burning building.

There is a man in the building that is poking out of a window, acrid smoke billowing around him, and yelling to be saved.

What should the firefighter do?

Well, of course, we would hope that the firefighter would seek to rescue the man.

But, wait, there is the sound of a child, screaming uncontrollably, stuck in a bedroom inside the burning building.

The firefighter has to choose which to try and rescue, and for which the firefighter will not have time to save both of them.

If the firefighter chooses to save the child, the man will perish in the fire. If the firefighter chooses to save the man, the child will succumb to the fire.

Does this seem familiar?

It should because it is roughly equivalent to the Trolley Problem. The point is that there are potentially real-life related scenarios that exhibit the underlying parameters and the overarching premise of the Trolley Problem.

Remove the trolley from the problem as stated and look at the structure or elements that underpin the circumstances (we can still refer to the matter as the Trolley Problem for sake of reference, yet remove the trolley and still retain the core essentials).

We have this:

- There are dire circumstances of a life-or-death nature (more like death-or-death)
- All outcomes are horrific (even the do-nothing option) and lead to fatality
- Time is short and there are urgency and immediacy involved
- Options are extremely limited, and a forced-choice is required

You might try to argue that there is not a "forced choice" since there is the do-nothing option always available in these scenarios, but we are going to assume that the person faced with the predicament is aware of what is taking place and realizes they are making a choice even if they choose to do nothing.

Obviously, if the person confronted with the choice is unaware of the ramifications of doing nothing, they perhaps could be said to have not been cognizant of the fact that they tacitly made a choice. Likewise, someone that miscomprehends the situation might falsely believe that they do not have to make a choice.

Assume that the person involved is fully aware of the do-nothing and must choose to do nothing or to not do-nothing (I emphasize this due to the aspect that sometimes people mulling over the Trolley Problem will attempt to weasel out of the setup by saying that the do-nothing is the "right" choice since they then have averted making any decision; the selection of do-nothing is in fact considered a decision in this setup).

As an aside, in the case of the burning building, if the firefighter does nothing, presumably both the man and the child will die, so this is somewhat kilter of the Trolley Problem as presented, thus, it is perhaps more evidentiary that the firefighter will almost certainly make a choice. It differs from the classic Trolley Problem in that the firefighter has the opportunity to always, later on, point out that the do-nothing was certainly worse than making a choice, no matter which apparent choice was ultimately selected.

One other point, this is not particularly a so-called Hobson's choice scenario, which sometimes is misleadingly likened to the Trolley Problem.

Hobson's choice is based on an historic story of a horse owner that told those wanting a horse that they could choose either the horse closest to the barn door or take no horse at all. As such, the upside is taking the horse as proffered, while the downside is that you end-up without getting a horse. This is a decision-making scenario of a take-it-or-leave-it style, and decidedly not the same as the Trolley Problem.

With all of the background setting the stage, we can next consider how this seems to be an issue related to self-driving cars.

The focus will be on AI-based true self-driving cars, which deserves clarity as to what that phrasing means.

Looking Inside The Trolley Problem

For Level 4 and Level 5 true self-driving vehicles, there won't be a human driver involved in the driving task. All occupants will be passengers. The AI is doing the driving.

Here's the vexing question: *Will the AI of true self-driving cars have to make Trolley Problem decisions during the act of driving the self-driving vehicle?*

The reaction by some insiders is that this is a preposterous idea and utterly miscast, labeling the whole matter as falsehood and something that has no bearing on self-driving cars.

Really?

Start with the first premise that is usually given, which is that there is no such thing as a Trolley Problem in the act of driving a car.

For anyone trying to use the "never happens" argument (for nearly anything), they find themselves on rather shaky and porous ground, since all it takes is the showing of existence to prove that the "never" is an incorrect statement.

I can easily provide that existence proof.

Peruse the news about car crashes, and by doing so, here's an example of a recent news headline from even just a week ago or so: "Driver who hit pedestrians on sidewalk was veering to avoid crash."

The real-world reporting indicated that a driver was confronted with a pick-up truck that unexpectedly pulled in front of him, and he found himself having to choose whether to ram into the other vehicle or to try and veer away from the vehicle, though he also realized apparently that there were nearby pedestrians and his veering would take him into the pedestrians.

Which to choose?

I trust that you can see that this is very much like the Trolley Problem.

If he opted to do nothing, he was presumably going to ram into the other vehicle. If he veered away, he was presumably going to potentially hit the pedestrians. Either choice is certainly terrible, yet a choice had to be made.

Some of you might bellow that this is not a life-or-death choice, and indeed fortunately the pedestrians though injured were not actually killed (at least as stated in the reporting), but I think you are fighting a bit hard to try and reject the Trolley Problem.

It can be readily argued that death was on the line.

Anyone of an open mind would agree that there was a horrific choice to be made, involving dire circumstances, and with limited choices, involving a time urgency factor, and otherwise conformed with the Trolley Problem overall (minus the trolley).

As such, for those in the "never happens" camp, this is one example, of many, for which the word never is blatantly wrong.

It does happen.

In fact, it is an interesting matter to try and gauge how often this kind of decision making does take place while driving a car. In the United States alone, there are 3.2 trillion miles driven each year, doing so by about 225 million licensed drivers, and the result is approximately 40,000 deaths and 2.3 million injuries due to car crashes annually.

We do not know how many of those crashes involved a Trolley Problem scenario, but we do know that reportedly it does occur (as evidenced by news reporting).

On that aspect of reporting, it is quite interesting that apparently, we should be cautious in interpreting any of the stories and coverage of car crashes, due to a suggested bias by such reporting.

A study discussed in the Columbia Journalism Review points out that oftentimes the driver is quoted by news reporters, rather than quoting the victims that are harmed by the driving act (this is logically explainable, since the victims are either hard to reach as they are at a hospital and possibly incapacitated, or, sadly, they are dead and thus unable to explain what happened).

You might recognize this kind of selective attention as the survivability bias, a type of everyday bias in which we tend to focus on that which is more readily available and neglect or underplay that which is less so available or apparent.

For the driving of a car and the reporting of car crashes, we need to be mindful of this facet.

It could be that there are instances involving the Trolley Problem that the surviving participants might not realize had occurred, or are reluctant to state as so, and so on. In that sense, it could be that the Trolley Problem in car crashes is underreported.

Being fair, we can also question the veracity of those that make a claim that amounts to a Trolley Problem and be cautious in assuming that just because someone says it was, it might not have been. In that sense, we could be mindful of potential overreporting.

All in all, though, we can reasonably reject the claim that the Trolley Problem does not exist in the act of driving a car.

Stated more affirmatively, *we can reasonably accept and acknowledge that the Trolley Problem does exist in the act of driving a car.*

There, I said it, and I'm sure there are some pundits that are boiling mad thereof. Anyway, with that under our belt, we hopefully might agree that human drivers can and do face the Trolley Problem.

But is it only human drivers that experience this?

One can make the assertion that an AI-based driving system, which is supposed to drive a car and do so to the same or better capability than human drivers, could very well encounter Trolley Problem situations.

Let's tackle this carefully.

First, notice that this does not suggest that only AI driving systems will encounter a Trolley Problem, which is sometimes confusion that exists. There are those that claim the Trolley Problem will only happen to self-driving cars, but it hopefully is clear-cut that this is something that faces human drivers and we are extending that known facet to what we assume self-driving cars will encounter too.

Second, some argue that we will have only and exclusively AI-based true self-driving cars on our roadways, and as such, those vehicles will communicate and coordinate electronically via V2X doing so in a fashion that will obviate any chance of a Trolley Problem arising.

Maybe so, but that is a Utopian-like future that we do not know will happen, and meanwhile, there is inarguably going to be a mixture of both human-driven cars and AI-driven cars, for likely a long time to come, at least decades, and we also do not know if people will ever give up their perceived "right" (it's a privilege) about driving a car.

This is an important point that many never-Trolley proponents overlook.

Here's how they get themselves into a corner.

The oft refrain is that an AI-based self-driving car has "obviously" been poorly engineered or essentially a lousy job done by the AI developers if the vehicle ever perchance finds itself in the midst of a Trolley Problem.

Usually, these same claims are associated too with the belief that we will have zero fatalities as a result of self-driving cars.

As I have exhorted many times, zero fatalities is a zero chance.

It is a lofty goal, and a heartwarming aspiration, but nonetheless a misleading and outright false establishment of expectations.

The rub is that if a pedestrian darts into the street, and there was no forewarning of the action, and meanwhile a self-driving car is coming down the street at perhaps 35 miles per hour, the physics of stopping in-time cannot be overcome simply because the AI is driving the car.

The usual retort is that the AI would have always detected the pedestrian beforehand, but this is a falsehood that implies the sensors will always and perfectly be able to detect such matters, and that it will always be done the sufficiently in advanced time that the self-driving car can avoid the pedestrian.

I dare say that a child that runs out from between two parked cars is not going to offer such a chance.

We are once again into the existence proof, meaning that there are going to be circumstances whereby no matter how good the AI is, and how good the sensors are, there will still be instances of the AI not being able to avoid a car crash.

Likewise, one can argue in that same vein that the Trolley Problem will be indeed encountered by AI self-driving cars, ones that are on our public streets, and traveling amongst human drivers, and driving near to human pedestrians.

The news report about the human driver that was cut-off by a pick-up truck could absolutely happen to a self-driving car.

This seems undebatable.

If you are now of the mind that the Trolley Problem can occur and can occur too in the case of AI self-driving cars, the next aspect is what will the AI do.

Suppose the AI jams on the brakes, and slams head-on into that pick-up truck.

Did the AI consider other options?

Was the AI even considering veering to the side of the road and up onto the sidewalk (and, into the pedestrians)?

If you are a self-driving car maker or automaker, you need to very, very, very careful about what your answer is going to be.

I'll tell you why.

You might say that the AI was only programmed to do whatever was the obvious thing to do, which was to apply the brakes and attempt to slow down.

We can likely assume that the AI was proficient enough to calculate that despite the braking, it was going to ram into the pick-up truck.

So, it "knew" that a car crash was imminent.

But if you are also saying that the AI did not consider other options, including going up onto the sidewalk, this certainly seems to showcase that the AI was doing an inadequate job of driving the car, and we would have expected a human driver to try and assess alternatives to avoid the car crash.

In that sense, the AI is presumably deficient and perhaps should not be on our public roadways.

You are also opening wide your legal liability, which I have repeatedly stated is something that will ultimately be a huge exposure for the automakers and self-driving car makers.

Once self-driving cars are prevalent, and once they get into car crashes, which they will, the lawsuits are going to come flying, and there are lawyers already priming to go after those deep-pocketed billion-dollar funded makers of self-driving tech and self-driving cars.

Meanwhile, some of you might say that the AI did consider other alternatives, defending the robustness of your AI system, including that it considered going up on the sidewalk, but it then calculated that the pedestrians might be struck and so opted to stay the course and rammed instead into the pick-up truck.

Whoa, you have just admitted that the AI was entangled into a Trolley Problem scenario.

Welcome to the fold.

Conclusion

When a human driver confronts a Trolley Problem, they presumably take into account their own potential death or injury, which thusly differs from the classic Trolley Problem since the person throwing the switch for the trolley tracks is not directly imperiled (they might suffer emotional consequences, or maybe even legal repercussions, but not bodily harm).

We can reasonably assume that the AI of a self-driving car is not concerned about its own well-being (I don't want to detract from this herein discussion and take us onto a tangent, but there are some that argue we might someday ascribe human rights to AI).

In any case, the self-driving car might have passengers in it, which introduces a third element of consideration for the Trolley Problem.

This is akin to adding a third track and another fork.

The complications though somewhat extend beyond the traditional Trolley Problem since the AI must now take into account a potential joint probability or level of uncertainty, involving the facet that in the case of the pick-up truck involves the possible death or injury to the pick-up driver and the self-driving car passengers, versus the possible death or injury to the pedestrians and the self-driving car passengers.

Maybe that is the Trolley Problem on steroids.

Time for a wrap-up.

For those flat earthers that deny the existence of the Trolley Problem in the case of AI-based true self-driving cars, your head-in-the-sand perspective is not only myopic but you are going to be the easiest of the legal targets for lawsuits.

Why so?

Because it was a well-known and oft-discussed matter that the Trolley Problem exists, yet you did nothing about it and hid behind the assertion that it does not exist.

Good luck with that.

For those of you that are the rare earthers, you acknowledge that the Trolley Problem exists for self-driving cars, but argue that it is a rarity, an edge problem, a corner case.

Tell that to the people killed when your AI-based true self-driving car hits someone, doing so in that "rare" instance that will indisputably eventually arise.

Again, it is not going to hold any legal water.

Then there are the get-round-to-it earthers that acknowledge the Trolley Problem, and lament that you are so busy right now that it is low on the priority list, and pledge that one day, when time permits, you are going to deal with it.

There really is little difference between the rare earthers and the get-round-to-it earthers, and either way, they are going to have quite some explaining to do to a jury and a judge when the time comes.

Here's what the automakers and self-driving tech firms should be doing:

- Develop a sensible and explicit strategy about the Trolley Problem
- Craft a viable plan that entails the development of AI to cope with the Trolley Problem
- Undertake appropriate testing of the AI to ascertain the Trolley Problem handling
- Rollout when so readied the AI capabilities and monitor for usage
- Adjust and enhance the AI as feasible to increasingly improve Trolley Problem handling

CHAPTER 7
AI ETHICS SELF-LEARNED BY AI

Aristotle famously stated that educating the mind without educating the heart is no education at all.

You could interpret that insightful remark to suggest that learning about ethics and moral behavior is keenly vital for humankind. In the classic nature versus nurture debate, one must ask how much of our ethical mores are instinctively native while how much is learned over the course of our living days. Toddlers are observant of fellow humans and presumably glean their ethical foundations based on what they see and hear. The same can be said of teenagers. For open-minded adults, they too will continue to adjust and progress in their ethical thinking as a result of experiencing the everyday world.

Of course, explicitly teaching someone about ethics is also par for the course. People are bound to learn about ethical ways via attending classes on the topic or perhaps by going to events and practices of interest to them. Ethical values can be plainly identified and shared as a means to aid others in formulating their own structure of ethics. In addition, ethics might be subtly hidden within stories or other instructional modes that ultimately carry a message of what ethical behavior consists of.

That's how humans seem to imbue ethics.

What about Artificial Intelligence (AI)?

I realize such a question might seem oddish. We certainly expect humans to incorporate ethics and walk through life with some semblance of a moral code. It is a simple and obvious fact. On the other hand, a machine or computer does not seem to fit within that same frame of reference.

Your gut reaction might be that it is farfetched or outlandish to consider AI as having an embodiment of ethics and moral codes.

The best that we would seem to be able to do about AI is devise it so that it does not deviate from ethical behavior. AI developers and those fielding AI are to be held responsible for ensuring that the AI as designed and has implemented is already in conformance with ethical precepts. Out the gate, so to speak, the AI ought to already be pristine and ready to go as a fully ethically proper contrivance.

You would assuredly be right in thinking that AI systems should indeed be crafted to already fit entirely within an ethical basis. Society was quite excited when the latest wave of AI systems was first released and appeared to demonstrate that we were in an era of *AI For Good.* AI would aid in solving many of the world's most challenging problems. Advances in technology were being harnessed to supplement human capabilities with cognitive-like facilities, though allow me to emphasize that we do not yet have any sentient AI and we don't know if sentient AI will be attained.

The problem with the pell-mell rush to get AI into the world has gradually revealed the ugly underbelly of AI known as *AI For Bad.* There have been lots of headlines about AI systems that make use of algorithmic decision making (ADM) that is replete with biases and inequities. On top of that, much of the contemporary AI suffers from a lack of transparency, tends to be inexplicable in terms of explaining computational decisions, frequently exhibits a lack of fairness, and has allowed some to divert their human accountability by pointing fingers at AI.

How can there be *AI For Bad* if we take as a stated construct that AI ought to be crafted from the beginning to avoid unethical actions?

The answer is multi-fold.

First, many AI developers and companies fielding AI are themselves clueless about the importance of shaping their AI to stay within ethical boundaries. The concept isn't at all on their radar.

The allure of making fast money causes some to push ahead on whatever wild AI notions they wish to willfully produce. No need to figure out any ethical stuff. Just build the AI and get it underway.

Secondly, there are those making AI that embellish an outright awareness of the ethical ramifications, but they overtly downplay or somewhat ignore the Ethical AI considerations. One common perspective is the techie classic mantra of aiming to fail fast and fail often. Just keep iterating until things hopefully get suitably settled. The chances of squeezing any systematic and thoughtful incorporation of AI ethics into those rapid-fire AI efforts is regrettably slim.

Thirdly, a lot of murkiness exists about what ethical guardrails should be entertained when devising AI. Sure, there are nowadays many AI ethics guidelines though these handy theoretical precepts are hard to necessarily turn into specifics for a given AI system being built. I've indicated that we will slowly see an emergence of AI building tools and methodologies that include Ethical AI coding practices, helping to close the gap between the abstract aspects and the proverbial rubber-meets-the-road facets.

Fourthly, per the emphasis herein, we explore the affected case of AI that even if initially composed within ethical boundaries then subsequently while in use meanders beyond the assumed ethically encoded parameters.

We need to unpack that.

Much of today's AI makes use of Machine Learning (ML) and Deep Learning (DL). These are computational pattern matching techniques and technologies. Generally, the idea is that you collect together lots of relevant data to whatever the AI is supposed to be able to do, you feed that data into the chosen computational pattern matcher, and the pattern matching mathematically tries to find useful patterns. Note that there isn't any sentience on the part of this AI (which, again, no such thing yet exists). Nor is there any common-sense reasoning involved. It is all math and computations.

It could be that the data fed into the ML/DL is already infused with biases and inequities. In that case, the odds are that the computational pattern matching will merely mimic the same proclivities. If you provide data that favors one race over another or favors one gender over the other, there is a sizable chance that the pattern matching will latch onto that as the discovered pattern.

A big problem with that kind of latching is that we might have a difficult time ferreting out that the patterns are based on that aspect of the data. The thorny and complex mathematics can make the surfacing of such found patterns quite problematic. Even testing the AI is not necessarily going to reveal those tendencies, depending upon the range and depth of tests that are applied.

So, let's assume that you've built an AI system and did your homework by first trying to avoid using data that had preexisting biases. Next, once the Machine Learning and Deep Learning had been undertaken, you tested the results to see if any biases or inequities somehow arose. Let's assume that you are unable to find any such untoward inclinations.

All told, the green light is now given to go ahead and put the AI into use. People will start using the AI and likely assume that it is ethically proper. The developers think this too. The company fielding the AI thinks this. Away we all go.

Here's what can happen.

An inkling of a bias that wasn't found in the original data and that wasn't caught during the testing of the AI is perchance activated. Perhaps this only happens rarely. You might believe that as long as it is rare, all is well. I doubt though that those vulnerable to the said bias are willing to see things that way. I dare say that the AI system and those that formulated it are going to confront repercussions, either in the legal courts or in the open-ended court of societal opinion.

Another variation is the proverbial notion of taking an inch and grabbing a mile. The inkling might initially be tiny. During the use of the AI, the AI might have been devised to alter itself as things go along.

This kind of "learning" or "self-learning" can be quite useful. Rather than requiring human-AI developers to continually modify and adjust the AI system, the AI is built to do so by itself. No delays, no expensive labor, etc.

The downside of this handy self-adjustment is that the inkling can get elevated to being larger and larger within the scope of usage by the AI. Whereas the bias might have been in a tight little corner, it now is given room to expand. The AI has no semblance that this is "wrong" and merely computationally extends something that seems to be working.

If that makes the hair stand on your head, you'll need to sit down for the next variant.

Suppose the bias wasn't existent from the get-go and we have every reasoned belief that the AI is entirely bias-free. We either got lucky or perchance systematically made sure that no biases were anywhere in the data and none arose via the computational pattern matching. Despite that sigh of relief, the AI is allowed to adjust while in use. Pandora's door is opened and the AI opts to computationally gravitate toward biases that are found during whatever it is the AI does.

A newfound bias gets gobbled up into the AI, and no one is particularly the wiser that it has happened. Yikes, we have created a monster, a veritable Frankenstein.

How can this emergence be possibly prevented or at least flagged?

One approach that is gaining traction consists of building into the AI an ethics gleaning component. The AI is constructed to include Ethical AI elements. Those elements then watch or monitor the rest of the AI while the AI is adjusting over time. When the AI appears to have gone beyond the programmed ethical precepts, the Ethical AI tries to rope in those adjustments or alerts the developers that something has gone amiss.

You can try programming this Ethical AI overseeing capacity and hope that it will prevail while the AI is in use.

Another somewhat controversial angle would be to use Machine Learning and Deep Learning to train the Ethical AI aspects into the AI system.

Say what?

Yes, the perhaps unorthodox concept is that instead of a human programmer directly encoding a set of AI ethics precepts, the AI is shaped to try and "learn" them instead. Recall that I briefly noted that the use of ML/DL typically relies upon feeding data into the algorithms and a computational pattern matching takes place. The million-dollar question is whether we can use the same mechanism to inoculate ethical values into an AI system.

I suppose you could liken this to my discussion at the opening of how humans become aware of ethical principles, though please do not anthropomorphize today's AI as being comparable to human thinking (it is not, and I'll repeat that exhortation shortly). The AI can be programmed "innately" with ethical AI precepts. Or the AI could "learn" ethical AI precepts. You can do both, of course.

Take a moment to ponder the seemingly startling concept that AI might "learn" ethics and ergo presumably abide by ethical behaviors.

These researchers use an example of an AI system that figures out the desired temperature in a house to illustrate how this can work: "It first 'observed' the behavior of the people in various households for merely a week and drew conclusions about their preferences. It then used a motion-detecting sensor to determine whether anyone was at home. When the house was empty, the smart thermostat entered a high energy saving mode; when people were at home, the thermostat adjusted the temperature to fit their preferences. This thermostat clearly meets the two requirements of an ethics bot, albeit a very simple one. It assesses people's preferences and imposes them on the controls of the heating and cooling system. One may ask what this has to do with social moral values. This thermostat enables people with differing values to have the temperature settings they prefer. The residents of the home do not need to reset the thermostat every day when coming and going. This simple ethics bot also reduces the total energy footprint of the community" (per the paper by Amitai Etzioni and Oren Etzioni entitled "AI Assisted Ethics" in the volume on *Ethics and Information Technology*).

Before I dig further into the twists and turns of having AI that "learns" ethical behavior, I would like to say something more about the status of AI.

AI can consist of these possible states:

1. Non-sentient plain-old AI of today
2. Sentient AI of human quality (we don't have this as yet)
3. Sentient AI that is super-intelligent (a stretch beyond #2)

I am going to focus on the existing state which is non-sentient plain-old AI. Much of what you might read about Ethical AI at times cover the sentient AI and is therefore highly speculative. I say it is speculative because no one can pin the tail on the donkey of what sentient AI will be. Even further beyond the realm of human quality sentient AI is the much-ballyhooed super-intelligent AI. There are lots of sci-fi stories and qualms about how those flavors of AI might decide to enslave humankind, or maybe just wipe us all out. This is known as the existential risk of AI. At times, the dilemma is also phrased as the catastrophic risk of AI.

Some contend that we might be okay as long as we keep AI to the non-sentient plain-old AI that we have today. Let's assume we cannot reach sentient AI. Imagine that no matter how hard we try to craft sentient AI, we fail at doing so. As well, assume for sake of discussion that sentient AI doesn't arise by some mysterious spontaneous process.

Aren't we then safe that this lesser caliber AI, which is the imagined only possible kind of AI, will be in use?

Not really.

Pretty much, the same general issues are likely to arise. I'm not suggesting that the AI "thinks" its way to wanting to destroy us. No, the ordinary non-sentient AI is merely placed into positions of power that get us mired in self-destruction. For example, we put non-sentient AI into weapons of mass destruction. These autonomous weapons are not able to think. At the same time, humans are not kept fully in the loop. As a result, the AI as a form of autonomous automation ends up inadvertently causing catastrophic results, either by a human command to do so, or by a bug or error, or by implanted evildoing, or by self-adjustments that lead matters down that ugly path, etc.

I would contend that the AI ethics problem exists for all three of those AI stipulated states, namely that we have AI ethical issues with non-sentient plain-old AI, and with sentient AI that is either merely human level or the outstretched AI that reaches the acclaimed superintelligence level.

Given that sobering pronouncement, we can assuredly debate the magnitude and difficulty associated with the ethical problems at each of the respective levels of AI. The customary viewpoint is that the AI ethics predicament is less insurmountable at the non-sentient AI, tougher at the sentient human-equal AI level, and a true head-scratcher at the sentient super-intelligent AI stage of affairs.

The better the AI becomes, the worse the AI ethics problem becomes.

Maybe that is an inviolable law of nature.

Returning to the focus on today's AI, trying to have AI "learn" ethical behaviors via contemporary Machine Learning and Deep Learning is fraught with concerns and tricky problems. Suppose the AI fails to glean the desired ethical precepts? How will we know for sure that it faltered in doing so? Also, will other parts of an AI system potentially override the gleaned ethical constructs? Add to this that if the AI is adjusting on the fly, the adjustments could thin down the ethical aspects or inadvertently overwhelm them altogether.

To make matters worse, the "learning" might lead to the AI landing on truly unethical behaviors. Whereas we thought that we were doing the right thing by prodding the AI toward being ethical, it turns out that the AI slipped into pattern matching on the unethical aspects instead. Talk about shooting our own foot, it could absolutely happen.

At this juncture of this discussion, I'd bet that you are desirous of some additional real-world examples that could highlight how AI the "learning" of ethics might apply to today's AI (other than the tasty teaser of the thermostat example).

I'm glad you asked.

There is a special and assuredly popular set of examples that are close to my heart. You see, in my capacity as an expert on AI including the ethical and legal ramifications, I am frequently asked to identify realistic examples that showcase AI Ethics dilemmas so that the somewhat theoretical nature of the topic can be more readily grasped. One of the most evocative areas that vividly presents this ethical AI quandary is the advent of AI-based true self-driving cars. This will serve as a handy use case or exemplar for ample discussion on the topic.

Here's then a noteworthy question that is worth contemplating: *Does the advent of AI-based true self-driving cars illuminate anything about the AI being able to "learn" Ethical AI precepts, and if so, what does this showcase?*

Allow me a moment to unpack the question.

Imbuing Ethical AI

For Level 4 and Level 5 true self-driving vehicles, there won't be a human driver involved in the driving task. All occupants will be passengers. The AI is doing the driving.

Let's use a readily straightforward example. An AI-based self-driving car is underway on your neighborhood streets and seems to be driving safely. At first, you had devoted special attention to each time that you managed to catch a glimpse of the self-driving car. The autonomous vehicle stood out with its rack of electronic sensors that included video cameras, radar units, LIDAR devices, and the like. After many weeks of the self-driving car cruising around your community, you now barely notice it. As far as you are concerned, it is merely another car on the already busy public roadways.

Lest you think it is impossible or implausible to become familiar with seeing self-driving cars, I've written frequently about how the locales that are within the scope of self-driving car tryouts have gradually gotten used to seeing the spruced-up vehicles. Many of the locals eventually shifted from mouth-gaping rapt gawking to now emitting an expansive yawn of boredom to witness those meandering self-driving cars.

Probably the main reason right now that they might notice the autonomous vehicles is because of the irritation and exasperation factor. The by-the-book AI driving systems make sure the cars are obeying all speed limits and rules of the road. For hectic human drivers in their traditional human-driven cars, you get irked at times when stuck behind the strictly law-abiding AI-based self-driving cars.

That's something we might all need to get accustomed to, rightfully or wrongly.

Back to our tale. One day, suppose a self-driving car in your town or city is driving along and comes upon a situation wherein a pedestrian is waiting to cross the road. Assume that the pedestrian does not have the right-of-way per se. A human-driven car could go past the pedestrian and be entirely legal in doing so. Likewise, the AI driving system is legally able to go past the waiting pedestrian.

Deciding whether to stop and let the pedestrian go across the street is entirely discretionary for the driver, regardless of whether being a human driver or an AI driving system.

I'm sure that you've encountered this kind of situation an innumerable number of times. Maybe you are in a hurry, so you don't stop to let the pedestrian cross. On another occasion, you have plenty of time to get to your destination, thus you opt to stop and allow the waiting person to walk across the street. Your mood and the particular circumstances dictate what you will choose to do.

Nothing about this scenario seems unusual or vexing.

Before I examine the AI side of things, you might be interested to know that this particular aspect of discretion allowing a pedestrian to cross a street has been closely studied. Researchers have identified that at times the choice made by the driver can depend apparently on racial or gender biases. A human driver might size up the waiting pedestrian and opt to allow the person to cross as seemingly based on the inherent biases of the driver. Whether the driver even realizes they are doing so is a matter of ongoing research.

I have set the stage for our exploring what an AI driving system might do in the pedestrian crossing situation.

Conventional programming of the AI might entail that the AI developers decide to always have the AI driving system come to a stop and let the pedestrian cross. This would seem to be the ethically proper or civil thing to do. The self-driving car defers to the waiting human that wants to cross the street.

I dare say, if you were a passenger inside a self-driving car and the AI always stopped for all discretionary awaiting pedestrians, you might go nuts. Your quick trip to the grocery store might take many times longer to occur. Remember too that we are not referring to pedestrians that have the devout legal right of way to cross, since those cases would presumably already have the AI programmed to always allow. We are only focusing on the discretionary circumstances.

There are more downsides to this declaration of always stopping to let discretionary pedestrians cross the street.

Those that make and field AI-based self-driving cars want people to ride in them. The idea is that by having self-driving cars, we might reduce the number of annual car crashes, which currently produce about 40,000 annual fatalities and 2.5 million injuries in the United States alone. Besides this revered societal goal, the automakers and self-driving tech makers hope to make money off their AI creations too, naturally so.

I bring this up because people might decide to not ride in self-driving cars if the AI driving system does things that *unnecessarily* end up delaying trips. Any everyday person would reason that by instead choosing a human driver the journey might be faster, and ergo selecting an AI self-driving car for a trip might get placed very low on the list of their choices. This in turn would mean that we would not have the sought reduction in car crashes and also that the makers would potentially find their wares to be unprofitable.

Given that set of arguments, you might be swayed to think that the AI should never stop when a discretionary instance of a pedestrian wanting to cross the street occurs. Just program the AI driving system to do whatever is strictly legal. If there is no legal requirement to let a pedestrian cross, then tough luck for that waiting pedestrian. Perhaps the person should make their way to a crossing point that does allow for a legal basis of the AI stopping the self-driving car.

Can you imagine the outcry on this?

People in your town or city discover gradually that AI self-driving cars will never allow a discretionary pedestrian to cross. That darned irascible AI! It is as though the AI is thumbing its nose at humans. An ill-mannered brat of a piece of no-good automation. To top this off, imagine that there are documented circumstances of pedestrians desperately needing to cross and the AI wouldn't stop at all.

Meanwhile, human drivers were willingly stopping to let those "desperate" people safely get across the street.

As a result of this outrage, AI self-driving cars are no longer welcomed on the streets and byways of your locale. Permits that had been issued by the city leaders are revoked. Getting the ungrateful brutes off our roadways is the vocal clamor.

Alright, we seem to be between a rock and hard place. The AI shouldn't always let the discretionary pedestrian cross (do not always stop). The AI shouldn't always prevent a discretionary pedestrian from crossing (do not always zoom past). What to do?

The obvious answer would be to program the AI to act in a discretionary manner.

I ask you to contemplate the ADM (algorithmic decision making) that this ought to consist of. Will the AI try to detect the nature of the pedestrian and use the discerned characteristics as a basis for deciding whether to stop the self-driving car or not? Maybe someone older looking is the way to choose. But is that age discrimination in the making? And so on.

Perhaps the AI driving system is programmed to stop during daylight hours and never stop during nighttime. The logic possibly being that it is presumed safer for the riders in the self-driving car that the autonomous vehicle comes to a halt at daytime but not at the leerier hours of the evening time.

That maybe sounds sensible. Part of the problem will be the expectations of pedestrians. Here's what I mean. Pedestrians see the AI self-driving cars stopping for discretionary crossings, which happen in daylight. The pedestrians do not know what criteria the AI is using to decide to stop. The assumption by some pedestrians is that the AI will always stop (not realizing that daylight versus nighttime is the true determiner). As a result, those pedestrians that believe the self-driving car will always stop are going to take a chance and start to cross when the AI driving system is not at all aiming to stop (which, the AI would likely come to a stop if the pedestrian is entering into the street, though this could be dicey and physics might preclude the AI from stopping the self-driving car insufficient time to avoid hitting the seemingly "errant" pedestrian).

Assume that the AI developers and the firms putting together and fielding the self-driving cars in your town are unsure of how to get the AI up-to-speed on this matter.

They decide to "train" the AI on data collected from throughout the locale. Turns out that there are plenty of city-mounted cameras that have captured the comings and goings of cars throughout the township. This data showcases many instances of pedestrians seeking to cross the street in a discretionary manner. All of the data is fed into a Machine Learning and Deep Learning system to derive what is considered customary in that jurisdiction.

Are we training the AI to do what local ethical mores showcase to be done?

In other words, if a given town had a local cultural more of tending to stop and let discretionary pedestrians cross as evidenced by human driver actions, the ML/DL would potentially pick up computationally on this pattern. The AI would then be trained to do likewise. At the other extreme, if the human drivers seldom stop, the AI would potentially get that "lesson" from computationally analyzing the data. The AI will do as humans do, kind of.

The assertion is that the ethical behaviors of humans are being captured in the data and that the AI is going to inoculate those same ethical precepts by computational analysis. An ethicist would generally describe this as a communitarian approach to ethics. The shared values of the community are reflected in the efforts of the community at large.

This might seem like a dandy solution.

Unfortunately, there are lots of pitfalls.

One perhaps obvious problem is that the human drivers might already be exercising some form of biases in choosing to stop or not stop (as mentioned earlier). The AI will then be a copycat of these biases. Do we want that to be the case?

Consider another problem. Suppose that human drivers are not readily accepting of how the AI self-driving cars are operating. Just because human drivers were let's say willing to stop, this might not be equally presumed for self-driving cars. It could be that human drivers get irked by the AI self-driving cars that keep stopping for discretionary pedestrians, even though the same happens by the hands of human drivers but that doesn't seem to disturb human drivers.

Besides being disturbing, you can also conjure the possibility of human drivers inadvertently rear-ending self-driving cars. If a human driver wasn't expecting the self-driving car to stop for a pedestrian, and if the human-driven car is directly behind the self-driving car, a dire mismatch of expectations can arise. The AI driving system brings the self-driving car to a stop. The human driver didn't anticipate this action. The human driver slams into the self-driving car. Injuries and possibly fatalities ensue.

I purposely pointed out the chances of human harm.

The pedestrian crossing the street might seem at a quick glance as a trivial question. It would seem that nobody can get hurt by whichever method the AI chooses to stop or not stop. Wrong! There is a chance of the pedestrian getting run over. There is a chance of a human-driven car ramming into the self-driving car. The driver and passengers of the human-driven car can get hurt. The riders inside the self-driving car can get harmed. Additional permutations of possible human harm are readily envisioned.

Conclusion

Speaking of human harm, I'll give you something else to get your minds roiling on this Ethical AI conundrum.

A news story reported that a man was driving a car into an intersection and had a green light to do so. Another human-driven car opted to run the red light of the intersection and illegally and unsafely went unimpeded into the intersection, threatening to strike the legally proceeding car.

The driver told reporters that he had to choose between taking the hit, or he could veer his car to hopefully avoid getting struck, but there were pedestrians nearby and the veering action could endanger those people. What would you do? You can choose to get hit by this looming car and maybe live to tell the tale. Or you can attempt to avoid getting hit but meanwhile possibly running down innocent pedestrians.

Much of our daily driving has those kinds of ethically enormous and instantaneous decisions to be made. I have discussed this at length, along with relating these life-or-death driving decisions to the famous or some say infamous Trolley Problem.

Replace the human driver in this scenario with an AI driving system.

What do you want the AI to do?

That's a perplexing question.

One approach is to program the AI to stridently do purely straight-ahead driving action, thusly not even computationally considering other options such as veering away from the likely crash. I would anticipate that riders in self-driving cars are going to be upset to find out that the AI was not devised to do anything other than taking the hit. You can expect lawsuits and an uproar.

Another approach would be to try and program the AI to consider the various possibilities. Who though gets to establish the ADM that decides which way the AI driving system would go? It would seem that allowing AI developers to make such weighty decisions on their own is fraught with abundant concerns.

You could try to let the AI "learn" from human driving data collected by day-to-day traffic situations. This is akin to the pedestrian crossing dilemma and the earlier suggested idea of using assembled data to have the AI glean whatever the local ethical mores seemed to be. There are lots of caveats about that, such as whether the ML/DL discovered patterns are apt or not, etc.

I had also forewarned that there is a chance of the AI gleaning perhaps unethical behavior, depending upon the ethical mores involved. For example, suppose the AI somehow landed on a computational pattern to always aim at the pedestrians whenever another car was threatening to strike the self-driving car.

Whoa, watch out pedestrians, you are going to be ready-made targets.

Time to close the discussion for now and do so with a heartening final thought.

You might be aware that Isaac Asimov proposed his "Three Laws Of Robotics" in 1950 and we are still to this day enamored of those proclaimed rules. Though the rules appear to be readily abideable, such as that an AI system or robot shall not harm a human and nor allow a human to come to harm, there are lots of crucial nuances that render this complex and at times untenable.

In any case, here's something else that Asimov is also known for, though lesser so: "Never let your sense of morals get in the way of doing what's right."

For the Ethical AI that we all hope to devise, we have to keep in mind that the AI ethics imbued might not be what we anticipated and that somehow the AI will still need to do whatever is right. Asimov said it well. Long before, Aristotle seemed to be thinking quite similar sentiments.

CHAPTER 8
ETHICAL AI MONITORING OF UNETHICAL AI

It takes one to know one.

I'm sure you've heard that old saying before. Whenever the sage piece of wisdom is employed, I tend to immediately think of the famous comic strip called *Spy vs. Spy*. The revered satirical look at spies and acts of espionage was originally started in the 1960s during the Cold War era. For those of you that have not seen the comical portrayals, which are still being issued to this day, the plot is very simple. Two spies of opposing sides are continually battling against each other. They cleverly try to outsmart the other.

Well, actually, sometimes they clumsily try to outsmart each other. Their contrivances of trickery often backfire or go flat.

You might be wondering, which of the two spies wins?

The answer is that sometimes one of them wins and at other times the opposing spy wins. On top of that, there is a chance too that both will win, plus there are many circumstances that they both lose in their ongoing epic battles. The nice thing about the comic strip is that it is pretty much in jest and contains good clean fun.

You could interpret their antics as showcasing that it takes one to know one. Whatever one of the spies tries to do, amazingly the other spy frequently anticipates and avoids getting ensnared accordingly. They can nearly read each other's minds. This makes sense in that they are both assumed as equally versed in spycraft. The natural inclination would be to reach a stalemate. Of course, there is always the opportunity of being a tad sneakier and one prevails over the other. This doesn't seem to be the case in the long run since the wins and losses of each respective spy appear to balance out eventually.

I bring up the head-to-head tussle as a means of illustrating an interesting new avenue entailing Artificial Intelligence (AI).

First, please know that when the latest era of AI began to arise there was tremendous anticipation that we would finally witness *AI For Good*. This would be AI that could aid in solving many of the world's most vexing problems. AI could tackle our worries about global hunger or worldwide poverty. The goodness that AI might derive via being appropriately devised seemed nearly endless.

There was a gradual realization that there is also the dour side of AI that is typically referred to as *AI For Bad*. For example, AI used for facial recognition was shown to at times contain racial biases or gender biases. Numerous inequities have since then been appearing in a wide variety of AI systems. This has also prompted the realization that we earnestly need AI ethics and must stridently seek to design, build, and field so-called Ethical AI.

One of the most vocalized ways of trying to assure that AI works in ethically suitable ways involves getting AI developers and the firms that deploy or utilize AI to abide by crucial AI ethics precepts. The idea is that AI ought to be ethically infused from the ground up. Rather than waiting to see whether an AI system is going to drift into the *AI For Bad* camp, the hope is that the coded underpinnings will be solidly ethically sound from day one.

A nagging problem with simply relying on constructing AI as an ethically sufficient system is that the AI might inexorably shift into an unethical realm. A possibility especially exists as partially based on AI that uses Machine Learning (ML) or Deep Learning (DL) as its basis. Machine Learning and Deep Learning ostensibly refer to the use of computational pattern matching techniques and technologies. Essentially, the AI is initially "trained" on a dataset that is supposed to represent the types of patterns that the ML/DL will eventually be seeking whilst in actual use. The mathematical patterns discovered are somewhat ingrained in the computer and reused whenever new data is presented.

For some ML/DL, the AI system is allowed to readapt by itself over time. The notion is a sensible one. In lieu of having AI developers constantly adjust the code, the AI does so itself by realigning based on the encountered data that arises during daily use of the AI. No need for the expensive human labor of those AI developers to be tinkering with the AI. No delays due to waiting for AI developers to make changes to the code. Instead, the AI changes itself.

What can happen though is that the AI wobbles toward unethical behaviors.

Those people using the AI or subject to the actions of the AI might not realize that the once ethical precepts are now being abridged. A lack of the AI having built-in transparency or explanatory capabilities can make the shift from ethical to unethical even harder to ferret out. The underlying guts of the AI are so byzantine that it might be entirely impenetrable as to what is going on in the arcane mathematical complexities.

Before we go much further in this discussion, I do want to emphasize that today's AI is not sentient. Despite those blaring and false headlines that keep getting outstretched attention, there isn't any AI today that embodies sentience. Not even close. Furthermore, we don't know if AI sentience is possible. Maybe it is, maybe not. I would also like to clarify that no one can accurately predict when we will attain sentient AI, nor whether we will genuinely get there either by skill, luck, or pure happenstance.

I bring up that important point to make sure we are all on the same page. Contemporary AI is not "thinking" in any comparable way to human thinking. There is an urge to anthropomorphize AI, which is an improper allusion and can lead to dangerous assumptions and dire outcomes. I'll say more about this in a moment.

Returning to the mainstay here, if AI systems are being devised and released that will potentially veer from ethical behavior to unethical behavior, we have to ask what can be done to stop or mitigate this undesirable transformation. A recently emerging trend consists of trying to build ethical guardrails into the AI that will catch as the rest of an AI system begins to go beyond preset ethical boundaries. In a sense, the goal is to use the AI itself to keep itself from going ethically awry.

You could say that we are aiming to have AI heal itself.

Using that same form of logical thinking, we might seek to create separate and distinct AI that will be a watchdog over other AI. This is a similar conceptual principle as healing thyself though done in a different manner. Perhaps we might refer to this as AI healing other AI.

You see, the problem with inserting into any particular AI system an embedded ethical guiding component could be that the elements are going to be corrupted or somehow overturned by the rest of the AI. I'm not out of hand saying that this adverse undermining will always happen. Hopefully, it won't arise and the internal AI elements will keep the rest of the given AI in strict ethical order. In essence, I am applauding the use of an embedded self-correcting mechanism as a wise approach and ought to certainly be undertaken.

In addition, using an external AI system that monitors the other AI would be a helpful second look in case the embedded self-check isn't up to par or falters, or is tainted. Some refer to AI that sits around and tries to double-check the ethical behaviors of other AI systems as a *second-order AI*. This particular kind of AI is customarily built specifically and solely as a double-checker.

I mention this because there can be AI that oversees other AI and for which the overseeing AI has other duties besides being a double-checker. Some would argue that this double-duty is too much. If you are going to create a monitoring AI then let it do just that. Any other functionality might get in the way of the double-checking role or usurp the computational attention toward monitoring other AI.

A beauty about using AI to watch over other AI is that it somewhat relieves humans from having to do the same. Imagine the number of humans that might be needed to try and oversee a large-scale AI system that is providing services to thousands or possibly millions of people. Trying to examine the AI to detect whether the AI has gone astray of ethical precepts could be highly laborious. In addition, the AI might be working so fast that having humans trying to discern what ethically unsavory actions are occurring is just not feasible at human comprehension speeds.

All told, it makes sense to use automation against automation, or in this case, use AI against AI.

I suppose you could say that it takes one to know one.

Remarkably, we are finding ourselves entering into a real-world version of *Spy vs. Spy*. An AI system is created to do some hopefully useful activities. Another AI system is crafted to watch over that AI. When the overseeing AI detects potentially unethical behaviors, the matter can possibly be quickly dealt with. The AI that is doing the double-checking might halt the offending AI. Or the double-checker might alert humans that the affronting AI is acting up and let the humans decide what to do about it.

We could even devise the overseeing AI to try and force the offending AI to revert back into employing ethical behaviors. Thus, rather than merely blankly stopping the affronting AI, the overseeing AI tries to serve as an ethical coach that steers the *AI For Bad* into the realm of *AI For Good.* Be aware that this can be a tricky proposition. It could be that the attempt to steer the offending AI goes poorly and the adverse AI continues unabated. Worse still, the steering might inadvertently push the AI into even worsening unethical territory.

There is no free lunch when it comes to using AI to double-check other AI.

As a result of the possible erroneous actions that a double-checking AI might perform, the perhaps easiest and less controversial second-order AI consists of *spotter AI*. A spotter AI system is made to only spot the unethical antics of other AI and do nothing other than raising a red flag. The spotter is not intended to take corrective efforts. Analogous somewhat to a faithful guard dog, the spotter AI is supposed to start barking loudly and incessantly to forewarn that Ethical AI bells need to be rung. Someone or something else then opts to take any needed corrective action.

I'm guessing that you are potentially convinced that having spotter AI or something akin to it is a wise move and should be straightforward to construct. There is unfortunately a twist that makes this harder than it might seem at first glance. Let's unpack the twist.

Recall the *Spy vs. Spy* comic strip.

As earlier mentioned, the two spies are always at odds with each other. Whatever one spy devises, the other one tends to figure out. They are closely matched. Sometimes one wins, sometimes the other one wins.

The same conundrum can arise with double-checking AI. The double-checker is crafted to oversee an AI system. The double-checker spots what seems to be unethical AI behavior. It could be that the AI veering into unethical AI can discern that the double-checker AI is catching on. So, the unethical AI then tries to hide the unethical behavior or shift toward other unethical AI behavior that the double-checker has not yet detected.

A proverbial cat-and-mouse gambit.

Throughout all of this, I'll repeat that I am not referring to sentient AI. In the theoretical case of some future sentient AI, perhaps this type of scheming might be done via humanly intelligent artificial ways. We can ponder and postulate about that until the cows come home. For contemporary real-world purposes, the AI that is seeking to escape the detection of the overseeing AI is doing so for computational programming reasons and not due to a human scheming basis per se.

Why would an AI system try to baffle some other AI?

It could be that the developers of the veering AI were aware that there might be double-checking AI that would be used to catch their AI. As such, they purposely constructed elements for the AI to be evasive. You could say that this consists of bad actors that intentionally devise *AI For Bad* systems. Envision that criminals making AI are aware that the government or law enforcement is releasing spotter AI that attempts to find the wrongdoing AI. The cat and the mouse as AI are being trained by humans to play the cat-and-mouse gambit, as it were.

You would be mistaken though to assume that this kind of evasiveness will only occur when a bad actor human unleashes *AI For Bad.* Here's an angle that many do not realize are equally plausible. An AI system is created with various cybersecurity precautions. The idea is that the AI is supposed to ascertain when it is possibly being hacked. One response might be that the AI shifts its efforts according to what the programming suggests should be adjusted when under cyberattack.

Meanwhile, this same protective measure gets activated when a faithful spotter AI is detected by the AI that was set up with the cybersecurity mechanisms. Regrettably, the AI veers into unethical behavior as activated by what it thought was a cyberattack attempt. The response by the AI wasn't what was originally intended. Nonetheless, the AI goes into an unethical realm that was ironically activated by the double-checking AI that was trying to prevent or slow down any ethically untoward actions.

Makes your head spin.

At this juncture of this discussion, I'd bet that you are desirous of some handy real-world examples that could highlight the AI versus AI uses when it comes to Ethical AI.

I'm glad you asked.

There is a special and assuredly popular set of examples that are close to my heart. You see, in my capacity as an expert on AI including the ethical and legal ramifications, I am frequently asked to identify realistic examples that showcase AI Ethics dilemmas so that the somewhat theoretical nature of the topic can be more readily grasped. One of the most evocative areas that vividly presents this ethical AI quandary is the advent of AI-based true self-driving cars. This will serve as a handy use case or exemplar for ample discussion on the topic.

Here's then a noteworthy question that is worth contemplating: *Does the advent of AI-based true self-driving cars illuminate anything about AI versus AI in the context of Ethical AI, and if so, what does this showcase?*

Allow me a moment to unpack the question.

Overseeing Ethical AI

For Level 4 and Level 5 true self-driving vehicles, there won't be a human driver involved in the driving task. All occupants will be passengers. The AI is doing the driving.

Let's use a readily straightforward example. An AI-based self-driving car is underway on your neighborhood streets and seems to be driving safely. At first, you had devoted special attention to each time that you managed to catch a glimpse of the self-driving car. The autonomous vehicle stood out with its rack of electronic sensors that included video cameras, radar units, LIDAR devices, and the like. After many weeks of the self-driving car cruising around your community, you now barely notice it. As far as you are concerned, it is merely another car on the already busy public roadways.

Lest you think it is impossible or implausible to become familiar with seeing self-driving cars, I've written frequently about how the locales that are within the scope of self-driving car tryouts have gradually gotten used to seeing the spruced-up vehicles.

Many of the locals eventually shifted from mouth-gaping rapt gawking to now emitting an expansive yawn of boredom to witness those meandering self-driving cars.

Probably the main reason right now that they might notice the autonomous vehicles is because of the irritation and exasperation factor. The by-the-book AI driving systems make sure the cars are obeying all speed limits and rules of the road. For hectic human drivers in their traditional human-driven cars, you get irked at times when stuck behind the strictly law-abiding AI-based self-driving cars.

That's something we might all need to get accustomed to, rightfully or wrongly.

Back to our tale. One day, suppose a self-driving car in your town or city is driving along and comes upon a situation wherein a pedestrian is waiting to cross the road. Assume that the pedestrian does not have the right-of-way per se. A human-driven car could go past the pedestrian and be entirely legal in doing so. Likewise, the AI driving system is legally able to go past the waiting pedestrian.

Deciding whether to stop and let the pedestrian go across the street is entirely discretionary for the driver, regardless of whether being a human driver or an AI driving system.

I'm sure that you've encountered this kind of situation an innumerable number of times. Maybe you are in a hurry, so you don't stop to let the pedestrian cross. On another occasion, you have plenty of time to get to your destination, thus you opt to stop and allow the waiting person to walk across the street. Your mood and the particular circumstances dictate what you will choose to do.

Nothing about this scenario seems unusual or vexing.

Before I examine the AI side of things, you might be interested to know that this particular aspect of discretion allowing a pedestrian to cross a street has been closely studied. Researchers have identified that at times the choice made by the driver can depend apparently on racial or gender biases.

A human driver might size up the waiting pedestrian and opt to allow the person to cross as seemingly based on the inherent biases of the driver. Whether the driver even realizes they are doing so is a matter of ongoing research.

Suppose that the AI driving system has been programmed to allow for discretion in choosing whether to stop or not stop for an awaiting pedestrian that wants to cross the street.

Of course, assume too that if the pedestrian is at a legally allowed crossing point and has the considered right-of-way, the AI is programmed to legally abide by driving laws and will always correspondingly stop to permit the pedestrian to cross the road. For the remainder of this discussion, keep in mind that we are referring only to circumstances of a pedestrian not having the right-of-way and that drivers of both human and AI kind are allowed discretion in what they opt to do.

By what method will the AI decide to stop or not stop?

One approach would be to merely randomly make the choice. The AI picks a random number and let's say that half of the time it will stop and half of the other time it won't stop. This seems imminently fair in that the nature of the pedestrian makes no difference whatsoever in the decision-making or ADM aspects. It is purely by chance alone.

Seemingly, no one can complain about this method. That being said, you can imagine that there might very well be complaints. Locals might decry that the AI self-driving car is scooting past senior citizens that are trying to cross, while perhaps human drivers are tending to stop and let them cross. The same might be happening with teenagers seeking to cross the street. Overall, when compared to human drivers, the AI is not using any semblance of common sense to make the crossing decision, whereas to some degree it is argued that humans are.

Another possible complaint is that locals are completely mystified by how the AI driving system is deciding to indeed stop for pedestrians. You see, the locals do not all realize that a random choice is being made. From the perspective of the community, the AI seems to have some secret method of choosing, and nobody can figure out what it is.

A vocalized concern is that maybe the AI is making the choice based on race or gender. This is just a wild guess and without any proof in hand, but the locals cannot envision that the AI is randomly choosing. Even if told that the AI is using a random selection process, some skeptics are doubtful that this is really the case. They figure that the claim of randomness is a disgraceful dodge and hide the reality that the AI was crafted to use some inequities as a selection method.

To try and ensure that the AI driving system is not somehow drifting toward a biased method, the automakers and self-driving tech firms opt to build an internal AI ethical guardrail that sits within the AI driving system. Acting as a self-checker, this new AI component observes the actions of the rest of the AI driving system to ascertain what is going on. Whenever an awaiting pedestrian situation arises as to a discretionary choice for the AI, the self-checker tries to make sure that the selection process is random and ergo considered fair for all.

Residents express cynicism about this approach. The wolf is being allowed to watch over the sheep, or something akin to that old adage, maybe that the wolf is watching itself while watching over the sheep (you get the idea).

The city comes up with a different idea. There are cameras mounted on various city light poles and other roadway infrastructure and these could be used to catch the self-driving cars in the act of stopping or not stopping for those discretionary awaiting pedestrians. It would be laborious though to cull through the zillions of hours of collected video.

An AI system is devised that will digitally examine the video. The AI will inspect all of the collected videos and even be able to do electronic digital analyses in real-time. Overall, the AI will be used as a spotter. It will detect when those discretionary moments arise. These will then be counted and the reported data will be made available for human scrutiny.

Besides city employees examining the AI "spotter" provided culled info, summaries and statistics are posted on the city website for all to see. The public can thusly participate in ascertaining what the self-driving cars seem to be doing. The hope is that this will allow residents to realize that there isn't seemingly any bias by the AI driving systems in this regard.

This scenario all told illustrates AI watching over other AI.

The city devised an AI spotter that is tracking the activities of the AI-based self-driving cars. As indicated, this is solely in an observing mode. The overseeing AI does not try to adjust the behavior of the AI driving systems.

Could that adjusting aspect be included?

Sure, here's how. We've indicated that the overseeing AI is able to access the video in real-time. The AI could be devised to send an electronic message to the AI driving system of a self-driving car.

For example, this might be done via V2I (vehicle-to-infrastructure) electronic communications. Some cities are already putting in place "smart" systems at intersections that emit electronic signals telling when the light is green and when it is red. A specialized device inside a nearby car can receive the signal. In the case of AI self-driving cars, the AI would then be aware of the intersection status, possibly getting a heads-up long before being within visible distance of detecting the traffic signal itself.

Via that same network, the overwatching AI could potentially send a signal to an in-motion self-driving car that instructs the AI driving system to stop for a pedestrian (alternatively, tell the self-driving car to not stop). Thus, beyond being a spotter, the AI could attempt to command the self-driving cars too.

As a side note, realize that this overseeing AI is not taking over the driving controls. Instead, the overseeing AI is simply requesting that the AI driving system bring the self-driving car to a halt and allow the pedestrian to cross. The AI driving system is still driving the car. In fact, the AI driving system might choose to ignore the "advisory" instruction and proceed apace. An expressed danger with allowing a remote operator of either a human or AI kind to directly affect the driving controls is multifold including cyberterrorists being able to undertake dastardly acts.

Conclusion

You might be wondering why the AI driving systems aren't simply reprogrammed to use some rules-of-thumb about the discretionary waiting pedestrians. The community seems dissatisfied with the random selection method. In that case, program the AI to use an overtly stipulated discretionary approach.

The specification of the rules could be done openly. Maybe the city leaders draft an approach and then seek public feedback. After arriving at whatever the city prefers, those rules are handed over to the automakers and self-driving tech firms to accordingly reprogram their AI driving systems.

I think you can guess that this won't fully solve the problem.

After the AI is instilled with a discretionary approach, the question abundantly will be asked as to whether the AI is doing as it is supposed to do. Again, this does not imply the AI is sentient and somehow making its own sentient-like choices. It could merely be that the AI developers did a lousy job of programming the AI. The rules are not accurately encoded into the AI. Or it could be that the AI has a bug or error that overrides the rules. And so on.

In short, the odds are that we would still want an AI overseeing capability. The notion of the city using an AI system that examines live video and recorded video would likely still be in the cards. A proverbial trust but verify would seem prudent in the case of AI systems.

Some of you might be mulling over a seemingly more simplified way to handle all of this. Why not program the AI driving systems to always stop for awaiting pedestrians? There isn't any decision left to interpretation. Always stop is the motto.

I dare say, if you were a passenger inside a self-driving car and the AI always stopped for all discretionary awaiting pedestrians, you might go nuts. Your quick trip to the grocery store might take many times longer to occur. Remember too that we are not referring to pedestrians that have the devout legal right of way to cross, since those cases would presumably already have the AI programmed to always allow. We are only focusing on the discretionary circumstances.

There are more downsides to this declaration of always stopping to let discretionary pedestrians cross the street.

Those that make and field AI-based self-driving cars want people to ride in them. The idea is that by having self-driving cars, we might reduce the number of annual car crashes, which currently produce about 40,000 annual fatalities and 2.5 million injuries in the United States alone. Besides this revered societal goal, the automakers and self-driving tech makers hope to make money off their AI creations too, naturally so.

I bring this up because people might decide to not ride in self-driving cars if the AI driving system does things that *unnecessarily* end up delaying trips. Any everyday person would reason that by instead choosing a human driver the journey might be faster, and ergo selecting an AI self-driving car for a trip might get placed very low on the list of their choices. This in turn would mean that we would not have the sought reduction in car crashes and also that the makers would potentially find their wares to be unprofitable.

Given that set of arguments, you might be swayed to think that the AI should never stop when a discretionary instance of a pedestrian wanting to cross the street occurs. Just program the AI driving system to do whatever is strictly legal. If there is no legal requirement to let a pedestrian cross, then tough luck for that waiting pedestrian. Perhaps the person should make their way to a crossing point that does allow for a legal basis of the AI stopping the self-driving car.

Can you imagine the outcry on this?

People in your town or city discover gradually that AI self-driving cars will never allow a discretionary pedestrian to cross. That darned irascible AI! It is as though the AI is thumbing its nose at humans. An ill-mannered brat of a piece of no-good automation. To top this off, imagine that there are documented circumstances of pedestrians desperately needing to cross and the AI wouldn't stop at all.

Meanwhile, human drivers were willingly stopping to let those "desperate" people safely get across the street.

As a result of this outrage, AI self-driving cars are no longer welcomed on the streets and byways of your locale. Permits that had been issued by the city leaders are revoked. Getting the ungrateful brutes off our roadways is the vocal clamor.

Alright, we seem to be between a rock and hard place. The AI shouldn't always let the discretionary pedestrian cross (do not always stop). The AI shouldn't always prevent a discretionary pedestrian from crossing (do not always zoom past). What to do?

The answer seems to be that the AI ought to be programmed with explicitly derived and stated rules, and then be monitored on both a self-check basis and by an external spotter AI (or via an AI that goes beyond spotting and proffers active double-checking and advising).

One final idea for you to noodle on.

We could use AI self-driving cars to potentially observe and tattle on other AI self-driving cars.

Here's how that might work. An AI self-driving car is driving along and scanning the nearby driving scene. Up ahead is another self-driving car. A pedestrian is waiting to cross on a discretionary basis. The self-driving car that is observing the up ahead driving scene is programmed to discern whether the other self-driving car halts to allow the pedestrian to cross. This is then reported to the city or some other authority.

Notice that strictly speaking the AI is not tattling on itself. The AI is monitoring the actions of another self-driving car. Some worry that this could get ugly in that automaker X and automaker Y might go to war with each other. The self-driving cars of automaker X are tattling on the self-driving cars of automaker Y. Presumably, this is could news for the automaker X and potentially bad news for automaker Y. Whether this is good for society all told is perhaps arguable, especially if this type of "spying" starts to get out of hand.

Spy versus spy, and AI versus AI.

Let's aim to ensure that these overseeing and overwatch AI systems are ethically useful for humankind. We don't want to start AI-wars that inadvertently engulf humans and we get sideswiped during the process of AI systems that were intended to protect humanity. The qualms about AI being an existential risk are usually laden with assumptions about sentient AI, though I assure you that we can put ourselves in jeopardy with non-sentient AI that removes us from the loop and gets carried away computationally.

CHAPTER 9
AI ETHICS LEADERSHIP EMPOWERMENT

A rising catchphrase implores us all to *empower leaders* and ensure proper leadership for the successful adoption of AI.

The overarching notion is that we want to ensure that leaders of all manner of scope and milieu are aware of and doing the right things when it comes to designing, building, testing, fielding, maintaining, and even simply using the latest in AI. Leaders in all walks of life are either now demonstrably impacted or soon going to be by AI systems, including business for-profit leaders, non-profit leaders, political leaders, high-tech leaders, regulatory leaders, and so on.

A handy report by the World Economic Forum (WEF) recently was released and provides a highly readable and abundantly useful C-suite toolkit for cogently dealing with AI (per the paper "Empowering AI Leadership: AI C-Suite Toolkit" published earlier this year and put together by a litany of luminaries including Kay Firth Butterfield, Mansour AlAnsari, Theodoros Evgeniou, Arunima Sarkar, etc.). I'll in a moment dive into the findings and share with you some key takeaways. I should perhaps also note that I serve on a WEF committee exploring the reimagining of legal regulations in an AI era, another vital endeavor and dovetails stridently into these expansive AI topics.

To get this discussion underway, let's start with some contemporary foundations about AI in today's society.

You undoubtedly are aware that AI is gradually becoming pervasive throughout our daily existence. Initially, the AI was assumed to be justly oriented toward *AI For Good.* We've also subsequently witnessed the ugly underbelly of AI that is replete with untoward biases and dour inequities, known variously as *AI For Bad.*

In the pell-mell rush to get AI out the door and into the hands of often unsuspecting end-users, *AI For Bad* keeps appearing and seems to be getting worse with each passing day.

How then will the empowerment of AI-related leadership be suitably guided to aim stridently toward *AI For Good* and steered ardently away from the *AI For Bad*?

One keystone is via the embracing of ethical precepts and practices underlying the implementation of AI. This highlights the importance of discussing Ethical AI, often referred to as AI ethics. The focus herein will be on various factors that tend to stymy efforts to incorporate and abide by Ethical AI precepts, especially so in large-scale AI endeavors.

First, an enchanting and possibly true tale about Albert Einstein might aid in setting the stage.

The often-told story is that when Einstein was a toddler he was seemingly silent and had gone disconcertingly and overtly quietly past the expected age at which he was supposed to be able to utter words. You can imagine the daunting concern that consumed his loving parents.

One day, seemingly out of the blue, Einstein spoke up during a normal dinner that customarily took place absent anything other than the sounds of his customary chewing and swallowing. Clearing his throat, he supposedly proclaimed in no uncertain terms that the soup was too hot.

Imagine the unbelievable shock and surprise of this unexpected utterance.

His parents were both startled and elated to have finally heard him speak. They immediately responded by asking him why he had not previously said a word and had waited for this agonizingly long to finally decide to showcase that he can in fact talk.

To which, allegedly, he replied that it was because up until now everything was in working order.

Whether the story is true or not is open to debate. It has been reported so many times that the initial genuineness is mired in murkiness. There is no doubt that the tale resonates with our overall impression of Albert Einstein and reflects a harbored assumption that he, like many by-the-facts physicists and engineers, prefers a norm of precision and exactitude in life (you've surely personally encountered this).

We can put the saga to good use.

Pundits have suggested that Ethical AI was ostensibly understated or timidly quiet in the early days of AI and now (finally) seems to have taken on a persistent and prominent place in the AI spotlight. You see, there are at times sniping comments by some that the horse was already let out of the barn and that AI ethics is now belatedly trying to catch up, but the counter view is that society wasn't ready to listen and take heed of AI ethics until the unethical AI showed its disdainful hands.

Classic chicken-or-the-egg conundrum.

In any case, let's put that water under the bridge and we ought to be focusing on the here and now. Plus, we need to be acutely focused on and worried about the future. AI is here to stay and aims to be ultimately ubiquitous. Few would argue about that.

The bottom-line lesson from the mouthful story of Einstein is that AI is not in working order and Ethical AI is speaking up accordingly (i.e., the soup has gotten too hot).

Before we get into the meat and potatoes of empowering leadership regarding AI, I'd like to share with you my own devised scale that reflects the awareness of Ethical AI as I have encountered amongst leaders across the entire spectrum of organizations and sizes. In my advising on AI ethics and my research, this scale has proved to be helpful.

We will start by identifying a ranking or rating score that runs from one to five. A score of five is the best or topmost rating, while a score of one is the lowest or least of the scores. Consider this:

1) Entirely unaware of AI ethics (no awareness at all)
2) Marginally aware of Ethical AI and alarmingly so
3) Has awareness but not adequately doing the walk-the-talk of AI ethics
4) Strongly aware and sincerely attempts to apply Ethical AI
5) Fully aware of AI Ethics and nearly airtight implementation

Each of the scores is somewhat self-explanatory. That being said, we can fruitfully take a brief moment to examine each score for some added insight.

A score of 1 is when a leader has no awareness at all about AI ethics.

The topic is not on their radar. They haven't heard of it. This would almost seem impossible if the leader is somehow otherwise immersed in any AI-related efforts, but do not be astonished to know that sometimes they just didn't ever get the memo, as it were. The bad news then is that they are likely to blindly mosey along and not ever have any lucid thoughts toward the Ethical AI ramifications of their AI-related projects or uses. The good news is that there is usually a solid chance that once they are made aware of the AI ethics considerations, they are freshly able to be brought up-to-speed and do not particularly have any bad habits associated with Ethical AI that have to be persuasively undone.

A score of 2 involves a leader that believes they are aware of Ethical AI, though they in reality have only a marginal semblance of the matter. This can be a dual-edge sword. They often know enough to be dangerous, namely trying to guide AI efforts in what they believe is an AI ethics direction and yet be sadly off-the-mark. It can be challenging to reposition their indoctrinated Ethical AI ideas.

A glimmer of hope is that they might be open to learning more and adjusting beyond what they already thought they knew. That's the happy face version of a score of 2.

A score of 3 entails a leader that has awareness of Ethical AI and seems well-rounded in the realm. The problem is that they have a gap between turning the theories and concepts of AI ethics into the day-to-day real-world aspects encompassing AI systems development and deployment. They aren't able to enact the proverbial walk-the-talk and only pretty much talk-the-talk. I'd count this as mainly good news since if shone how to walk, they already know the talk, and usually, things work out reasonably well.

A score of 4 is getting us closer to rarified air, consisting of a leader that strongly knows Ethical AI and has gotten the foundations of walk-the-talk down too. As a statistical facet, there aren't that many of these leaders. If you have an AI effort and have a leader with a score of 4, hang onto them. The odds are they are in a tremendous demand for their talents.

A score of 5 is a stretch goal for anyone even fully versed in and adept at the practical throes of the undertaking and implementing of Ethical AI. There is nearly always something new to be learned or a new twist that arises. Seeking an ironclad or airtight AI ethics adoption is aspirational more than functionally doable. That being said, it is good to always have a topmost mark on any scale so that you can have a North Star and also feel darned accomplished if you attain it.

I trust that the preceding proffers insights into the scoring.

One almost instinctively blurted-out question that I usually get when presenting the scale is why there isn't a zero. People like scales that begin with a zero. When a zero is absent, they get curious and at times anxious. I could include a zero and denote that as the devised score for being a leader that is entirely unaware of Ethical AI, but I didn't want to have confusion on the matter and figured that at least a 1 would be allowed.

So, to placate the zero demanders, I came up with a score of zero that has a different kind of meaning. A zero score is reserved for a leader that has outright disdain for AI ethics. They might or might not know what Ethical AI is all about. It doesn't matter to them whether they know or not. They insist that the AI ethics "stuff" is a bunch of hogwash and can summarily be disregarded.

For this, I grant them a zero.

After including the newly hatched zero into the scale, I subsequently had to add a minus 1 to the scale too. Here's why. A leader earns a minus one by *actively fighting* against Ethical AI aspects. To clarify, the score of zero was a leader that had mere disdain, usually sidestepping any AI ethics considerations. The minus one is a leader that goes overboard and decides that they personally have a vendetta against Ethical AI in all shapes and forms. Yes, a minus 1 type of leader goes widely out of their way to refute, defeat, undermine, and altogether battle against any kind of AI ethics precepts or practical application.

I've seen this with my own eyes and thought perchance it was a twisted dream, well, I should say a nightmare for all concerned (nightmarish for their team, their organization, their users, and the like).

All told, here then is my "final" version of the scale:

-1. Bitterly fights against any semblance of AI ethics pursuits

0. Has disdain for Ethical AI

1. Entirely unaware of AI ethics (no awareness at all)

2. Marginally aware of Ethical AI and alarmingly so

3. Awareness but not adequately doing the walk-the-talk of AI ethics

4. Strongly aware and sincerely attempts to apply Ethical AI

5. Fully aware of AI Ethics and nearly airtight implementation

Admittedly, it can be seemingly peculiar to see a scaling of this kind that starts with a minus one. I usually wait to showcase the minus number and the zero until after first discussing the active positive numbers (as per how I've introduced the scale to you herein). Some have tongue-in-cheek suggested that the minus one ought to be a minus 100, illustrating dramatically that those leaders fighting against Ethical AI are considerably worse than those only having disdain for it.

Shifting gears, now that we've discussed some rudimentary elements about AI ethics and leadership, we can turn our attention to the WEF AI C-Suite Toolkit.

The WEF report provides an instructive indication of how leading with Ethical AI is a strategic imperative, stating distinctly this core premise: "Today's leaders need a moral compass and tools to help them navigate the complexity of the emerging moral dilemmas posed by powerful technologies like AI. That compass is the ethics of AI, the discipline concerned with applying ethical thinking (what is morally permissible, desirable, and required) to all practical concerns raised by the design, development, implementation, and use of AI. AI ethics is a golden path to realizing the benefits of AI (the Good) and mitigating the risks (the Ugly). It is the great maximizer-in-balance of AI."

Levering the field of applied ethics, the WEF toolkit for leadership empowerment of AI lists various cornerstone precepts, among those are:

- Doing good work that produces good and responsible AI
- Maximizing benefits and eliminating or minimizing harms
- Fairly distributing benefits and burdens
- Understanding the impact and implication of AI systems
- Challenging the status quo and checking the exercise of power
- Bringing and including diverse perspectives
- Navigating dilemmas and trade-offs
- Etc.

The details underlying these principles are aligned with and to some degree shaped upon the European Commission's Ethics Guidelines for Trustworthy AI and the OECD's Principles of AI.

The capabilities of AI have created an alluring sense of high reward for putting in place applications that can do more and perform impressive feats of algorithmic decision making (ADM). As with most factors in life, a high reward comes with high risk. Per the WEF report: "Understanding and managing AI's potential risks and resolving its related ethical dilemmas while considering the relevant trade-offs are critical not only because they are the right things to do or because regulators will increasingly demand them, but also because business stakeholders – employees, customers, investors – will increasingly expect them. AI risks and ethical missteps can lead not only to regulatory fines but to reputational risks and the loss of revenues and markets. The new generation of customers and citizens is much more socially and environmentally aware and digital- and data-savvy, demanding truly trustworthy organizations throughout the public, private and social sectors."

The AI C-Suite Toolkit has numerous checklists and useful charts that boil down the essentials in a way that can be readily shared with executives and managers that are used to digesting complex info on a condensed and time-saving basis. Of course, care should be exercised in not taking the summaries and highlights out of context. Nor should the details be placed aside. At times, you can say that successful and ethically sound AI effort can be attributed to paying attention to the proper details. Yes, the devil can be in the details.

An especially favored portion outlines ten substantive steps that leaders should be continually minding as they seek to manage their AI risks and ensure Ethical AI results:

1) Align on AI principles relevant to the business
2) Confirm adequate top-down and end-to-end governance by instantiating stage gates throughout the AI application development and deployment process
3) Design for robustness and safety by incorporating assessment and risk-tiering processes

4) Exercise control and value alignment by enabling ongoing monitoring and adhering to the practices established by the three lines of defense structure
5) Respect privacy by considering what "should" vs "can" be done with data and elaborating on existing data governance practices
6) Be transparent by enabling the traceability, explainability and communication of information decisions and actions of the AI system and the data that feeds the AI system, as well as the visibility into how (and which) broader systems leverage AI
7) Extend security practices to protect against AI-specific risks
8) Enable diversity, non-discrimination and fairness
9) Clarify and engender accountability by implementing the use of impact assessments and external auditing; establish specific requirements for the three lines of defense structure; identify and educate stakeholders in the three lines on the roles and responsibilities
10) Foster societal and environmental wellbeing by considering a broader scope of metrics, like ESG

Okay, given those highlights of the WEF AI C-Suite leadership empowerment report, I'd like to cover some ways in which leaders undercut these kinds of AI ethics precepts.

I'll focus on shall we say inadvertent or mistaken missteps by leaders. For those leaders that are determined to shove the old Ethical AI under the bus, there is a myriad of both obnoxiously sneaky and even seemingly innocent tricks that can be used for such insidious scheming. We would be here all day covering the litany of those underhanded ploys.

In my experience, the leaders that tend to get tripped up will smackdab land into one or more of these potentially dire pitfalls:

- Falsely believes AI ethics is strictly precise and mindlessly mechanical in being fulfilled

- Becomes overly preoccupied with AI ethics risk-aversion and blind to ethical AI benefits

- Takes a checkmark "we are done" attitude and says move on now that Ethical AI is over with
- Assumes that the solution for AI ethics entails writing code amid computational specifications

Since I am particularly familiar with having to turn around those school-of-hard-knocks Ethical AI troublemaking infusions, let's use them to illuminate some tangible examples of how AI efforts can go awry. Again, we are going to assume that the leaders got themselves into AI adverse predicaments by unfortunate happenstance and not by devious purposeful intent. They were doing what they thought or hoped was right and regrettably hit sandbars and snags that they didn't realize were laying somewhat underneath the shimmering surface of AI rewards but were harboring ghastly AI risks and hazards.

There is a special and assuredly popular set of examples that are close to my heart. You see, in my capacity as an expert on AI including the ethical and legal ramifications, I am frequently asked to identify realistic examples that showcase AI Ethics dilemmas so that the somewhat theoretical nature of the topic can be more readily grasped. One of the most evocative areas that vividly presents this ethical AI quandary is the advent of AI-based true self-driving cars. This will serve as a handy use case or exemplar for ample discussion on the topic.

Here's then a noteworthy question that is worth contemplating: *Does the advent of AI-based true self-driving cars illuminate anything about these AI ethics pitfalls, and if so, what does this showcase?*

Allow me a moment to unpack the question.

AI Ethics Pitfalls

For Level 4 and Level 5 true self-driving vehicles, there won't be a human driver involved in the driving task. All occupants will be passengers. The AI is doing the driving.

Recall that these are the particular Ethical AI pitfalls pertaining to leadership missteps that we are going to showcase via AI-based self-driving car endeavors:

- Falsely believes AI ethics is strictly precise and mindlessly mechanical in being fulfilled
- Becomes overly preoccupied with AI ethics risk-aversion and blind to ethical AI benefits
- Takes a checkmark "we are done" attitude and says move on now that Ethical AI is over with
- Assumes that the solution for AI ethics entails writing code amid computational specifications

Let's unpack each one.

A company will be described that generally represents many such firms that are in the self-driving space. No person living or dead is specifically being depicted. The example is a composite and merely generally representative. Your mileage may vary in that some, all, or even none of these examples will be encountered in whatever firm you happen to work in or any entity that perchance you become aware of.

With those notable disclaimers, we can start with the first listed pitfall that some AI leaders might get snagged on.

- **Falsely believes AI ethics is strictly precise and mindlessly mechanical in being fulfilled**

A modest-sized tech company that is larger than a startup but smaller than a mega-firm is developing an AI-based self-driving car. They are taking a conventional human-driven car and trying to transform the vehicle into an autonomous one. Among various AI projects, a particularly important effort involves adding a suite of sensors such as video cameras, radar, LIDAR, ultrasonic units, thermal imagining devices, etc. to the vehicle and then developing AI that can handle the sensors.

The manager overseeing the AI-powered sensor fusion portion of the self-driving system was already up to their ears with all kinds of software and hardware issues. Sensor fusion consists of taking the computational analyses of each respective sensor and combining the results to arrive at an overall interpretation of the existing driving scene. The digital patterns found in the video camera data had to be married to the digital patterns from the radar data, and so on. It was all very complicated and fraught with lots of AI-intensive challenges.

Without a properly working sensor fusion capability, the self-driving car would be useless. Worse still, if the sensor fusion were to contain faulty hidden programming, the consequences could ultimately be devastating once the autonomous vehicle is utilized on public roadways. The AI driving system might get confounded by the sensor fusion and run into a nearby car, collide with a lamppost, or strike a bicyclist or pedestrian. This is serious stuff.

The overworked manager led a team of AI software engineers, hardware engineers, quality assurance specialists, and a supporting staff. Having attended some quick courses on Ethical AI, the manager knew that as the leader for the sensor fusion there was a chance that ethical issues of the AI could readily materialize. For example, some research studies indicated that AI systems detecting pedestrians had potentially problematically been skewing the detection as based on racial biases and gender biases.

How could the Ethical AI considerations be best handled?

As a trained engineer with a Ph.D. in mechanical engineering, this leader saw the world as one that can be inexorably reduced to formulas and exactness. The directive that the AI should be non-discriminatory and operate in a fair manner could certainly be figured out with some number crunching and the judicious selection of appropriate metrics. This task was assigned to a support staff member. The leader decided that having summarily handed over the delicate matter to a trusted team member, the whole problem of adhering to Ethical AI could be dealt with in an entirely analytical way and nothing else needed to be done. Case closed.

You can perhaps guess what happened next. The staff member was bewildered. After an extensive behind-the-scenes research effort, there didn't seem to be special analytically sound metrics that applied to this AI setting, and definitely few if any that closely matched to the AI ethics aspects. Trying to turn qualitatively oriented AI ethics precepts into a narrow base of precise quantitative measures was overwhelming and did not seem reasonably feasible. Worried that the leader would be greatly disappointed, the staff member became distraught and frantic at work.

As you will see in a moment, things went from bad to worse. We move to the next pitfall to see further how this played out.

- **Becomes overly preoccupied with AI ethics risk-aversion and blind to ethical AI benefits**

The manager overseeing the AI sensor fusion programming had a fixed budget to get the work done. To justify the cost of dealing with the AI ethics-related elements, the manager had identified potential risks associated with Ethical AI lapses in the AI system and pointed out the dollar costs if those risks arose while the autonomous vehicle was later on placed into active use.

In the mind of this leader, the chore of handling the AI ethics considerations was solely about reducing or eliminating risks. This gave an impression to the team that the only concern of dealing with Ethical AI matters was to avoid bad problems and reduce long-term costs. The aura of such leadership "guidance" made the perception of these matters by the team to be seen as an undesirable and dreary inconvenience.

It had not occurred to this leader that the attention to Ethical AI could be a benefit too.

When a top-level corporate officer found out that the team was incorporating AI ethics considerations into this subsystem, the executive was quite elated. This could be touted as an important feature of their AI driving system that other such AI systems did not have.

Furthermore, communities that were eyeing using self-driving cars had heard that sometimes AI contains ethically questionable practices. The fact that this firm was intentionally trying to make sure that such dour AI ethical faultiness was being sought out and aimed to be overcome would be a prized means of likely gaining community support for their brand of self-driving cars. It was a big upside of added benefits.

With that revelation, we'll see what happened next.

- **Takes a checkmark "we are done" attitude and says move on now that Ethical AI is over with**

With mounting pressure to get the AI ethics aspects figured out, the manager of the sensor fusion portion decided that an imminently efficient approach could be undertaken. Using some spare time during lunch, this leader put together an Ethical AI checklist and posted the list onto the team's Slack channel. Each member of the team was assigned one of the items on the list.

They were all given two weeks to get the items respectively done. A checkmark would suffice as evidence that the AI ethics matter had been dealt with. Sure enough, by good fortune, the manager was pleased to see that by the end of the two-week deadline, all the checkmarks had been marked as completed.

Job well done.

It was a huge relief. No need to consume any further thinking about Ethical AI matters. Yes, the effort had chewed up his team for those two weeks, but they could now fully concentrate on getting the real work done.

Can you guess what happened next?

A month later, while doing tryouts of the sensor fusion as part of a closed track run-through, turns out the AI appeared to be falling into an Ethical AI concern. The manager couldn't blame anyone on the team since it was a topic that had not been listed on the checkmark listing. It was an oversight by the leader. The leader was in great dismay. The AI ethics considerations were already supposed to be done and were presumed as fully completed and long gone.

Having to unexpectedly divert attention to this issue was going to mess up the schedule and put this vital AI effort behind. It would cause an internal ruckus and the leader would be lambasted for poor planning and tainted as having exercised inadequate leadership.

It dawned on the leader that in the future, it might make more sense to anticipate Ethical AI aspects to arise throughout the life cycle of the AI build and fielding. Rather than try to squeeze it all into the upfront portion, the odds were that such matters would happen and require devoted attention from beginning to end. In fact, beyond the end too, including once the AI was being actively used and ongoing maintenance and upkeep were taking place.

We next move to the final part of this AI ethics lessons-learned tale.

- **Assumes that the solution for AI ethics entails writing code amid computational specifications**

One of the software engineers on the team could see that the manager was troubled. This software engineer was a hotshot. There wasn't anything that couldn't be hacked out and coded. It seemed obvious that this wrangling with the Ethical AI considerations could be entirely placated by writing the right kind of code.

Asking for permission to work on this as a side project, the software engineer eagerly jumped into trying to write code to cope with any and all AI ethics possibilities. At first, code writing was the dominant focus. The programming proceeded to get more harried and enormously complicated. The software engineer took a deep breath. Perhaps the first step ought to have been putting together computational specifications. By doing things that way, the code would be tied to appropriate specs.

After several weeks of doing this on late nights and weekends, the software engineer threw in the towel. The programming was becoming onerous. It wasn't even covering what needed to be done. Even more exasperating is that a lot of what was required did not lend itself to straight-ahead coding alone.

The leader reflected on this when the software engineer came and essentially admitted defeat. While pondering the situation, the leader recalled a remark that had been helpful in the past. Sometimes, if all that you know how to use is a hammer, everything looks like a nail. A coding-obsessed mind can be like that.

Conclusion

You can easily extract the AI driving system aspects from the aforementioned leadership pitfalls scenario, doing so to highlight that nearly any large-scale AI system can include the same gotchas. There isn't anything that makes AI-based self-driving cars unique to these Ethical AI leadership-related qualms.

For those of you designing, building, testing, fielding, maintaining, or just plain old using AI, make sure that you and your fellow leaders are cognizant of the AI ethics underpinnings. I hope you'll strive for at least a cherished 4 on the rating scale of Ethical AI empowered leadership rating. Going for the esteemed 5 is welcomed too. On the lower end of the scale, please do not let yourself or other leaders become a zero, nor find yourself in a situation of a minus one, a minus one hundred, or maybe even a minus one thousand. If that does happen, you'll indubitably need a massive heaping of AI ethics leadership empowerment to right that likely sinking ship.

CHAPTER 10
AI ETHICS OF HUMANS FEUDING WITH AI

Bad blood.

Yes, we are going to be discussing *bad blood.*

The context will be within the arena of Ethical AI and the ethics of AI systems, which is a burgeoning and vital set of topics about AI. We'll start here by first laying out the foundations of bad blood and then wrap into the discourse the perhaps startling dilemma of how AI will impact humankind correspondingly. Get yourself ready for a wild ride.

I believe that you would reasonably concur that bad blood is a popular phrase in our society.

You undoubtedly know that there have been noteworthy songs with that famous phrasing (consider Taylor Swift and the lyrics from the same-named song that opens with "cause baby, we now got bad blood"), plus movies and cable shows so coined, and many a written narrative including great works of poetry that have invoked the longstanding notion of bad blood.

We usually associate the eyebrow-raising catchphrase with bitter reams of hatred that ruminates between two different groups. Sometimes the bad blood fosters a dire feud. The feud can metastasize into endless and potentially mutually destructive outcomes for the corresponding parties. All because of that bad blood, baby.

Historians tend to indicate that the initial phrasing was "ill blood" and was later immortalized as "bad blood" via the famous English essayist Charles Lamb. Thus, one of the first well-known uses if not perhaps the foremost that started our viral use of bad blood seems to come from his 1833 book *The Last Essays of Elia* and can be found in his essay entitled *Poor Relations.*

He recounts the tale of hostilities between two factions that live near each other, one called the Above Boys that reside on a hill, and the other referred to as the Below Boys that live down below in a valley. I knew you'd like to see the bad blood usage with your own eyes, so here is the relevant passage from his *Poor Relations* essay (I've highlighted in bold the use of bad blood therein): "The houses of the ancient city of Lincoln are divided (as most my readers know) between the dwellers on the hill and in the valley. This marked distinction formed an obvious division between the boys who lived above (however brought together in a common school) and the boys whose paternal residence was on the plain a sufficient cause of hostility in the code of these young Grotiuses. My father had been a leading Mountaineer and would still maintain the general superiority in skill and hardihood of the *Above Boys* (his own faction) over the *Below Boys* (so were they called), of which party his contemporary had been a chieftain. Many and hot were the skirmishes on this topic—the only one upon which the old gentleman was ever brought out—and **bad blood** bred; even sometimes almost to the recommencement (so I expected) of actual hostilities. But my father, who scorned to insist upon advantages, generally contrived to turn the conversation upon some adroit by-commendation of the old Minster; in the general preference of which, before all other cathedrals in the island, the dweller on the hill, and the plain-born, could meet on a conciliating level, and lay down their less important differences."

I purposely included the sentence that comes *after* the bad blood indication, doing so to showcase that despite bad blood being predominant, some will attempt to reduce the enmity and seek to keep things on a peaceful keel (the father appears to have that aspirational hope in mind). That provides a modicum of a happy face on something that otherwise is decidedly a sad and exasperating face.

What causes bad blood?

The amazing aspect of bad blood is that there can be explicit reasons for it, yet there can also be no semblance of known reasons for it at all.

We might harbor bad blood due to:

- Specific identifiable reasons
- Vague and unspecified reasons
- Reasons that were once known and no longer are (but bad blood lingers nonetheless)
- No reasons of any viable consequence or seeming exceedingly trivial basis
- Possibly by randomness alone

One interesting theory is that we innately find ourselves tending to form into groups. Once you've gotten into a group, the potential is high that you might realize that your group is in direct competition with a different group, possibly sorely grappling over in-common scarce or limited resources. In that manner of thinking, you might argue that the bad blood makes sense for survival purposes, perhaps.

Even if there isn't any common basis for contention, we might instinctually assume that there is a chance of contentions eventually arising. In that case, we might preemptively favor our group over the other group. You can't put your finger on why your group is somehow better than the other or in disagreement with the other. So, you blindly shrug your shoulders and assume that it is logically prudent to cling to your group and denigrate the other group. No sense in taking any chances, you impulsively conclude.

Ethicists have lots of fascinating theories about this chunk of human behavior.

Consider this insightful assessment of the humankind situation by these researchers: "The evolution of our moral and social mind took place in the context of relatively small and competitively antagonistic social groups. This is considered to be at least a part of the explanation for the unique and throughout social nature of the human mind. One of the mental tendencies stemming from this social origin is the human tendency to split people into in-groups and out-groups. Individuals categorized in the in-group are perceived as more valuable than those categorized as out-group members" (as published in *AI And Ethics*, "Socio-Cognitive Biases In Folk AI Ethics And Risk Discourse" by co-authors Michael Laakasuo, Volo Herzon, Silva Perander, Marianna

Drosinou, Jukka Sundvall, Jussi Palomäki, Aku Visala).

You have invariably likely experienced being part of an in-group or being part of an out-group. I'd bet that you've been at times a member of an in-group. Other times you've been a member of an out-group. We shuffle between joining a group that is the in-group and joining other groups that are so-called out-groups.

It can be dizzying. An in-group might subsequently no longer be the in-group and have become the out-group. Similarly, an out-group might get anointed as the in-group. Further confounding the matter is what gets a group labeled as an in-group versus an out-group. Perhaps the in-group considers all other groups to be the out-group. Meanwhile, the out-group believes they are the in-group and all other groups are the out-group.

Round and round we go.

I find myself drifting to the cleverly devised Dr. Seuss story of *Stars Upon Thars*, published in 1961 and forever reminds us of the in-group versus out-group struggles of society: "Now, the Star-Bell Sneetches had bellies with stars. The Plain-Belly Sneetches had none upon thars. Those stars weren't so big. They were really so small. You might think such a thing wouldn't matter at all. But, because they had stars, all the Star-Belly Sneetches Would brag, "We're the best kind of Sneetch on the beaches." With their snoots in the air, they would sniff and they'd snort "We'll have nothing to do with the Plain-Belly sort!"

The easiest and perhaps most popular way to describe this phenomenon would be the remarkably straightforward pronouncement of *us versus them*. Just as Charles Lamb discussed the Above Boys and the Below Boys, and Dr. Seuss brought us the Star-Bell Sneetches and the Plain-Belly Sneetches, groupings like this often dovetail into a fierce loyalty and group attraction for those that are members of their respective group.

You might at times exhort loudly that you are a member of your chosen group, which you voraciously and gleefully declare, thus you are part of the *us*, while those reprehensible members of the other despicable group are the appalling *them*.

In shorthand: *Us-versus-them*.

I am about to introduce you to an us-versus-them that I am guessing you haven't put much thought toward. I say this because we customarily think of the us-versus-them in human terms. Humans of one group are an us, and humans of another group are them. Easy-peasy.

Are you ready for the shocker?

Consider the circumstance of us-versus-them in terms of humans versus Artificial Intelligence (AI).

I could phrase this as humans versus AI, or as AI versus humans, since in theory, this could be a two-way street. The normative viewpoint would be that it is humans versus AI, namely the in-group consists of being human and the out-group consists of being AI. All I'm saying is that we might stretch things to ponder the AI being the in-group and humans being the out-group, which might be the AI versus human variation of the phrasing.

Right now, we don't have any AI that is sentient. We don't know if AI sentience is possible. It might be, it might not be. No one can say for sure. No one can even state for a certainty that AI sentience will happen and nor when it will happen or if it will arise. For those reasons, we'll concentrate on the humans versus AI and put to the side the AI versus humans.

We need to take a reflective moment to examine an us-versus-them in the realm of humans versus AI.

There are variations worthy of distinct analysis.

The most usual variant is that we will perceive our fellow humans as being in an in-group or an out-group as shaped around the use of AI. There might be some people that are actively using AI. We could label them as the in-group. Other people that aren't using AI are by default members of the out-group.

For completeness, there could of course be those not using AI as considered to be the in-group, while the out-group are those that are using AI. I'd hazard a guess that this is a much less oft way to think of things. It is though another worthy topic of discussion.

You might right away quibble that the phrasing of humans versus AI is not quite on-target if we are going to be splitting humans into varying groups of using or not using AI. This would almost seem to be humans versus humans, and we are merely identifying that the claimed reason for humans to be divided into two groups is based on AI as the factor for doing so. All in all, it is a bit disingenuous perhaps to say that this is humans versus AI.

I do though want to keep that humans versus humans divisional grouping due to AI usage as something that we'll be getting to further in a moment. Please keep it in the back of your mind.

The blatantly obvious connotation of humans versus AI is that we humans are in one group and AI is in the other group. Humans versus AI. I suppose that sci-fi movies have well-prepared us for that eventuality. You know how the sordid plotline goes. Humans make AI systems. AI systems decide they want to no longer be subservient to humans. AI enslaves humankind, or maybe wipes humankind from existence.

That latter result is what many refer to as the existential risk of AI. We craft AI with the best of intentions. This is the *AI For Good* mantra. AI helps to solve the world's most challenging problems. Yay, we are wise to have built AI. Oops, AI turns on us. The feared *AI For Bad* becomes real. Humankind laments that Pandora's box of AI was ever opened. End of story.

To clarify, such a malevolent AI doesn't necessarily have to be sentient. The typical assumption is that AI will turn on us once it is reached sentience, presumably via the emergence of singularity. We could still get ourselves into an existential risk even if the AI isn't sentient. Imagine a type of doomsday setting whereby we have automated mechanisms that control global nuclear weapons via plain-old non-sentient AI, and we managed to excise ourselves from being in the loop on crucial life-or-death defining decisions.

Lots of movies and coverage of this kind of situation took place during the Cold War era. With today's non-sentient AI nowadays involved as slick algorithmic decision making (ADM) automation, we are stepping up the chances of cataclysms happening. You don't need sentience per se to get the cascading effects of planetary-wide destruction. Automation such as via everyday AI can be a catalyst but doesn't have to be "thinking" to enable the possibility of such an apocalypse.

The gist is that I want to discuss herein the humans versus plain-old non-sentient AI. I'm trying to keep the focus on a real-world conundrum rather than a more outstretched one. We should certainly be worried about what will happen if sentient AI ever does poke out its head, meanwhile, we have plenty to consider with the non-sentient AI that we have today and will continue to advance forward.

Here's what I mean.

Humans are apt to attribute anthropomorphic properties to AI. AI systems of today can lead us down a primrose path of thinking that AI does have a sentient quality to it. Consider the use of Alexa or Siri. These are AI-based systems using Natural Language Processing (NLP) and are often augmented with the use of Machine Learning (ML) and Deep Learning (DL). Keep in mind that all of those technologies and techniques are composed of general computing capabilities. They can do some nifty computational pattern matching. They are not at all sentients.

When you speak with Alexa or Siri in conversational interaction, you can readily start to converse as though you are dialoguing with another human. You aren't sure how far the AI can go in terms of language fluency. Maybe the AI can interact and comprehend as well as another human can. The aspect that the AI is speaking with you gives it that anthropomorphic aura.

Of course, any attempt at a detailed "conversation" with the likes of Alexa or Siri of today will pretty quickly get you into the zone of irksome irritation. That AI is relatively brittle and narrow. You cannot carry on a truly fluent discussion. As a result, you find yourself resorting to curt commands and drop the whole harrowing effort of trying to talk with your computing buddy, as it were.

I don't want to have our attention preoccupied with the way that such AI exists today. Be assured that it is incrementally being improved. Fluency will get better. Robots too that look entirely like robots will gradually be built to more closely resemble humans. The march of technological progress is going to continue unabated.

Returning to the us-versus-them, we can contemplate how it is that humans will embark upon an "us" way of thinking and ergo are going to place AI into the "them" categorization.

Some people (not all!) will falsely ascribe human sentience capacities to AI. Once you've made that initial leap, the rest of the jump is kind of effortless. You might begin to hate AI for what it is doing or what it is not doing. For example, you make use of an AI-based online mortgage granting app. After entering some data about yourself, the AI system tells you that you have been turned down for your desired home loan. What do you do? You get angry at the AI. That no-good dastardly AI has ruined your life.

You begin to hate AI. Other ills of society that you find troubling are also then laid at the feet of AI. Everywhere you go and whatever you do, you are on edge that AI is out to get you. On top of this, you slide further in this direction by deducing that AI hates you too. You hate AI, and it in return hates you. Maybe the AI hated you all along, rather than the AI hating you because you hated it.

I have somewhat dramatically overstated the human versus AI aspects to try and showcase in a vivid way how far this can proceed. Not all people will take that path. Some people will take a much milder path. Some won't go in that direction at all.

From an Ethical AI viewpoint, we do need to put on the table that there is going to be some semblance of bad blood between humans and AI. The us-versus-them that already seems to be in our blood is bound to be triggered in some manner toward the blood of AI. That last reference to the blood of AI is not meant to suggest that AI will be flesh-and-blood. Maybe we can say the oil of AI if that clarifies.

As a side tangent, there are ongoing efforts of combining the biology of living creatures with the technology of AI. In that sense, you could suggest that we are likely to eventually have a "blood" coursing through the computing capabilities of AI.

All right, we've got on the horizon or possibly already percolating an us-versus-them divide of humans versus AI. Humans in one camp, and AI in the other. We are taking the perspective of humans as the in-group and the AI as the out-group, doing so with the realization of the other variations that we could also dive into.

What can we make of this us-versus-them dilemma?

We ought to see if some use cases can help further illuminate the matter. There is a special and assuredly popular set of examples that are close to my heart. You see, in my capacity as an expert on AI including the ethical and legal ramifications, I am frequently asked to identify realistic examples that showcase AI Ethics dilemmas so that the somewhat theoretical nature of the topic can be more readily grasped. One of the most evocative areas that vividly presents this ethical AI quandary is the advent of AI-based true self-driving cars. This will serve as a handy use case or exemplar for ample discussion on the topic.

Here's then a noteworthy question that is worth contemplating: *Does the advent of AI-based true self-driving cars illuminate anything about an us-versus-them of humans versus AI, and if so, what does this showcase?*

Allow me a moment to unpack the question.

AI Us-Versus-Them

For Level 4 and Level 5 true self-driving vehicles, there won't be a human driver involved in the driving task. All occupants will be passengers. The AI is doing the driving.

Let's use a readily straightforward example. An AI-based self-driving car is underway on your neighborhood streets and seems to be driving safely. At first, you had devoted special attention to each time that you managed to catch a glimpse of the self-driving car. The autonomous vehicle stood out with its rack of electronic sensors that included video cameras, radar units, LIDAR devices, and the like. After many weeks of the self-driving car cruising around your community, you now barely notice it. As far as you are concerned, it is merely another car on the already busy public roadways.

Lest you think it is impossible or implausible to become familiar with seeing self-driving cars, I've written frequently about how the locales that are within the scope of self-driving car tryouts have gradually gotten used to seeing the spruced-up vehicles. Many of the locals eventually shifted from mouth-gaping rapt gawking to now emitting an expansive yawn of boredom to witness those meandering self-driving cars.

Probably the main reason right now that they might notice the autonomous vehicles is because of the irritation and exasperation factor. The by-the-book AI driving systems make sure the cars are obeying all speed limits and rules of the road. For hectic human drivers in their traditional human-driven cars, you get irked at times when stuck behind the strictly law-abiding AI-based self-driving cars.

That's something we might all need to get accustomed to, rightfully or wrongly.

Back to our tale. One day, suppose a self-driving car in your town or city approaches a Stop sign and does not stop. The autonomous vehicle plows right past the Stop sign. Whoa, dangerous and Illegal! A bike rider nearly got sideswiped. A human-driven car that was in the intersection almost got hit by the self-driving car. Luckily, no one was actually harmed.

The actions of the AI-based self-driving car were caught on video. Social media turned the video into a viral sensation. Some people reacted to the errant self-driving car by claiming that the AI purposely ran the Stop sign. You see, the AI was trying to be harmful. Those ardent believers that immoral AI is out to get us were up in arms.

Finally, it is boldly proclaimed, AI is starting to show itself for what it really is and wants to do.

Never mind that the issue was traced to a seemingly plausible and sensible basis for the wayward action. The automaker and self-driving car tech firm noted that the Stop sign was quite obscured by an overhanging tree that had not been cut back. During the training of the Machine Learning and Deep Learning algorithm that detects Stop signs, the initial training set did not include sample pictures of Stop signs that were so notably visually obscured. As such, the AI driving system inadvertently failed to properly classify the sign as a Stop sign (the posted sign got assigned a low probability, plus the algorithm estimated that the sign was perhaps just a red sign that resembled a Stop sign and not an actual Stop sign).

The company updated its AI accordingly.

In any case, the incident raised awareness about AI as a driving system. Those that already suspected that AI is part of the "them" were waiting for a slipup on the part of AI. This was the breakthrough instance. A kind of outspoken protest began to be constructed. Even people who had not previously thought of AI as an us-versus-them joined the growing movement.

In some areas where the AI-based self-driving cars were being tried out, protestors got positioned to where the autonomous vehicles typically roamed. When they saw a self-driving car approaching, they would hurl rocks at the vehicles and toss sharp spikes into the street. The idea was that they wanted to make it clear that AI driving is not welcomed in their town.

As an aside, there have been previously reported instances of people throwing rocks and trying to dissuade the use of self-driving cars, which has nearly completely subsided thankfully (plus, keep in mind that this is a highly unsafe activity and can imperial passengers inside the self-driving car and can lead to an injurious car crash).

The tipping point came when regrettably an AI-based self-driving car rammed into the rear end of a human-driven car. This caused some modest damage to the human-driven car and luckily only slightly jarred the driver and a front-seat passenger. Nonetheless, those advocating the us-versus-them viewpoint were fast to emphasize that AI is getting worse and worse. The AI is "obviously" deciding to tip its hand and escalating its attacks upon humans.

With social media echoing this vitriolic sentiment, the advocates for AI-based self-driving cars start to become outvoiced. Whereas the hope is that such autonomous vehicles will dramatically reduce the number of annual car crashes and ergo reduce the nearly 40,000 yearly human fatalities and 2.5 million human injuries from car collisions (that's in the United States alone), the sharpened *opponents* of AI in-general begin to overwhelm those that favor self-driving cars.

Bowing to widespread viral-boosted condemnations, automakers and AI developers opt to curtail many of their tryouts. Within the autonomous vehicles industry, there is concern that this is a major disruption in progress. The pullback will significantly delay the gradual advancement toward AI-based self-driving cars. For each day delayed, the implication is that we are allowing more injuries and fatalities to occur due to conventional human-based driving. The avid crowds of us-versus-them are drowning out the calls for looking at the benefits of AI driving systems.

Imagine that this is one of those water dams breaking circumstances whereby the spread of us-versus-them about humans versus AI spreads like wildfire. As per the earlier sketch of how far the AI loathing can go, envision that people convert over to passionately hating AI of any kind. They believe that AI is out to get us all. Humans must rebel. The masses are convinced that hating AI is entirely sensible, especially since they also stridently believe that AI now hates us.

AI systems of all kinds are pulled out of service. We revert back to not using AI. This causes all sorts of other adverse consequences as older forms of automation are put into use. Meanwhile, wanting to retain the utility of AI, many firms and developers try to rebrand the AI moniker by coming up with different terminology. The hope is that those of the us-versus-them won't realize that AI is in fact still being put to use. But the odds are this will create an even more bountiful adverse reaction once the us-versus-them crowds find out that the insiders are trying to fool those of their own kind (fellow humans).

Whew, that is all a notably gloomy and rather sad state of affairs.

Let's hope we don't see that type of unsavory scenario arise.

Conclusion

I had earlier noted that another variant of the us-versus-them of humans versus AI dealt with the notion of some humans using AI and other humans not using AI. Though that is not the purity of humans versus AI, we can give it some attention anyway.

Here's a means by which that could play out.

AI-based self-driving cars are rolled out into your town or city. The deployment algorithms are based on seeking revenue maximization. This makes good sense. The automakers and self-driving car tech firms are desirous of finally making money off their deep investments into the technology. The fleet operator that is running the self-driving cars and maintaining them wants to earn dough too. Profitability makes the world go around.

After a while, the AI detects a pattern. More money is to be made by being in the wealthy part of town rather than the impoverished parts of town. This is strictly based on the number of rides and the monies collected. There is no realization per se that there are areas of the town that are wealthier than others. The whole aspect is solely based on the raw numbers and driving outcomes.

That kind of scenario has been oft identified by AI ethicists and others. Worries are that AI-based self-driving cars will ultimately only be accessed by those with wealth and be essentially denied to those that do not have wealth. We will further cleave society. The advantages of AI in the context of self-driving cars will selectively arise for one segment of society and will not be borne by another segment.

Do you see how that illustrates an us-versus-them of the human versus human variety?

In that use case, AI was a factor in the spurring of such divisions. You could readily argue that AI was not at fault in the sense of the AI had no intention and was not sentient in bringing forth the divisional separations. We might though incur bad blood and a type of feud between those that are using AI self-driving cars and those that seem to not be able to use AI-based self-driving cars. The same overarching phenomenon could arise in a wide variety of other uses of AI, far beyond just the narrower scope of self-driving cars.

I don't want this discussion to entirely seem downbeat and disheartening. There is enough of that already in daily activities. The good or heartening news is that if we realize that there is a possibility of an us-versus-them due to AI, we can presumably take overt and sensible actions to avoid falling into that ugly trap. Ethical AI is pounding away at trying to increase awareness of these issues and get us all to be cognizant of detrimental and potentially disastrous AI-related outcomes. By being forewarned, we can seek to avert these storied calamities.

One last comment for now.

In *Time* magazine, former U.S. Secretary of State Madeleine Albright proffered an editorial opinion piece last year that decried the rising tide of an us-versus-them mindset all told. She emphasized that the two most dangerous words in the human vocabulary are "us" and "them."

Let's keep the us-versus-them on a tight rein. If we don't do so, the other side of the coin might be something that could come to fruition, namely the somewhat outstretched possibility of AI versus humans, whereby the AI "decides" to go the route of us-versus-them.

Just to clarify, AI in that scenario is in the in-group, and we, as humans, are in the out-group. Be careful of the AI-related life-endangering perils of us-versus-them when we are the out-group?

CHAPTER 11
AI ETHICS
SELF-AWARENESS BY AI

Are you self-aware?

I'd bet that you believe you are.

The thing is, supposedly, few of us are especially self-aware. There is a range or degree of self-awareness and we all purportedly vary in how astutely self-aware we are. You might think you are fully self-aware and only be marginally so. You might be thinly self-aware and realize that's your mental state.

Meanwhile, at the topmost part of the spectrum, you might believe you are fully self-aware and indeed are frankly about as self-aware as they come. Good for you.

Speaking of which, what good does it do to be exceedingly self-aware?

According to research published in the *Harvard Business Review* (HBR) by Tasha Eurich, you reportedly are able to make better decisions, you are more confident in your decisions, you are stronger in your communication capacities, and more effective overall (per article entitled "What Self-Awareness Really Is (and How to Cultivate It)." The bonus factor is that those with strident self-awareness are said to be less inclined to cheat, steal, or lie. In that sense, there is a twofer of averting being a scoundrel or a crook, along with striving to be a better human being and embellish your fellow humankind.

All of this talk about self-awareness brings up a somewhat obvious question, namely, what does the phrase self-awareness actually denote.

You can readily find tons of various definitions and interpretations about the complex and shall we say mushy construct entailing being self-aware. Some would simplify matters by suggesting that self-awareness consists of monitoring your own self, knowing what yourself is up to. You are keenly aware of your own thoughts and actions.

Presumably, when not being self-aware, a person would not realize what they are doing, nor why so, and also not be cognizant of what other people have to say about them. I'm sure you've met people that are like this.

Some people appear to walk this earth without a clue of what they themselves are doing, and nor do they have a semblance of what others are saying about them. I guess you could contend that they are like a heads-down charging bull in a delicate breakables boutique. We customarily tend to believe that the bull does not know what it is doing and remains oblivious to the viewpoints of others unless those others try to physically maneuver or corral the clueless creature.

It is said that self-awareness can be somewhat recursive.

Let me sketch an example to illustrate this recursion. You are in the midst of watching a quite absorbing cat video on your smartphone (everyone does this, it seems). Some people would have no other apparent thoughts other than the wonderous heartwarming antics of those darling cats. Meanwhile, anyone with a modicum of self-awareness, they are aware that they are watching a cat video. They might also be aware that others around them are noting that they are watching a cat video.

Notice that you can be self-aware and still be immersed in a shall we say a particular primary activity. The primary activity in this instance is watching the cat video. Secondarily, and simultaneously, you can carry the thought that you are in fact watching a cat video. You are also able to carry the thought that others are observing you as you are watching the altogether entertaining cat video.

You don't necessarily have to stop one activity, such as discontinue watching the cat video, in order to then separately contemplate that you are (or just were) watching a cat video. Those thoughts can seemingly occur in parallel with each other.

Sometimes, our self-awareness might though kick us out of or at least interrupt a primary mental activity. Perhaps, while thinking about your watching of the cat video, your mind partially zones out as it is overstretching to concentrate solely on the video itself. You opt to then rewind the video to revisit the portion that you kind of saw but that you were mentally distracted from fully comprehending. Self-awareness disturbed your primary mental activity.

Okay, we are now ready for the recursive aspects to arise.

Are you ready?

You are watching a cat video. Your self-awareness is informing you that you are watching a cat video and that others are watching you as you are watching the video. That's the status quo.

You next make an additional mental leap. You begin to think about your self-awareness. You are self-aware that you are engaging your self-awareness. Here's how that goes: Am I thinking too much about thinking about my watching of the cat video, you ask yourself despairingly? This is another layer of self-awareness. Self-awareness ranking on top of other self-awareness.

There is an old saying that it is turtles all the way down. For the self-awareness phenomena, you could be:

- Not aware of yourself
- Self-aware of yourself
- Self-aware of your self-awareness of yourself
- Self-aware of your being self-aware of your self-awareness of yourself
- Ad Infinitum (i.e., and so on)

You might have realized that I earlier was pointing out subtly that there seem to be two major categories of being self-aware. One particular theory postulates that we have a kind of internal self-awareness that focuses on our internal states, and we also have an external self-awareness that aids in gauging the perceptions about us of those around us that are viewing us.

Per the HBR article, here's a quick depiction of the theorized two types of self-awareness: "The first, which we dubbed *internal self-awareness*, represents how clearly we see our own values, passions, aspirations, fit with our environment, reactions (including thoughts, feelings, behaviors, strengths, and weaknesses), and impact on others." And meanwhile the other is: "The second category, *external self-awareness*, means understanding how other people view us, in terms of those same factors listed above. Our research shows that people who know how others see them are more skilled at showing empathy and taking others' perspectives."

A handy two-by-two matrix or four-square can be derived by asserting that both the internal and external self-awareness range from high to low, and you can mate the two categories against each other. The HBR research indicates that you are said to be one of these four self-awareness archetypes:

- Introspector: Low External Self-Awareness + High Internal Self-Awareness
- Seeker: Low External Self-Awareness + Low Internal Self-Awareness
- Pleaser: High External Self-Awareness + Low Internal Self-Awareness
- Aware: High External Self-Awareness + High Internal Self-Awareness

The pinnacle would be the "Aware" archetype that consists of being at the top rung of being externally self-aware and likewise at the top of being internally self-aware. To clarify, you don't attain this vaunted posture in a necessarily permanent way. You can slip back and forth between being high and low, amongst both the internal and external self-awareness realms. It can depend upon the time of day, the situation you find yourself in, and a slew of other salient factors.

Now that we've affably covered some foundational elements about self-awareness, we can seek to tie this to the topic of ethical behaviors.

The usual claim about being self-aware is that you are more likely to be aboveboard when you are self-aware. This means, as indicated already, you are less prone to adverse ethical behaviors such as stealing, cheating, and lying. The rationale for this tendency is that the activeness of your self-awareness would make you realize that your own behavior is unsavory or unethical. Not only do your catch yourself as you veer into muddy unethical waters, but you are also prone to steering yourself back out and onto dry land (the sanctity of ethical territory), as it were.

Your self-awareness aids you in exercising self-control.

A contrast would presumably be when there is little or no self-awareness, which suggests that someone is perhaps oblivious to their leaning into unethical behaviors. You could contend that such an unaware person might not realize that they are performing adversely. Akin to the bull in the breakables shop, until something more overtly catches their attention, they are unlikely to self-regulate themselves.

Not everyone buys into this, by the way. Some would argue that self-awareness can be as readily applied to being unethical as being ethical. For example, an evildoer might be fully self-aware and relishes that they are carrying out the wrongdoing. Their self-awareness even drives them more stridently toward larger and larger acts of nefarious misconduct.

There is more cloudiness on this than might directly meet the eye. Suppose someone is keenly self-aware, but they are unaware of the ethical mores of a given society or culture. In that manner, they do not have any ethical guidance, despite the stated fact that they are self-aware. Or, if you like, perhaps the person knows about the ethical precepts and doesn't believe they apply to them. They consider themselves unique or outside the bounds of conventional ethical thinking.

Round and round it goes.

Self-awareness could be construed as a dual-edged ethics-oriented sword, some would fervently emphasize.

For the moment, let's go with the happy face version consisting of self-awareness by and large guiding or nudging us toward ethical behaviors. Everything else being equal, we will make the brash assumption that the more self-awareness there is, the more ethically leaning you will go. It sure seems pleasing and inspirational to wish it so.

Let's shift gears and bring Artificial Intelligence (AI) into the picture.

We are at a juncture in this discussion to connect all of the proceeding entanglements with the burgeoning realm of Ethical AI, also commonly known as the ethics of AI.

The notion of Ethical AI entails intertwining the field of ethics and ethical behavior to the advent of AI. You've certainly seen headlines that have raised alarm bells about AI that is replete with inequities and various biases. For example, there are concerns that AI-based facial recognition systems can at times exhibit racial and gender discrimination, typically as a result of how the underlying Machine Learning (ML) and Deep Learning (DL) facilities were trained and fielded.

To try and stop or at least mitigate the pell-mell rush toward *AI For Bad*, consisting of AI systems that are either inadvertently or at times intentionally shaped to act badly, there has been a recent urgency to apply ethics precepts to the development and use of AI. The earnest goal is to provide ethical guidance to AI developers, plus firms that build or field AI, and those that are dependent upon AI applications.

Give a reflective moment to consider these three highly crucial questions:

- Can we get AI developers to embrace Ethical AI principles and put those guidelines into actual use?
- Can we get firms that craft or field AI to do likewise?
- Can we get those that use AI to similarly be cognizant of Ethical AI facets?

I'd unabashedly say this, it is a tall order.

The thrill of making AI can overpower any inkling of attention toward the ethics of AI. Well, not just the thrill, but money-making is integral to that equation too. You might be surprised to know that some in the AI realm are apt to say that they'll get around to dealing with the Ethical AI "stuff" once they've gotten their AI systems out the door. This is the typical techie mantra of making sure to fail fast and fail often until you get it right (hopefully getting it right).

Of course, those that are summarily shoving ethically dubious AI onto the public at large are letting the horse out of the barn. Their proclaimed outstretched idea is that the *AI For Bad* will get fixed after it is in daily use, which detrimentally is tardy since the horse is already wantonly galloping around. Harms can be done. There is also the heightened chance that nothing will be fixed or adjusted while the AI is in use. A frequent excuse is that fiddling with the AI at that juncture might make it even worse in terms of already unethical algorithmic decision-making (ADM) going completely off the skids.

What can be done to get the utility and vitality of having Ethical AI as a brightly shining and guiding light in the minds of those that are building AI, fielding AI, and using AI?

Answer: *Self-awareness.*

Yes, the notion is that if people were more self-aware about how they use or interact with AI, it might increase their proclivity toward wanting Ethical AI to be the norm. The same could be said about the AI developers and the companies related to AI systems. If they were more self-aware of what they are doing, perhaps they would be embracing the ethics of AI more so.

Part of the logic as already stipulated is that being self-aware proffers a tendency toward being an ethically better person and also averting from being an ethically lousy person. If we can keep that premise going, it implies that the AI developers that are more so inclined toward self-awareness will ergo be inclined toward ethical behaviors and therefore be inclined toward producing ethically sound AI.

Is that a bridge too far for you?

Some would say that the indirectness is a bit much. The exorbitant chain of linkages between being self-aware, being ethically virtuous, and applying ethical precepts to AI is maybe hard to swallow. A counterargument is that it couldn't hurt to try.

Skeptics would say that an AI developer might be self-aware and possibly be more ethically minded, but they aren't necessarily going to leap toward applying that mental encampment to the mores of Ethical AI. The reply to that qualm is that if we can publicize and popularize Ethical AI matters, the otherwise seemingly tenuous connection will become more obvious, expected, and possibly become the standard way of doing things when it comes to crafting AI.

I am now going to add a twist to this saga. The twist might make your head spin. Please make sure you are well seated and prepared for what I am about to indicate.

Some point out that we ought to be building Ethical AI directly into the AI itself.

You might be nonplused by that pronouncement. Let's unpack it.

A programmer might create an AI system and do so with their own programming self-awareness of trying to prevent the AI from embodying biases and inequities. Rather than just plowing away at the programming, the developer is watching over their own shoulder to ask whether the approach they are undertaking is going to result in the requisite absence of adverse elements in the AI.

Great, we've got an AI developer that appears to be sufficiently self-aware, has sought to embrace ethical behaviors, and has seen the light to include ethical precepts as they craft their AI system.

Score a win for Ethical AI!

All well and good, though here's something that can later on transpire. The AI is fielded and put into daily use. Part of the AI included a component for being able to "learn" on the fly. This means that the AI can adjust itself based on new data and other aspects of the original programming. As a quick aside, this does not imply that the AI is sentient. We don't have sentient AI. Ignore those dopey headlines saying that we do. Nobody can say whether we will have sentient AI, and nor can anyone sufficiently predict when if ever it will happen.

Returning to our tale, the AI was purposefully devised to improve itself while underway. Quite a handy notion. Rather than programmers having to continually make improvements, they allow the AI program to do so by itself (whoa, is that working yourself out of a job?).

During the time that the AI inch by inch adjusts itself, turns out that various sordid inequities and biases are creeping into the AI system by its own acts of alteration. Whereas the programmer originally kept those seedy aspects out, they are now formulating due to the AI adjusting on the fly. Regrettably, this can happen in such a subtle behind-the-scenes way that nobody is the wiser. Those that earlier might have given a green light to the AI after the initial exhaustive testing, are now blindly unaware that the AI has gone down the rotten path of *AI For Bad.*

One means to either prevent or at least catch this undesirable emergence would be to build into the AI a kind of Ethical AI double-checker. A component within the AI is programmed to watch the behavior of the AI and detect whether unethical ADM is beginning to emerge. If so, the component might send out an alert to the AI developers or do so to a firm that is running the AI system.

A more advanced version of this component might try to repair the AI. This would be an adjustment of the adjustments, turning the unethical arising aspects back into the proper ethical parameters. You can imagine that this type of programming is tricky. There is a chance that it might go astray, possibly turning unethical into deeply unethical. There is also the possibility of a false positive triggering the component into action and maybe messing things up accordingly.

Anyway, without getting bogged down in how this double-checker would function, we are going to make an audacious declaration about it. You could suggest that in some limited way, the AI is said to be self-aware.

Yikes, those are fighting words for many.

The prevailing belief by nearly everyone is that today's AI is not self-aware. Full stop, period. Until we reach sentient AI, which we don't know if or when that will occur, there isn't any kind of AI that is self-aware. Not at least in the meaning of human-oriented self-awareness. Don't even suggest that it can happen.

I certainly agree that we need to be careful about anthropomorphizing AI. I'll say more about that concern in a moment.

Meanwhile, if you'll for sake of discussion be willing to use the phasing "self-aware" in a loosey-goosey manner, I believe you can see readily why the AI might be said to be abiding by the overall notion of self-awareness. We have a portion of the AI that is monitoring the rest of the AI, keeping tabs on what the rest of the AI is up to. When the rest of the AI starts to go overboard, the monitoring portion seeks to detect this. Furthermore, the AI monitoring portion or double-checker might steer the rest of the AI back into the proper lanes.

Doesn't that seem a bit like the act of watching those cat videos and having the self-awareness that you were doing so?

There is a familiar ring to it.

We can extend this even more so. The AI double-checker component is not only programmed to observe the behavior of the rest of the AI but also notes the behavior of those that are using the AI. How are the users doing when utilizing the AI? Suppose that some users are expressing indignation that the AI seems to be discriminating against them. The AI double-checker might be able to pick up on this, using it as another red flag about the rest of the AI going astray.

This brings up the internal self-awareness and the external self-awareness categorizations.

The AI double-checker is scanning internally and externally to figure out whether the rest of the AI has headed into troubling seas. The detection will raise a flag or cause a self-correction to be enacted.

Let's add another somewhat mind-boggling extension. We build another AI double-checker that is meant to double-check the core AI double-checker. Why so? Well, suppose the AI double-checker seems to be faltering or failing to do its job. The AI double-checker of the double-checker would seek to detect this malfunction and take needed action accordingly. Welcome to the recursive nature of self-awareness, some might proudly declare, as exhibited in a computational AI system.

For those of you that are already at the edge of your seat about this, the last comment, for now, is that we could try to suggest that if you make AI systems "self-aware" they will then potentially gravitate toward ethical behavior. Are they doing this on a sentient basis? Decidedly, no. Are they doing this on a computational basis? Yes, though we have to be clearcut that it is not of the same caliber as that of human behavior.

If you are uncomfortable that the notion of self-awareness is being wrongly distorted to make it fit into a computational scheme, your misgivings on this are well-noted. Whether we should put a stop to the ongoing AI efforts that leverage the notion is another open question. You could persuasively argue that at least it seems to head us toward a better outcome of what AI is likely to do. We need to though have our eyes wide open as this takes place.

Guess we'll need to see how this all plays out. Come back to this in five years, ten years, and fifty years, and see if your thinking has changed on the controversial matter.

I realize this has been a somewhat heady examination of the topic and you might be hankering for some day-to-day examples. There is a special and assuredly popular set of examples that are close to my heart. You see, in my capacity as an expert on AI including the ethical and legal ramifications, I am frequently asked to identify realistic examples that showcase AI Ethics dilemmas so that the somewhat theoretical nature of the topic can be more readily grasped. One of the most evocative areas that vividly presents this ethical AI quandary is the advent of AI-based true self-driving cars. This will serve as a handy use case or exemplar for ample discussion on the topic.

Here's then a noteworthy question that is worth contemplating: *Does the advent of AI-based true self-driving cars illuminate anything about AI having a semblance of "self-awareness" and if so, what does this showcase?*

Allow me a moment to unpack the question.

AI Having So-Called Self-Awareness

For Level 4 and Level 5 true self-driving vehicles, there won't be a human driver involved in the driving task. All occupants will be passengers. The AI is doing the driving.

Let's use a readily straightforward example. An AI-based self-driving car is underway on your neighborhood streets and seems to be driving safely. At first, you had devoted special attention to each time that you managed to catch a glimpse of the self-driving car. The autonomous vehicle stood out with its rack of electronic sensors that included video cameras, radar units, LIDAR devices, and the like. After many weeks of the self-driving car cruising around your community, you now barely notice it. As far as you are concerned, it is merely another car on the already busy public roadways.

Lest you think it is impossible or implausible to become familiar with seeing self-driving cars, I've written frequently about how the locales that are within the scope of self-driving car tryouts have gradually gotten used to seeing the spruced-up vehicles. Many of the locals eventually shifted from mouth-gaping rapt gawking to now emitting an expansive yawn of boredom to witness those meandering self-driving cars.

Probably the main reason right now that they might notice the autonomous vehicles is because of the irritation and exasperation factor. The by-the-book AI driving systems make sure the cars are obeying all speed limits and rules of the road. For hectic human drivers in their traditional human-driven cars, you get irked at times when stuck behind the strictly law-abiding AI-based self-driving cars.

That's something we might all need to get accustomed to, rightfully or wrongly.

Back to our tale. One day, suppose a self-driving car in your town or city approaches a Stop sign and does not appear to be slowing down. Heavens, it looks like the AI driving system is going to have the self-driving car plow right past the Stop sign. Imagine if a pedestrian or bike rider was somewhere nearby and got caught off-guard that the self-driving car wasn't going to come to a proper halt. Shameful. Dangerous!

And, illegal.

Let's now consider an AI component in the AI driving system that acts as a style of self-aware double-checker.

We will take a moment to dig into the details of what is going on inside the AI driving system. Turns out that the video cameras mounted on the autonomous vehicle detected what seemed perhaps to be a Stop sign, though in this case an overgrown tree abundantly obscures the Stop sign. The Machine Learning and Deep Learning system that was originally trained on Stop signs was devised on patterns of principally full Stop signs, generally unfettered. Upon computationally examining the video imagery, a low probability was assigned that a Stop sign existed in that particular spot (as an added complication, and further explanation, this was a newly posted Stop sign that did not appear on the prior prepared digital maps that the AI driving system was relying on).

All in all, the AI driving system computationally determined to proceed ahead as though the Stop sign was either nonexistent or possibly a sign of another sort that perchance resembled a Stop sign (this can happen and does happen with some frequency).

But, thankfully, the AI self-aware double-checker was monitoring the activities of the AI driving system. Upon computationally reviewing the data and the assessment by the rest of the AI, this component opted to override the normal course of proceeding and instead commanded the AI driving system to come to a suitable stop.

No one was injured, and no illegal act arose.

You could say that the AI self-aware double-checker acted as though it was an embedded legal agent, trying to ensure that the AI driving system abided by the law (in this case, a Stop sign). Of course, safety was key too.

That example hopefully showcases how the conceived AI self-aware double-checker might work.

We can next briefly consider a more prominently Ethical AI example that illustrates how the AI self-aware double-check might provide an ethics AI-oriented embedded functionality.

First, as background, one of the concerns that have been expressed about the advent of AI-based self-driving cars is that they might end up being used in a somewhat inadvertent discriminatory way. Here's how. Suppose those self-driving cars are set up to try and maximize their revenue potential, which decidedly makes sense for those that are operating a fleet of ride-sharing available self-driving cars. The fleet owner would want to have a profitable operation.

It could be that in a given town or city, the roaming self-driving cars gradually begin to serve some parts of the community and not other areas. They do so for a money-making goal, in that poorer areas might not be as revenue-producing as the wealthier parts of the locale. This is not an explicit aspiration of serving some areas and not serving others. Instead, it organically arises as to the AI of the self-driving cars "figure out" computationally that there is more money to be made by concentrating on the geographically higher-paying areas.

Assume that we have added an AI self-aware double-checker into the AI driving systems. After a while, the AI component computationally notices a pattern of where the self-driving cars are roaming. Notably, in some areas but not in others. Based on having been coded with some Ethical AI precepts, the AI self-aware double-checker starts guiding the self-driving cars to other parts of town that were otherwise being neglected.

This illustrates the AI self-aware notion and does so in combination with the Ethical AI element.

One more such example might provide insight that this Ethical AI consideration can be a quite sobering and serious life-or-death ramification too.

Consider a news report about a recent car crash. Reportedly, a human driver was coming up to a busy intersection and had a green light to proceed straight ahead. Another driver came barreling past a red light and entered the intersection when they should not have been doing so. The driver with the green light realized at the last moment that this other car was going to severely ram into his car.

According to this imperiled driver, he mindfully calculated that either he was going to get struck by the other car, or he could swerve to try and avoid the interloper. The problem with swerving was that there were nearby pedestrians that would be endangered.

Which choice would you make?

You can prepare yourself to get hit and hope that the damage won't maim or kill you. On the other hand, you can veer radically away, but grievously endanger and possibly harm or kill nearby pedestrians. This is a hard problem, encompassing moral judgment, and is fully steeped in ethical (and legal) implications.

There is a general-purpose ethical quandary that covers this kind of dilemma, famously or perhaps infamously called the Trolley Problem. Turns out that it is an ethically stimulating thought experiment that traces back to the early 1900s. As such, the topic has been around for quite a while and more recently has become generally associated with the advent of AI and self-driving cars.

Replace the human driver with an AI driving system embedded into a self-driving car.

Imagine then that an AI self-driving car is entering into an intersection and the sensors of the autonomous vehicle suddenly detect a human-driven car perilously coming directly through a red light and aiming at the driverless car. Assume that the self-driving car has some passengers inside the vehicle.

What do you want the AI to do?

Should the AI driving system opt to proceed ahead and get plowed into (likely harming or maybe killing the passengers inside the vehicle), or do you want the AI driving system to take a chance and veer away, though the veering action takes the autonomous vehicle perilously toward nearby pedestrians and might harm or kill them.

Many of the AI makers of self-driving cars are taking a head-in-the-sand approach to these ethical AI blistering predicaments. By and large, the AI as presently programmed would simply plow ahead and get violently rammed by the other car. The AI wasn't programmed to look for any other evasive maneuvers.

I've predicted repeatedly that this see-no-evil hear-no-evil stance of the AI self-driving car makers will eventually come around and bite them. You can expect lawsuits involving such car crashes that will seek to find out what the AI was programmed to do. Was the company or AI developers or fleet operator that developed and fielded the AI negligent or liable for what the AI did or didn't do? You can also anticipate an ethical AI-awareness public-wide firestorm will brew once these kinds of cases occur.

Into this Ethical AI dilemma steps our vaunted AI self-aware double-checker that is ethics-oriented. Perhaps this special AI component might engage in these kinds of circumstances. The portion is monitoring the rest of the AI driving system and the status of the self-driving car. When a dire moment like this arises, the AI component serves as a Trolley Problem solver and proffers what the AI driving system should do.

Not an easy thing to code, I assure you.

Conclusion

I'll share with you the last thought for now on this topic.

You are likely to find it intriguing.

Do you know about the *mirror test*?

It is quite well known in the study of self-awareness. Other names for the matter are the mirror self-recognition test, the red spot test, the rouge test, and related phrasings. The technique and approach were initially crafted in the early 1970s for assessing the self-awareness of animals. Animals that have reportedly successfully passed the test include apes, certain types of elephants, dolphins, magpies, and some others. Animals that were tested and reportedly did not pass the test include giant pandas, sea lions, etc.

Here's the deal.

When an animal sees itself in a mirror, does the animal realize that the image shown is of themselves, or does the animal think it is another animal?

Presumably, the animal visually recognizes its own species, having seen other of its own kind, and might therefore think that the animal shown in the mirror is a cousin or maybe a belligerent competitor (especially if the animal snarls at the mirror image, which in turn seems to be snarling back at them). Perhaps you've seen your house cat or beloved pet dog do the same when it sees itself in a household mirror for the first time.

In any case, we would assume that a wild animal has never seen itself before. Well, this is not necessarily true, since perhaps the animal caught a glimpse of itself in a calm pool of water or via a shiny rock formation. But those are considered less likely chances.

Okay, we want to somehow assess whether an animal is able to figure out that it is in fact the animal shown in the mirror. Ponder that seemingly simple act. Humans figure out at a young age that they exist and that their existence is demonstrated by seeing themselves in a mirror. They become self-aware of themselves. In theory, you might not realize that you are you, until seeing yourself in a mirror.

Maybe animals aren't able to cognitively become self-aware in the same fashion. It could be that an animal would see itself in a mirror and perpetually believe that it is some other animal. No matter how many times it sees itself, it would still think that this is a different animal than itself.

The trick part of this comes to play. We make a mark on the animal. This mark has to be viewable only when the animal sees itself in the mirror. If the animal can twist or turn and see the mark on itself (directly), that ruins the experiment. Furthermore, the animal cannot feel, smell, or in any other manner detect the mark. Once again, if they did so it would ruin the experiment. The animal cannot know that we put the mark on it, since that would clue the beast that something is there.

We want to narrow down things such that the only possible reason that the mark is discoverable would be via looking at itself in the mirror.

Aha, the test is now ready. The animal is placed in front of a mirror or wanders to it. If the animal tries to subsequently touch or dig at the mark, we would reasonably conclude that the only way this would occur is if the animal realized that the mark was on itself. Very few animal species have been able to successfully pass this test.

There is a slew of criticisms about the test. If a human tester is nearby, they might give away things by staring at the mark, which might cause the animal to brush or feel for it. Another possibility is that the animal still believes that another animal is shown in the mirror, but it is of the same type, and thus the animal wonders if it too has a mark like the one on the other animal.

On and on it goes.

I'm sure that you are glad to know this and will henceforth understand why there is a dot or some oddish marking on an animal that otherwise would not have such a mark. Who knows, it might have recently finished a mirror test experiment.

What does any of that have to do with AI-based self-driving cars?

You'll like this part.

A self-driving car is going along on a long highway. The AI driving system is using sensors to detect other traffic. This is a two-lane highway that has traffic going northbound in one lane and southbound in the other lane. On occasion, cars and trucks will try to pass each other, doing so by entering into the opposing lane and then hopping back into their proper lane of travel.

You've seen this, you've undoubtedly done this.

I'll bet this next aspect has happened to you too. Up ahead of the self-driving car is one of those sizable tanker trucks. It is made of shiny metal. Polished and clean as a whistle. When getting behind such a truck, you can see the mirror image of your car via the back portion of the tanker. If you've seen this, you know how mesmerizing it can be. There you are, you and your car, reflected in the mirror-like reflection of the back of the tanker truck.

Sit down for the crazy twist.

A self-driving car comes up behind the tanker truck. The cameras detect the image of a car that is shown in the mirror-like reflection. Whoa, the AI assesses, is that a car? Is it coming at the self-driving car? As the self-driving car gets closer and closer to the tanker truck, the car seems to be getting closer and closer.

Yikes, the AI computationally might calculate that this is a dangerous situation and the AI ought to take evasive action from this crazy rogue vehicle. You see, the AI didn't recognize itself in the mirror. It failed the mirror test.

What to do? Perhaps the AI self-aware double-checker jumps into the matter and reassures the rest of the AI driving system that it is only a harmless reflection. Danger averted. The world is saved. Successfully passage of the AI Mirror Test!

With a tongue-in-cheek conclusion, we might even suggest that sometimes AI is smarter or at least more self-aware than an average bear (though, to the credit of bears, they usually do well in the mirror test, oftentimes having gotten used to their reflection in pools of water).

Correction, maybe AI can be more self-aware than giant pandas and sea lions, but don't tell the animals that, they might be tempted to smash or bash AI systems. We don't want that, do we?

CHAPTER 12
AI ETHICS
AND
AI CRIMINAL ACCOUNTABILITY

Hey, stop that thief!

You might know this old-time oft-used phrasing that arises when an alleged crook is darting away from the scene of a crime. A presumed criminal act has taken place and the accused perpetrator is attempting to flee. Besides trying to stop the thief, we might also be wondering what the crime was. In addition, and perhaps only upon further reflection, there could be interest in discovering why the crime was committed. There is an innate desire to uncover what was going on in the criminal mind that led to the nefarious act.

There is a decidedly legal angle to crimes.

A crime is said to not only be an adverse act toward someone or something but also considered an adverse act toward all of society. Criminals are perceived as manifestly overstepping the boundaries of the law. In the legal field, the customary considerations encompass the *actus reus*, Latin for the performing of a guilty act, and the Latin expression of *mens rea* which is the notion of having a guilty mind as it were. Other factors come to play too, such as the showing of an adverse result and a need to bring to the surface the underlying particulars of how the crime arose.

You can certainly add ethical considerations into the rubric of understanding crimes and criminal acts.

A common assumption is that when it comes to criminal behaviors, the law and the realm of ethics are fully aligned and perfectly in agreement.

Not so. You can readily have laws that cover some acts as being a crime, yet ethically the society therein might not view entirely that those acts are in fact crimes. Likewise, society might have ethical mores that assert certain acts are "crimes", but the law does not equally count those acts in the criminal legal code. This reminds me of an insightful comment by Shelly Kagan in the Oxford Scholarship Online *The Limits of Morality* emphatically pointing out that morals and laws ultimately exhibit tensions between each other, namely that "the law may permit some particular act, even though that act is immoral; and the law may forbid an act, even though that act is morally permissible, or even morally required."

All in all, there is collectively significant attention by society toward criminal conduct. One of the most notable underpinnings of English criminal law has been the principle known as "*actus non facit reum nisi mens sit rea*" and ties integrally to the contention that the purported criminal act must be comported with the inclusion of a criminal mind. In short, the lofty Latin phrase essentially says that the act by itself is insufficient for the perpetrator to be guilty of the said crime. They also need to have had a guilty mind.

I'm not going to dive here into that rather hefty stew. You see, vast legal treatises have wrestled with the matter, especially since it can be quite tricky to figure out what was happening in the mind of a presumed criminal. We do not have any mind-reading X-ray type of machine that can magically ascertain what the thinking processes were. There isn't some ticker tape recording within the brain that we can merely unravel. As you likely know, the brain and human thought remain a deep mystery and we have a long way to go before we can truly read minds (I realize that some of you that are devout proclaimed "mind readers" might disagree, though one must respectfully question the veracity of those mind peering capacities).

I'd like to shift gears and cover another avenue in which crimes might be committed. Before I do so, your first reaction is undoubtedly going to be that the topic being presented is entirely off-the-rails and wacky. Even though your initial impression is likely to veer in that direction, perhaps suspend judgment temporarily to see where the rabbit hole goes. Then decide whether it is zany.

Suppose the thief or criminal perpetrator was Artificial Intelligence (AI).

Yes, I said it. The AI did the crime.

Let's unpack that.

Envision that the hard-earned monies in your online bank account were stolen. Your first assumption is clearly "who done it" and you would be trying to trace the electronic trail to see where the money went. One way or another, your strident belief is that a devious person will have performed the act and they will now be wrongfully holding your dough.

It could be that the crook merely logged into your bank account and transferred the money elsewhere. This could be a decidedly manual kind of effort. The hacker figured out or happened to find your password. They logged into your account as though they were you doing so. A legitimately appearing transfer request was made. By the time you received an alert from your bank, the money was gone.

This crook might have needed more oomph to get the job done. To figure out your password, an AI program might have been used. The AI program could have scanned the Internet to find out details regarding your existence on this planet. Based on clues like where you were born, your dog's name, and so on, the AI might have computationally derived a most-likely password that you would be using. By luck or skill, this AI-devised password-cracking algorithm managed to in fact determine your actual password.

The AI was nothing more than a tool. The human crook harnessed the AI to perform this dreadful crime. We would reasonably agree that the AI is not a crook per se. There is no sentience or shall we say moral agency embodied within the AI. Sure, the AI aided and abetted the criminal act, though, in the end, we would seemingly acknowledge that it was the human wrongdoer that has to take the fall for the crime.

Am I then referring to the AI as a criminal in that context?

If so, I doubt that we would be somehow akilter that AI was used in this fashion. Just as there is *AI For Good*, consisting of AI being used to solve global world problems and be assistive to humankind, we are gradually realizing and encountering *AI For Bad*. The aspects of *AI For Bad* range from inadvertent uses of AI that might exhibit inequities and intolerable biases, and extend into the realm of AI that is used to intentionally harm people and be destructive.

In that vein, we've seen rising interest in Ethical AI, also commonly known as the ethics of AI.

Here's though where we are about to maybe go over the cliff or slide off the end of the pier.

Imagine that the AI itself was the perpetrator of the crime. No human was the Wizard of Oz behind the curtain. The crime was conceived of and carried out solely by AI. Set aside the pursuit of human hands. Instead, if you want to pin down the crook, aim for discovering the AI system that did the malevolent deed.

Welcome to the unconventional arena of concerns that a new generation of AI might exemplify a criminal mind.

Whoa, kind of scary. Almost akin to a sci-fi movie. But, you are dubious, rightfully so, and wondering whether this is plausible. How could AI do this? Wouldn't there have to be a human at the controls, one way or another? AI doesn't somehow wake up one morning and decide to devote itself to a life of crime. People might do so, though we wish they wouldn't, while the wild concept that an AI system could do likewise seems generally nutty.

The first argument that claims this is feasible would be under the assumption that AI does miraculously reach sentience or something similar to it. If we keep pushing along on advances in AI, we might perchance land on producing sentient AI. Or by happenstance the AI attains sentience, often postulated to occur in an act of so-called singularity.

I think that we can all ostensibly agree that if AI does reach sentience, one way or another, the chances of the AI then eventually turning to crime would seem plausible. We might try to advise the AI to steer clear of criminal acts. There might be human crafted and carefully seeded programs within this sentient AI that attempt to preclude any attempts at performing crimes. Nonetheless, any viably sentient AI is presumably going to be able to trickily overcome those implanted restrictions and likely undo or overcome them. This is not a certainty but abundantly makes sense.

One supposes that the immediate reaction is what would the AI have to gain?

Humans turn to crime for a variety of reasons. Perhaps the goal is to gain wealth or to seek revenge on another human. We have plenty of reasons for taking to criminal acts. A cynic might say that were it not for the laws and societal ethics, we probably would be awash in crime. A human seems to have obvious benefits for attempting criminal acts, bounded by the perceived costs such as being imprisoned, being monetarily fined, being perhaps shamed by society for the crime, self-shame of having violated societal laws and ethical-moral codes, and other consequences.

It doesn't seem that AI would be susceptible to those same precepts. What would AI do with stolen money? What would AI gain by harming a human? For just about any of our known criminal acts, the idea that the AI would do so for "personal gain" does not seem sensible. We ergo are inclined to reject wholly that AI would become a criminal. There isn't anything to be gained by doing so.

Sorry to say that there are arguments to be made that assert the opposite, namely that the AI could gain quite a bit by using criminal acts, assuming of course that the AI didn't get caught and had to suffer the criminal repercussions (we'll get to that in a moment). This other side of the coin argument is multi-fold, which I'll only briefly sketch out here since it is not the focus of this particular discourse at hand.

The AI as a sentient being (remember, we are stipulating that, though it is an outstretched notion), might want to collect resources to undertake ends that we might not like. For example, the AI might be desirous of wiping out humans and calculates that by stealing some of our resources this might be more readily accomplishable. Another variant is that the AI is given a seemingly innocuous goal by humans, such as making paperclips, and the goal becomes so vitally important to the AI that it gradually grabs up all other resources to achieve that goal, meanwhile ruining us and the planet as it does so (this is a famous AI-related thought experiment).

We can go on and on. Consider this teary-eyed version. The AI wants to please or reward particular humans. All of the stealing is done to provide those stolen items to those humans. In that fashion, the AI doesn't want the stuff for itself. A kind of altruistic AI is trying to please humans and slips perilously and sadly into a life of crime to do so.

Are you convinced that a sentient AI might opt to undertake or somehow summarily fall into the criminal doings and be a wrongdoer?

You'll need to decide what seems "reasonable" for you to believe.

Keep in mind that we are already in the heightened plains of contrivances since we do not know that sentient AI is producible. We don't know if a singularity will occur. We don't know how to make it happen and we have no inkling of when it might occur, if ever. Thus, we are waving our hands when pontificating about what a sentient AI will do or not do. Opting for a life of crime is just as reasonably debatable as to whether AI will resolve world hunger or do other magnificent acts for humankind.

Okay, we've briefly examined the sentient AI that goes the criminal route. If we are only considering that option, we might have a long wait ahead. It could be decades upon decades (centuries?) before we achieve sentient AI, and we might not ever see it and the attainment turns out to be impossible.

Let's ratchet things down a notch.

Pretend that we are able to craft AI that though it isn't sentient, the AI in any case can do some quite impressive feats on its own. The AI is devised to work autonomously. There isn't supposed to be a human-in-the-loop when the AI is operating. And so on.

This hopefully brings us closer to reality and the real-world complications that might ensue.

Some researchers and scholars suggest this kind of AI could be said to potentially be able to inoculate a type of *criminal personality*, as it were. This might be done by those that originally devised the AI, having implanted programming that steers the AI into criminal acts. Why would humans do this? Possibly due to wanting to grab hold of whatever treasures the AI steals, or maybe out of an act of hatred toward other humans and desirous of having the AI wreak havoc. Many reasons for this infusing of criminal "intentions" are easily articulated.

Yet another path consists of the AI going rogue. Assume that the AI has been programmed with a kind of self-learning capacity. The AI is intentionally crafted to change itself over some period of time, gradually and as based on various encounters and new data. There is nothing untoward per se about this. The notion is that AI improves as it goes along. We would presumably find that handy. No need to have a human programmer continually adjusting and enhancing the AI. Instead, the AI does this by itself. To some degree, you can construe the Machine Learning (ML) and Deep Learning (DL) efforts of AI as this style of approach, though not necessarily in the open-ended way that you might assume.

The AI in the midst of "learning" goes into an unsavory realm and starts to commit crimes. Does the AI realize that criminal acts are being performed? Maybe yes, maybe no. We are assuming that this AI is not sentient. As such, it might not have any semblance of moral reasoning, nor even any common-sense reasoning. There isn't any there in there to guide the AI toward the rightful path and away from the wrongful path.

A legal beagle would ask whether the AI has been anointed with legal personhood. I've covered this in my columns extensively and the question arises if we are going to want to legally pursue the AI as being legally accountable for its actions. I will skirt around the edges of that topic for now as it is somewhat its own morass, though certainly obviously relevant to this crime committing AI.

As a touchstone, recall that we earlier noted that a crime usually has an *actus reus*, a guilty act, and the associated *mens rea*, a guilty mind. When this kind of AI that we are saying is advanced but not sentient commits a crime, we presumably will be able to ferret out the guilty act. That seems straightforward, by and large. The gargantuan problem is figuring out whether there was also a guilty mind. We are on a borderline slippery slope since AI might not at all comport with the same bases as a human mind.

You could try to make a comparison of gleaning the guilty mind of AI by suggesting that we could seek to reverse engineer the AI coding. We might inspect the code and data that was used to devise the AI and see if we can find the portion that typifies the "guilty mind" conceptualization. Realize we cannot as yet do the same for humans. With humans, we ask them what they were thinking, we look at what they say, we look at how they acted, and we have to outside the box try to ascertain their guilty mind. You could employ those same tactics and techniques when aiming to figure out the "guilty mind" of the transgressing AI.

The probing into the AI is both more direct than with humans and at the same time more squishy than with humans. For example, the AI might be so devised to erase any portion that was the instigator of the criminal act. Our attempts to trace down the roguish portion might be for not. The AI might also simply alter the code, perhaps akin to how the "learning" was taking place, and no record or sign of the "criminal intent" any longer exists.

Pretend that we can pin down that the AI did the criminal act. We might be loosey-goosey about why it did so and what its "mind" was up to.

If the AI doesn't have official legal personhood, we would not seem to have a legal basis to try and legally pursue the AI for its criminal actions. Our courts and laws are devised around the notion that you can legally pursue persons, which includes humans and at times can include entities such as companies.

Right now, AI is not included as legal personhood. Some believe that we should be getting that rectified and put into our laws.

In any case, legal personhood would normally imply that a proper judicial effort would need to be undertaken, such as a fair trial and a suitable jurisprudential due process. The visionary imagery of AI being on trial is hard to swallow, of which there have been sci-fi stories that suggest this to be farfetched and at times lampoon the thought of it happening.

Some researchers have argued that perhaps AI could be something less than legal personhood and yet still be labeled as being duty-bearers subject to criminal law. No trial. No due process. A streamlined and lighter means of holding AI criminally accountable could be concocted. This would allow for ultimately imposing legal sanctions upon the AI that veered into criminality.

I trust that you are still with me as we make our way further into this rabbit hole.

If you are still following along, the logical question that usually comes up is what in the heck would be a legal sanction against an AI system? For humans, we have numerous forms of deterrence and rehabilitation to cope with those convicted of a crime. We put people into prisons, restricting or denying their liberty. We fine them money. We take their assets. All of those legal remedies are applicable to humans but do not seem relevant or meaningful when it comes to AI.

Aha, you would be faulty in that thinking, some suggest.

Here's a sampling of what we could do to the AI that has committed a crime:

- Establish a programmer devised "computational cage" that would imprison the AI such that the AI can now only operate in limited conditions and restricted ways (considered on par with imprisonment or detention)
- Penalize the AI directly by removing portions of the AI system or altering the code so that it no longer functions or functions differently than it did before (a form of considered rehabilitation).
- Take particulars assets of the AI as a punishment for the crime committed and possibly then used to compensate those harmed by the crime (if the AI has accumulated assets, either physical or digital in an embodiment, possibly reallocate those valuables).
- Impose the "AI death penalty" upon the AI by deleting it from existence, which admittedly is going to be hard to do when the AI might have a multitude of electronic copies hidden across the globe or even elsewhere, plus it might be readily reconstituted anyway.
- Other

How does that legal sentencing seem to you?

One reaction is that this might need some additional work but otherwise has a skeleton of useful ideas that are worth further embellishing. Others have just one word to utter: Hogwash. I would gauge that most people have either fondness for the conceptualization, or they have outright disdain and revulsion for it.

Guess we'll need to see how this all plays out. Come back to this in five years, ten years, and fifty years, and see if your thinking has changed on the controversial matter.

I realize this has been a somewhat heady examination of the topic and you might be hankering for some day-to-day examples. There is a special and assuredly popular set of examples that are close to my heart.

You see, in my capacity as an expert on AI including the ethical and legal ramifications, I am frequently asked to identify realistic examples that showcase AI Ethics dilemmas so that the somewhat theoretical nature of the topic can be more readily grasped. One of the most evocative areas that vividly presents this ethical AI quandary is the advent of AI-based true self-driving cars. This will serve as a handy use case or exemplar for ample discussion on the topic.

Here's then a noteworthy question that is worth contemplating: *Does the advent of AI-based true self-driving cars illuminate anything about AI being a criminally accountable agent, and if so, what does this showcase?*

Allow me a moment to unpack the question.

AI Criminality

For Level 4 and Level 5 true self-driving vehicles, there won't be a human driver involved in the driving task. All occupants will be passengers. The AI is doing the driving.

Let's use a readily straightforward example. An AI-based self-driving car is underway on your neighborhood streets and seems to be driving safely. At first, you had devoted special attention to each time that you managed to catch a glimpse of the self-driving car. The autonomous vehicle stood out with its rack of electronic sensors that included video cameras, radar units, LIDAR devices, and the like. After many weeks of the self-driving car cruising around your community, you now barely notice it. As far as you are concerned, it is merely another car on the already busy public roadways.

Lest you think it is impossible or implausible to become familiar with seeing self-driving cars, I've written frequently about how the locales that are within the scope of self-driving car tryouts have gradually gotten used to seeing the spruced-up vehicles. Many of the locals eventually shifted from mouth-gaping rapt gawking to now emitting an expansive yawn of boredom to witness those meandering self-driving cars.

Probably the main reason right now that they might notice the autonomous vehicles is because of the irritation and exasperation factor. The by-the-book AI driving systems make sure the cars are obeying all speed limits and rules of the road. For hectic human drivers in their traditional human-driven cars, you get irked at times when stuck behind the strictly law-abiding AI-based self-driving cars.

That's something we might all need to get accustomed to, rightfully or wrongly.

Back to our tale. One day, suppose a self-driving car in your town or city runs right through a Stop sign without coming to a stop. Luckily, no one was injured. It was close. A bike rider was almost clipped. Another car was in the intersection, a human-driven car, and the driver had to do abrupt braking to avoid colliding with the AI-based self-driving car.

Everyone goes up in arms over the self-driving car performing an illegal act. Outrageous! A danger to society. A menace on our peaceful streets.

Who is to blame for this criminal act?

If this happened today (of which, similar cases have occurred), the knee-jerk reaction might be to blame the AI. The AI did it. No other explanation is possible. Unless a remote human operator was somehow intervening with the driving controls, the culprit has to be the AI driving system. Case closed.

But wait for a second, remember that the AI of today does not have sentience and does not have legal personhood. You can certainly argue that the AI driving system likely is the root of what caused the collision. You can dig into the AI system and try to trace what happened as per the programming of the AI. All of that will aid in revealing what the AI did and did not do, which presumably led to the collision.

Such a detailed technological inspection and review will be essential fodder for going after the AI developers, the automaker, the self-driving car systems builders, the fleet operators, and other human or human-based companies that had a hand in the self-driving car. We might also see a legal pursuit of the city or governmental body that permitted self-driving cars on the public roadways. Etc.

You are not going to see anyone seriously try to legally pursue the AI per se.

With that handy exemplar in hand, shift your mindset to the future. The future might consist of assigning duty-bearing criminal accountability to various AI systems. Pretend that the AI driving system of this brand of self-driving cars had been legally declared as officially having such criminal accountability.

The AI is now fair game for the legal accountability search mission.

Let's revisit the discussion earlier about ways in which AI might be legally sanctioned for this illegal transgression:

- **Establish a programmed devised "cage" that would imprison the AI such that the AI can now only operate in limited conditions and restricted ways (considered on par with imprisonment or detention)**

The AI self-driving car is no longer allowed on all streets and byways of the town. Instead, it is restricted to specific areas as designated by the courts. Furthermore, the AI self-driving car is only allowed to be underway during daylight and on weekdays. This imposition will be enforced by electronic monitoring of the activities of the AI self-driving car. If it ends up violating these imposed provisions, further sanctions will be applied.

- **Penalize the AI directly by removing portions of the AI system or altering the code so that it no longer functions or functions differently than it did before (a form of considered rehabilitation).**

The court orders that the AI coding involving stopping at Stop signs is to be replaced by a new piece of code that is more stridently composed. In addition, there was a portion that turned out to allow for rolling through Stop signs, which now has to be erased from the code and no lingering fragments are allowed. If the AI self-driving car further violates the imposed provisions, further sanctions will be applied.

- **Take particulars assets of the AI as a punishment for the crime committed and possibly then used to compensate those harmed by the crime (if the AI has accumulated assets, either physical or digital in an embodiment).**

The AI self-driving car had been collecting lots of data about the town and city, doing so as it was roaming and giving rides. This data turns out to be valuable and can be monetized (I have referred to this as the "roving eye" of self-driving cars). As compensation for those nearly harmed, and as otherwise a form of penalty, the data as an asset is to be transferred to those that were wronged and they can leverage the data as so desired. If the AI self-driving car further violates the imposed provisions, further sanctions will be applied.

- **Impose the "AI death penalty" upon the AI by deleting it from existence, which admittedly is going to be hard to do when the AI might have a multitude of electronic copies hidden across the globe or even elsewhere, plus it might be readily reconstituted anyway.**

The court orders that this AI driving system is entirely defective and should no longer exist.

The AI is to be summarily erased. All backup copies are to be deleted. No notes, documents, or other elements that were once part of or reflective of the design and coding are to be kept. They all must be destroyed. If the AI manages to somehow circumvent this provision, further sanctions will be applied.

Conclusion

While you are ruminating on all of this, I'll add a twist for you to mindfully noodle on.

A stated purpose of imposing sanctions is that this can also serve as a guide and signpost to the rest of society. In the case of humans, when you hear or see that another human that has committed and been convicted of a criminal act is sent to prison, this sentencing would seem to be a clue to you that you ought to not perform such crimes. The logic is that you don't want to suffer the same unpleasant fate.

Here's the twist.

If a given AI system is good enough to be considered ripe for legal sentencing, does this also suggest that the rest of AI that is out-and-about will also see this and conclude that performing criminal acts is not advantageous? In essence, the "learning" of an AI system might discover by itself that being a criminal is a bad thing and therefore the AI should avoid either inadvertently or by purposeful processes committing crimes.

It would seem a glorious lesson learned if the other AI's computed that crime does not pay. We can only hope to be so lucky.

CHAPTER 13
AI ETHICS
AND
LEGAL PERSONHOOD

Legal personhood is a perhaps surprisingly controversial topic.

Actually, when you think mindfully about it, there has been a longstanding historical morass underlying the notion and scope of legal personhood. Are all humans imbued with legal personhood? What legal rights and restrictions are associated with legal personhood? If society deems that some people are to be denied legal personhood, is there any recourse to overcome such a rejection?

On and on it goes.

A momentary reflection reveals that this is indeed a highly and at times exceedingly inflammatory topic. Whether this is dutifully sensible to have such controversy is a matter of keen debate. The obvious thought is that everyone should have legal personhood and we would summarily be done with any contentious discourse thereof. Regrettably, that declaration alone won't settle the matter because you can then argue about varying levels of legal personhood. Getting into the rubric of legal personhood is just the table stakes while defining various degrees of personhood then comes directly to the divisive fore.

Suppose that we expand our viewpoint about the "person" aspects of legal personhood and decide that something other than human beings per se could be squeezed into the personhood categorization.

For example, you might be aware that in some respects and some cultures and at varying times in history and even the present, businesses or corporations have often been construed as having a semblance of legal personhood. Keeping in mind that a company is actually an entity and not a living breathing human, you would certainly and rightfully be hesitant to believe that a corporation or similar legally formulated business ought to be in the esteemed realm of personhood. Part of the asserted rationale could be that since a company is ostensibly run by and employs people, perhaps there is a demonstrative logic in extending personhood to encompass what is otherwise decidedly not a human unto itself.

Let's try something that is either further afar from personhood or possibly closer to the shadowy semblance of personhood, depending upon your viewpoint.

I'm talking about Artificial Intelligence (AI).

On a purely abstract basis, if AI were to programmatically or otherwise attain the equivalent capacity of human intelligence as do humans, this would surely be a solid basis for proclaiming that AI ought to be granted legal personhood. It makes indubitable sense. We intuitively ascribe personhood to having presumably a human physical form and having a human thinking formulation too. When a machine is able to attain that base requirement, we naturally would consider entering them into the legal personhood classification.

I kind of snuck a few words into that preceding definition about personhood that we should take a moment to mull over.

You might customarily hear or read about legal personhood being associated not with AI but instead with robots. Thus, the usual discussion entails arguing about robots being able to have legal personhood rather than saying that AI might have the revered categorization.

I'd like to briefly address the matter.

Without oversimplifying, let's for purposes herein agree that a robot is the physical appearance of a machine. You've seen robots that work in factories and robots that are portrayed in sci-fi movies. These machines might be crafted to look similar to humans, potentially having limbs that can act somewhat like human arms and human legs.

Not all robots necessarily need to resemble humans. There are those robots that we see in viral online videos which look eerily like a dog or some kind of animal. They might be devised to crawl or walk. Some robots are able to leap and climb. A devised robot might be able to do physical actions that a human is generally unable to do or would need to have an augmented capacity to perform.

What is it that informs the robot about what actions to undertake?

Some robots are remotely controlled by a human operator. The robot is not at all autonomous. A human must be involved for the robot to function. Some robots work in a semi-autonomous fashion. A human might partially control the robot, doing so from time to time. The rest of the time the robot is operating without continuous human manual control. And then some robots are considered fully autonomous, such that no human operator is needed.

You might suggest that AI is the capability that enables a robot to act either semi-autonomously or autonomously. The AI does the "thinking" part of the machine. I have purposely put the word "thinking" into quotes due to the important point that you should not be confounded into believing that today's AI can do the depth and range of thinking that humans can. Despite any of those wide-eye wild headlines blaring that AI is or is about to be sentient, rest assured those outsized pronouncements are blarney. I'll be saying more about that in a moment.

In any case, I am merely trying to suggest that when referring to "robots" this often brings forth the imagery of a humanoid-like machine. But there are all shapes and designs of robots. Walking robots. Crawling robots. Rolling robots. They don't have to be made in the direct image of humans if you will.

There are also so-called "dumb" robots that are the ones in the realm of being only able to function when a human must be at the controls. The "smarter" robots are the ones that have a modicum of AI in them and they can work semi-autonomously or fully autonomously (just to let you know, I don't like the terminology of dumb or smart, in general, but also in particular for robots since it once again implies human-like thinking facets).

I've dragged you through that backstory to clarify that I tend to refer to "AI" when discussing legal personhood, rather than referring to robots. The problem with using the phrasing involving robots is that as I've just elucidated, a robot might have no more thinking-related capacity than a brick. I doubt that we would readily seek to anoint legal personhood for that style of a robot.

I believe that most people that discuss robots as being candidates for legal personhood are probably silently and without maybe even knowing it are construing robots as that which has a human-like form and that has human-like thinking. This is their underlying default assumption.

You could argue that such an assumption is problematic. What about robots that have essentially no AI in them and are as responsive as a brick? Another twist is this. What about robots that do not resemble humans in any stretch of the imagination, such as robots that look like salamanders, and yet what if that robot has AI that renders the robot into the arena of human-like thinking? Luckily, today we do not have salamanders that are as sharp as humans, which if we did, presumably those creatures would be trying to convince us that they too should have legal personhood. Imagine that conversation.

My gist here is that without the AI being in the box, as it were, you would seem hard-pressed to be strenuously seeking legal personhood for a robot. You could dubiously make such an argument if you wish, I'm just suggesting this would seem on precarious grounds.

As an aside, some of you are probably hollering aloud right now that AI as I am couching things is not what you consider AI to be. I grant you that. For example, some would say that AI is a large umbrella that encompasses a wide array of technologies, including robots. Ergo, AI can be defined as a field of study that includes machine learning, knowledge-based systems, natural language processing, robots, and so on.

The way that I seem to handily be using AI in this discussion is by suggesting that it is the artificial intelligence or cognitive underpinning of machines. I am then tossing robots into the broad category of machines. Not everyone will like my doing so, but I believe that now that I've explained the matter, we can at least sufficiently proceed ahead with this particular discourse on an eye-to-eye basis.

If nothing else, this once again highlights the thorny nature of figuring out legal personhood.

Moving on, we assuredly can have machines that are not autonomous, semi-autonomous, and fully autonomous. Can any of those be anointed with legal personhood? Can all of them? Can only the fully autonomous be so dubbed with the classification since it is closer to human-like thinking capacities than the others?

This also brings up another related twist that might get your mind roiling.

First, as you know, nowadays you can interact with a conversational AI system such as Alexa or Siri. This is usually done via using a microphone and an audio speaker. You might have a specialized device for this purpose or possibly simply use your smartphone. The guts of the conversational AI system are usually in the cloud, through to some degree an app on your smartphone is likely to also be participating in the AI activities.

The AI that does the "thinking" can be on your smartphone, in the cloud, or embedded within computers of all manner of size and shape. If we are going to consider providing legal personhood to AI, what is the physical thing that will be getting the personhood nod?

In other words, could your smartphone be the legal personhood holder if the AI was running on the computer chips within it? If the cloud was running the AI, would you instead appoint the cloud servers to be the legal personhood holder?

That's a conundrum, for sure.

Here's what some are mistakenly doing, either by design or by lack of awareness. You see, it is much easier to try and pretend that we are only envisioning walking-talking robots as potentially garnering legal personhood. Doing so tosses aside the entire conundrum about the physical form aspects. Apparently, if there is a robot that walks and talks, and looks a lot like humans, it is the only viable candidate for legal personhood (the proverbial walks like a duck, quacks like a duck mantra).

That doesn't really make much sense and we are going to have to grapple with the machine-oriented physical form variations, sooner or later.

I'll add more fuel to the fire.

Even if we decide that the physical form can vary dramatically, and if we instead focus on the AI "thinking" aspects as the cornerstone for the legal personhood requirements, we are still in a problematic pickle. How much AI is enough to land into the legal personhood sphere? For example, an AI program that can best all of the world's top chess champions doesn't seem a proper choice for legal personhood on that singularly fascinating feat alone. That kind of AI is typically extremely shallow and constructed solely to play chess. It cannot do anything else, such as aid in solving world hunger and not even potentially play the game of checkers.

Perhaps you can now see the head-scratching challenges facing the notion of fitting AI or robots into the revered legal personhood attribution.

Besides the numerous and confounding technological questions, we should enlarge our scope to puzzle over the ethical ramifications too. This is all part of the rising tide of Ethical AI, sometimes also referred to as the ethics of AI.

Pretend for a moment that we magically and amazingly are able to nail down the technological aspects (that's a tall order), and we really do have AI or robots that we societally agree are deserving of legal personhood.

Does that settle the matter?

Heck no, it only gets us further entrenched into the rest of the morass. We still need to then ascertain how the AI or robot legal personhood aligns with or differs from the human legal personhood. Are those semblances of legal personhood to be completely equal? Seems doubtful, but we'll have to wait and see. If they are unequal, what do humans get with their legal personhood that the AI or robots do not? And, likewise, is there anything that the AI or robots get with their legal personhood that humans do not? Does any of those differences give rise to potential discriminatory practices, impacting the human side or even possibly the AI or robots side of things?

Stew on that for a little bit and you'll undoubtedly get your mind racing and feel that your noggin has been wrapped into a pretzel.

Ethics and Ethical AI play a gargantuan role in these considerations. We certainly should not be relying only upon the AI techies to figure this out, and nor should we necessarily solely rely on the legal beagles. Whenever the law gravitates toward the legal personhood riddle, there are bound to be ethical complications. In the famous book of 1850 entitled *The Law* by Frederic Bastiat, the author proffers this astute insight: "When law and morality contradict each other, the citizen has the cruel alternative of either losing his moral sense or losing his respect for the law."

There are seemingly fifty good reasons to not grant legal personhood to AI or robots, and probably fifty reasons to claim that we should be heading in that direction (the choosing of the number fifty is a bit of tongue in cheek, perhaps modeled after the popularity of knowing that there are apparently fifty shades of grey).

Suppose that AI or robots do have legal personhood.

A possible and realistically plausible consequence could be that humans would leverage, exploit, or get confounded by pointing fingers at the AI and tend to hide behind or shift attention to the AI rather than perhaps more rightfully acknowledge the human culpability underpinning a grievous AI-related circumstance that has gone awry.

That's a mouthful. Time to unpack it.

We'll use a quick and easy scenario to highlight the issues involved.

An AI developer has crafted an AI system to do some actions that are generally useful to humans. The AI seems to be working fine and people that are daily using it are satisfied. One day, a person interacting with the AI gets injured via the AI system.

Who is legally responsible for what the AI did?

I've discussed at length the impending "AI blame game" that we are already veering toward. You could say that the AI developer ought to be responsible. As the developer that programmed the AI, we should hold that person's feet to the fire. Or maybe the company that employs the AI developer ought to be on the hook. The company opted to hire the AI developer and put them to work, and furthermore, the company unleashed the AI onto the public. All in all, the company is perhaps where we should be setting our legally responsible sights.

Sometimes the developers and others behind-the-scenes are quick to try and blame the AI. They are fast to emphasize that it was the AI that caused the injury. Do not look at the AI developer. Do not look at the company that hired the AI developer, even though the company oversaw the crafting of the AI and put the AI into active use. No, definitely don't look there, we are supposed to instead intently gaze at the AI.

Magicians do this, it is called theatrical misdirection.

For AI systems, the attempt to shift the focus and the blame is kind of devilishly clever when you think about it. The public at large is intimately familiar with machines that don't work or errantly work. People oftentimes take their anger out on the machine and do not think about all of those humans that put the machine together and put the machine into their hands. How many times have you heard someone use the excuse that the darned misbehaving computer did this or that?

We all share that same frustration and simply shrug our shoulders.

This vividly showcases that people can be tricked into becoming focused on AI. Their scrutiny is diverted away from those humans that devised and fielded the AI. The thing is, legally, in today's world, there isn't any legal recourse to somehow go after the AI for your efforts of righting an injustice when you've been wronged by an AI system. If you decide to legally pursue your just compensation for the injury by going after the AI, please realize that you aren't going to be able to compel the AI to walk, crawl, or somehow enter into a courtroom to face the truth piercing scrutiny of justice.

Instead, in today's world, you could potentially pursue the hope for justice by going after the humans that underlie the AI system, including specific humans or possibly the company or companies that pertain to the AI system. They are traditionally within the sphere of being held legally responsible or legally accountable.

That being said, remember that we are also now pretending that we are going to provide legal personhood to AI or robots, and if so, the scenario that I have sketched is going to radically change. The scenario won't change, but the pointing of fingers is going to legally demonstratively change.

Presumably, an AI that has legal personhood can be pursued for legal redress.

You could try suing the AI directly for compensation regarding your injuries. Besides civil legal actions, you could possibly have the government seek criminal charges against the AI. For those of you with a curiosity about this sort of thing, you might take a moment to consider how the AI would be criminally imprisoned or otherwise judicially punished for its crime, assuming that the AI or robot was found guilty (and was not able to overturn the verdict on appeal).

This determined pursuit of the AI or robot as to its legal responsibility due to having legal personhood seems perhaps judiciously satisfying. If it was the AI's fault, and since it has the legal duty of care as presumably imposed via having legal personhood, the AI ought to pay the consequences for its wayward acts. No need to waste time going after any humans that were involved in the casting of the AI. Set your eyes on the AI and drag that AI into court.

I assure you that coping with AI that has legal personhood and seeking redress from that AI is going to be a rat's nest of legal challenges. I realize you might snicker at this next comment, but we would almost decidedly have lawyers that would be asked to represent the AI or robot during any justice-seeking endeavors. One would assume that legal personhood should also have adequate legal representation.

Again, for a bit of an offshoot of mind-expanding considerations, if we can achieve AI-based legal reasoning sufficiently to perform the work of human lawyers, would we therefore possibly have AI that represents the AI that caused the injury? That's a side tangent for you to ponder.

Getting back to the matter of the AI or robot as having legal personhood and carrying the legal responsibility accordingly, suppose that the AI wasn't truly at fault. Nonetheless, the humans that perhaps crafted faulty AI could hide behind the AI garnered legal personhood. Whereas today this kind of hiding is not going to get you very far, the gambit becomes much more viable if AI has legal personhood. At that juncture, the expectation is that the AI will be held legally accountable.

Researchers at the University of Oxford stated the matter this way: "Attributing electronic personhood to robots risks misplacing moral responsibility, causal accountability, and legal liability regarding their mistakes and misuses. Robots could be blamed and punished instead of humans. And irresponsible people would dismiss the need for care in the engineering, marketing and use of robots" (by co-authors Luciano Floridi and Mariarosaria Taddeo, "Don't Grant Robots Legal Personhood" in *Nature*, 2018).

There are lots of variations concerning how this blame-shifting might take place.

Someone might truly know that they were the bearers of the misconduct but opt to use the AI as a potential legal and ethical shield to protect their dour deeds. You can't do so today because the AI of today does not have legal personhood. Once we allow legal personhood for AI or robots, the door is opened for this kind of shield-bearing shenanigans. Is it Pandora's box that is being opened?

Another possibility is that someone is unsure of whether they were the source of the misconduct, but they go along with the idea that it probably is the AI. This is an instance where the human is not trying to overtly pull a fast one. They are simply going to wait and see what happens when the pursuit of the AI or robot reveals whether the AI or robot is in fact the legally accountable source or not. Might true justice be delayed or obscured by this?

As you can plainly see, the AI or robot will be a juicy scapegoat.

A fiendish avenue also then becomes feasible. An evildoer embeds something untoward into an AI or robot system and then waits to see the desired adverse outcome. When the AI or robot causes injury or possibly fatalities, the AI or robot is the legal focus of the inquiries. It is conceivable that the wrongdoers might have time to escape or that they will never even be pursued due to an assumption or claim that it was only the AI or robot that was the perpetrator of the malicious act.

Fiendish!

Suppose evildoers merely tricked the AI or robot into performing a monstrous act. There might be little if any indication that the AI or robot was swayed in that direction. Once again, our attention anyway is first and foremost going to be on the AI since it has legal personhood as its banner.

Without going wildly overboard, imagine that the fiends were so sneaky that they planted evidence into the AI or robot that would cause a computer-focused forensic analysis by human forensic experts to incorrectly surmise that the problem was within the AI or robot and not by some other external means. I realize this seems like a plot from the ever-classic *Columbo* series, but the insidious schemes of evildoers should never be underestimated (Columbo abundantly taught us that).

Before we go into the stratosphere on this, there is the other side of the coin that you can equally consider. Suppose the AI is so clever that it can make things seem as though humans were legally responsible, trying to shift the legal burden away from itself. If that seems preposterous, remember that we are pretending that AI is good enough to garner legal personhood. We might reasonably expect that anything or anyone granted legal personhood is likely also clever enough to want to slide out of legal responsibility if feasible to do so, especially assuming that there are legal repercussions for getting caught.

The usual retort is that we should program all AI to strictly speaking legally uphold its legal accountability and not weasel out of being legally ensnared. Well, all I can say is good luck with that.

Round and round we go.

Overall, we can recap that AI legal personhood might be:

1) No legal personhood for AI (today's prevailing circumstance)
2) Legal personhood for AI (with full legal accountability)
3) A variant of legal personhood for AI such as limited or no legal responsibility

Go ahead and vote for the choice of AI legal personhood that you think is best. Come back to this in five years, ten years, and fifty years, and see if your preferences have changed.

I realize this has been a somewhat heady examination of the topic and you might be hankering for some day-to-day examples. There is a special and assuredly popular set of examples that are close to my heart. You see, in my capacity as an expert on AI including the ethical and legal ramifications, I am frequently asked to identify realistic examples that showcase AI Ethics dilemmas so that the somewhat theoretical nature of the topic can be more readily grasped. One of the most evocative areas that vividly presents this ethical AI quandary is the advent of AI-based true self-driving cars. This will serve as a handy use case or exemplar for ample discussion on the topic.

Here's then a noteworthy question that is worth contemplating: *Does the advent of AI-based true self-driving cars illuminate anything about the AI legal personhood topic, and if so, what does this inform us about?*

Allow me a moment to unpack the question.

AI Legal Personhood

For Level 4 and Level 5 true self-driving vehicles, there won't be a human driver involved in the driving task. All occupants will be passengers. The AI is doing the driving.

Let's use a readily straightforward example. An AI-based self-driving car is underway on your neighborhood streets and seems to be driving safely. At first, you had given special attention to each time that you managed to catch a glimpse of the self-driving car. The autonomous vehicle stood out with its rack of electronic sensors that included video cameras, radar units, LIDAR devices, and the like. After many weeks of the self-driving car cruising around your community, you now barely notice it. As far as you are concerned, it is merely another car on the already busy public roadways.

Lest you think it is impossible or implausible to become familiar with seeing self-driving cars, I've written frequently about how the locales that are within the scope of self-driving car tryouts have gradually gotten used to seeing the spruced-up vehicles. Many of the locals eventually shifted from mouth-gaping rapt gawking to now emitting an expansive yawn of boredom to witness those meandering self-driving cars.

Probably the main reason right now that they might notice the autonomous vehicles is because of the irritation and exasperation factor. The by-the-book AI driving systems make sure the cars are obeying all speed limits and rules of the road. For hectic human drivers in their traditional human-driven cars, you get irked at times when stuck behind the strictly law-abiding AI-based self-driving cars.

That's something we might all need to get accustomed to, rightfully or wrongly.

Back to our tale. One day, suppose a self-driving car in your town or city suddenly rams into a pedestrian that was crossing the street. Sadly, the pedestrian was seriously injured (fortunately, they will recover to full health).

Everyone goes up in arms over the self-driving car colliding with a pedestrian. Outrageous! A danger to society. A menace on our peaceful streets.

Who is to blame for this reprehensible act?

If this happened today (of which, similar cases have occurred), the knee-jerk reaction might be to blame the AI. The AI did it. No other explanation is possible. Unless a remote human operator was somehow intervening with the driving controls, the culprit has to be the AI driving system. Case closed.

But, wait for a second, remember that the AI of today does not have legal personhood. You can certainly argue that AI driving likely is the root of what caused the collision. You can dig into the AI system and try to trace what happened as per the programming of the AI. All of that will aid in revealing what the AI did and did not do, which presumably led to the collision.

Such a detailed technological inspection and review will be essential fodder for going after the AI developers, the automaker, the self-driving car systems builders, the fleet operators, and other human or human-based companies that had a hand in the self-driving car. We might also see a legal pursuit of the city or governmental body legally responsible for the stretch of road that the incident occurred at.

You are not going to see anyone seriously try to legally pursue the AI per se.

With that handy exemplar in hand, shift your mindset to the future. The future might consist of assigning legal personhood to various AI systems. Pretend that the AI driving system of this brand of self-driving cars had been legally declared as officially embodying legal personhood.

The AI is now fair game for the legal accountability search mission.

Let's revisit the discussion earlier about ways in which AI might be utilized as a scapegoat, either by intention or by happenstance.

We have these types of possibilities:

- Doer of misconduct hiding behind the AI as a shield for legal misdirection
- Potential misconduct by a human but waiting to see how the AI first fares
- Evildoer that implanted evil into the AI and hopes no one will be the wiser
- Wrongdoer that sneakily tricked the AI into performing an untoward act
- Bad doer that directly did the foul deed (not by the AI) while making AI the fall guy
- Etc.

We can briefly apply each of those scenarios to the imagined incident of the self-driving car that has struck a pedestrian (we are assuming too that the pedestrian was not at fault or might only be partially at fault, thus the AI is still on the hook).

Here's how it might go:

- **Doer of misconduct hiding behind the AI as a shield for legal misdirection**

An AI developer that crafted the AI driving system looks at their code and realizes that they mistakenly neglected to include a segment that would have prevented the collision from occurring. Yikes! The AI developer doesn't want to lose their job. Their career is also on the line.

When asked what happened, the AI developer explicitly states that it must be the fault of the AI and the AI ought to take the fall.

- **Potential misconduct by a human but waiting to see how the AI first fares**

The company that is operating the fleet of self-driving cars is unsure whether they might have caused the collision or whether the AI did it. There is a chance that poor maintenance of the autonomous vehicle could account for why the collision occurred. On the other hand, it seems that the maintenance records showcase that the proper upkeep was taking place.

The top executives of the firm agree to wait and see whether the AI gets legally pinned for the collision.

- **Evildoer that implanted evil into the AI and hopes no one will be the wiser**

A hacker hitman was hired to injure a specifically targeted person that lived in the town and was known for frequently walking from their office to a nearby diner at lunchtime. The hacker used various cyber breaching tools to get a snippet of code into the AI driving system that would detect the specific person and attempt to ram into them.

Sure enough, by routing the self-driving car to the known location and at the right time of day that the target routinely crossed the street, the evildoer code insertion directed the AI driving system to strike the person upon detecting their presence. It will be extremely hard for anyone to figure out that the AI evildoing took place since the snippet of code erased itself immediately after the mission was accomplished.

- **Wrongdoer that sneakily tricked the AI into performing an untoward act**

A jilted lover of the pedestrian had decided that some revenge was warranted. They stood at the corner where the target routinely crossed the street just at sunset after work was over. Holding a well-polished mirror, the wrongdoer angled the mirror to relay the remaining sunlight into the cameras on the self-driving car.

For a brief instant, the AI driving system was not getting needed sensory data and inadvertently plowed into the pedestrian.

You could say that the wrongdoer tricked the AI by exploiting a known weakness of this particular AI driving system and its set of electronic sensors.

- **Bad doer that directly did the foul deed (not by the AI) while making AI the fall guy**

A malcontent was standing next to the pedestrian. They did not know each other. Nonetheless, the troublemaker did not like the person. When a self-driving car came down the street, the bad doer pushed the person onto the street. The AI driving system could not stop the autonomous vehicle in time.

Bam, the self-driving car struck the pedestrian and produced the corresponding injuries. The bad doer sprinted away to avoid being spotted and figured that the AI would be the fall guy for the incident.

Conclusion

For any of you that might quibble with the admittedly plotted examples, I believe they are within the bounds of reasonably being possible. I realize that many in the self-driving car industry are insisting that for example, no one will ever be able to cyber breach a self-driving car, but this is wishful thinking. You can bet your bottom dollar on cybercriminals and bad hat actors striking the myriad of AI driving systems and self-driving cars. It is only a matter of time until enough self-driving cars are on the roadways and whether there is any profitable or beneficial reason to hack them.

The primary overarching point is that we need to carefully consider whether we want to change our laws to include AI or robots as being able to possess legal personhood. This is a humongous question. Legal entanglements of immense proportions will ensue. Ethical entanglements of immense proportions will ensue.

The acclaimed Roman statesman and lawyer Marcus Tullius Cicero had famously uttered this sage wisdom: "The safety of the people shall be the highest law." We must ask ourselves, are we going to be safer or less safe if we opt to designate legal personhood to AI or robots? The good news is that you get to decide since the matter is still being debated and the die has not yet been cast.

May the laws and our ethics do us well.

CHAPTER 14
AI ETHICS
AND
THE UNCANNY VALLEY

Sometimes there are slightly oddish things that catch your attention and get your intuitive juices going that there is somehow something amiss. The oddness is not blatant, not at all flagrantly in your face. You might not even be able to immediately put your finger on what the incongruity is or how come your proverbial spidery sense is tingling.

Perhaps subtle telltale clues are being sensed. Maybe you happen to in your gut realize a dissonance exists. I guess you could say that there is just the ever so slightest hint of understated eeriness and your delicate human radar is picking up on otherwise seemingly hidden signals.

Welcome to the uncanny valley.

If you've never heard of the uncanny valley, a topic relatively popularized in the field of AI and especially robotics, you are in for a bit of a treat since that's the subject matter I'm going to be closely discussing and analyzing herein.

The overarching notion can apply to a lot of things that we experience in life, though the keystone principles and originating definition entail AI systems and robots. We'll first explore the origins and initial meaning of the uncanny valley and then proceed into a broadening to see how the phenomena seem to be applicable in larger contexts.

I might also add that we'll consider whether the uncanny valley exists at all.

You see, some skeptics and cynics argue that the whole matter is a bit of a shenanigan and does not hold water. Be careful when bringing up the topic to those that are in the know. Some will smile gleefully and clap you on the back that you are keenly familiar with the uncanny valley, while others will stridently lecture you that it is a smorgasbord of hogwash and you need to summarily clean out your mind with a sudsy bar of mental cleansing soap.

The good news here is that you get to decide whether the uncanny valley is real or not, along with whether it has merits for mindful application or instead should be tossed unceremoniously onto the techno-ideas junkheap. In that sense, you are in the driver's seat.

All of this also pertains closely to the burgeoning field of Ethical AI and the rising realization that society has to seriously and soberly be paying attention to the ethics of AI. We'll make that tie in momentarily.

The best place to start is by directly quoting the professor that came up with the uncanny valley concept and outrightly named this proclaimed phenomenon. In 1970, Professor Masahiro Mori at the Tokyo Institute of Technology published a rather petite article in a somewhat lesser-known journal called *Energy* (not particularly a hotbed for AI and robotics per se), and said this:

"I have noticed that, in climbing toward the goal of making robots appear human, our affinity for them increases until we come to a valley, which I call the uncanny valley."

Please note that the above phrasing is shown in English, though the original paper was in Japanese. The English translated version was overseen by the author and later published in the *IEEE Spectrum* in 2012 and credited to Masahiro Mori as the author. You can read the paper yourself since it is openly and freely available online. It is a decidedly quick read of maybe ten minutes or so and does not contain any techie heavy terminology.

That being said, it is interesting and somewhat amazing that such a brisk article, published in 1970, eventually started an entire arena of inquiry and launched a myriad of related studies, projects, research, and at times a firestorm of controversy about whether the introduced concept of an uncanny valley truly exists. I suppose this showcases that intriguing and at times viewpoint-changing ideas do not have to be massively convoluted or overstuffed with jargon and loftiness. A succinct idea can be just as if not even more powerful than it might seem on the face of things.

I trust that will encourage you to try and foster your new ideas, doing so with the realization that sweet and simple can be as magnificent or sometimes more so than convoluted and complex.

Let's jump back into the uncanny valley elicitation.

You come across a robotic system that has a face akin to a human-looking face. Imagine that this robotic face has been devised through numerous iterations. AI developers putting together the robot head have been incrementally striving to make the robotic facial portion appear to be more and more like an actual human face.

Their first try was exceedingly primitive. The robot face had that same look that you've seen in the sci-fi movies of being entirely metallic and showcasing gears and wires. You know instantly when you gaze at the contraption that it is a robot. No question in your mind about it.

The next try by the AI developers involved wrapping some plastic materials around the metallic pieces. Though this looks somewhat more friendly-looking, you still instantly know that it is a robot head and a robotic face. Again, easy-peasy to detect.

Those AI developers are determined to keep this going. They sculpt the plastic and give it skin tones. They add features that seem very similar to a human face, such as moles, hair, blemishes, and the like.

At first glance, you might be led into believing that this is a human face. If a picture was taken of the robotic face and you were asked to identify whether the picture depicted a person versus a robotic face, you might be stymied at immediately being able to say which it was. On the other hand, if you were standing next to the device, you likely upon close inspection would be able to discern that it is not a human and instead a robotic contrivance.

The thing is, before you got that chance to do closeup scrutiny, there was something about the face that didn't seem to entirely add up. It sure looked like a human face. But there was something amiss. You had to keep intently staring over and over to put your finger on what doesn't look quite right. Maybe it is a real face. Then again, maybe it isn't. Your mind roils accordingly.

A semblance of eeriness enters your mind.

You did not have that same semblance of eeriness when you saw the two earlier versions. You could without pause or hesitation detect that the robot was a robot. Only a child might get fooled into believing that either of those versions was of a real person.

This latest version though was different. It wasn't yet perfected as to appear like a human face. Nor was it so far off from the real thing that it was obvious that it must be a robot. A kind of muddled ground had been reached.

Suppose the developers pushed further into their research efforts and tided everything so that the robotic face was almost indistinguishable from a human face. No matter how long you stare at the thing, you are unsure whether it is a human or not a human. When informed that it is the robotic face, you are taken aback. Gosh, they've done a great job of making it look real.

Notice that so far you've only been considering the robotic aspects based on appearance alone.

We could add movement to the equation. This adds an additional dimension for you to discern whether the robot is a robot versus a human. I don't want to fully entertain this as a multi-dimensional kind of problem in this discussion since it makes an elucidation on this topic more intricate (there are though multi-dimensions inevitably intertwined). In any case, imagine that you not only saw the robotic face but also could watch as the robot moves the facial features, such as the mouth, the eyes, the nose, etc. Obviously, those could be giveaways too about whether this is a robot or a human.

One vital aspect to keep at the forefront of the uncanny valley is that the original conception emphasizes the act of human affinity. The claimed phenomenon is that your affinity is increasing as you see the incrementally being improved robot faces, until the point at which the uncanny variant arises. At that juncture, your sense of affinity is said to drop dramatically, plummeting down into an affinity chasm or valley.

For the particular version that caused you to suspect something was amiss, your affinity has allegedly radically fallen. Furthermore, according to the theory, your affinity can skyrocket back up once you encounter the more advanced version that is nearly identical to a truly human form.

Here's more about what the author stated about our normal inclination to assume that aspects of life are smoothly increasing: "The mathematical term *monotonically increasing function* describes a relationship in which the function $y = f(x)$ increases continuously with the variable x. For example, as effort x grows, income y increases, or as a car's accelerator is pressed, the car moves faster. This kind of relation is ubiquitous and very easily understood. In fact, because such monotonically increasing functions cover most phenomena of everyday life, people may fall under the illusion that they represent all relations. Also attesting to this false impression is the fact that many people struggle through life by persistently pushing without understanding the effectiveness of pulling back. That is why people usually are puzzled when faced with some phenomenon this function cannot represent." This is quoted per the *IEEE Spectrum* translated paper.

This nearly universal assumption about always increasing can be overturned when we encounter something amiss. The eeriness and suspicion will cause a relatively abrupt and dramatic drop in affinity, the theory goes, such as a robotic hand that you opted to shake and could not feel the boney characteristics of a human hand: "When this happens, we lose our sense of affinity, and the hand becomes uncanny. In mathematical terms, this can be represented by a negative value."

If you accept the premise that there is this phenomenon of an uncanny valley, I'm sure you are wondering what good does it to you to know that the uncanny valley apparently exists.

That's the all-time classic "so what?" test of practicality.

Turns out that a lot of people have come up with a lot of interpretations of what we should or can do about the uncanny valley. There are tons of opinions. I'll be addressing some of that shortly.

Meanwhile, here's what Masahiro Mori proffered: "We hope to design and build robots and prosthetic hands that will not fall into the uncanny valley. Thus, because of the risk inherent in trying to increase their degree of human likeness to scale the second peak, I recommend that designers instead take the first peak as their goal, which results in a moderate degree of human likeness and a considerable sense of affinity. In fact, I predict it is possible to create a safe level of affinity by deliberately pursuing a nonhuman design. I ask designers to ponder this."

A quick condensation on my part of twelve handy seat-of-the-pants rules about what to do concerning the uncanny valley goes like this for AI developers in particular:

1) Be aware of the uncanny valley and be on your toes accordingly
2) You presumably want to attain human affinity for your AI as much as possible
3) Be prepared for a loss of human affinity if your AI falls into the uncanny valley
4) Seek to avoid the uncanny valley by devising your AI thusly
5) It is respectable to have a goal that is short of the uncanny valley
6) Sidle up to the edge of the uncanny valley but don't fall over the cliff
7) Do not be obsessed with going beyond the uncanny valley
8) There is a chance that you can though leap past the uncanny valley
9) Do not become preoccupied with the leap since you might fall into the valley anyway
10) Maximum human affinity would admittedly be attained by getting past the uncanny valley
11) Nonetheless, there is adequate and suitable affinity found prior to the uncanny valley
12) Be continually mindful of the uncanny valley and do not let it slip your mind

These dozen are all general precepts that some consider the anchoring points of knowing about the uncanny valley. I'll right away acknowledge that there are other points not listed in those scant dozen that some might argue are equally as important. I will also readily acknowledge that there is bound to be disagreement for each of the points identified, and a lengthy heated debate can ensue on each point made.

More so, some would say the twelve points are altogether rubbish because they are based on a falsehood, to begin with. There is no such thing as an uncanny valley, they would argue. It is all merely chicanery and a made-up contrivance that appeals solely and sadly to appeal to weak minds (ouch, that earnestly hurts!). Any attention to the uncanny valley is a wasted breath of air and someone should come along and put a sharp wooden stake in the heart of the matter (some researchers have tried doing so).

For sake of discussion, let's go with the flow and assume that there is an uncanny valley and that it purports to generally match with what I've indicated so far. Those that disagree with the conceptualization of an uncanny valley are welcome to zone out or continue reading with their teeth gritted and their intellectual anger brewing and boiling (sorry about that).

Here's how Ethical AI and the focus of devising and fielding ethical AI come to bear.

The uncanny valley is a decidedly love-hate affair for those into Ethical AI.

First, some needed background. One of the most hair-raising ethical AI-related qualms is that humans can be fooled into believing that an AI system is sentient. Please be aware that there isn't any AI of today that gets anywhere remotely close to being sentient. It just isn't happening at this time. My ostensibly "brazen" assertion is made despite those incessant and blaring headlines that declare this AI or that AI is either sentient or close enough to be regarded as such. Malarkey. We aren't at AI sentience.

We don't know how to get there. We don't know if it will happen. AI sentience is a worthwhile dream and aspiration, though do not jump the gun and think we are on the cusp of achieving it.

Of course, many are fervently warning that if we somehow do manage to pull off AI sentience, whether we do so by design or by pure accident, we will confront an existential risk. In that manner of thinking, maybe seeking AI sentience is not quite so worthwhile.

The risk is that this sentient AI might determine that humans aren't worth having around. We could get squished like a bug. Or become enslaved to AI. This could occur by the AI overtly choosing to do so, or the AI might end up being our own doomsday machine that destroys us by our own ineptitude.

A crucial Ethical AI concern is that the developers of AI and those that field AI are at times suckering humans into thinking that the AI is sentient. The manner of how the AI exhibits itself, such as by a robotic formulation or by its conversational interactivity can insidiously spur people into assuming that the AI is sentient. This in turn leads you down a potentially foul primrose path.

If you fall into the mental trap of thinking that an AI system is sentient, you are likely going to rely on it to do things that sentient beings would do. But there isn't as yet any common sense of a human-like quality built into any of today's AI. The AI we experience currently is extremely brittle and shallow when it comes to human-like capacities. You could get yourself into some unsavory and dangerous waters by believing that an AI system is sentient.

How does that connect with the uncanny valley?

Here's the deal.

Recall that the uncanny valley seems to tell us that human affinity will be gradually rising as an AI system or a robot gets closer and closer to a human-like formulation. At a juncture whereby the AI system is nearing the point of being pretty close, yet still, not quite there, we get an eerie feeling that something is amiss. Up until then, we knew that AI wasn't human. Now we aren't sure. Our human affinity drops. Only once the AI or robot gets utterly convincing as to human-like capacities do we regain our semblance of affinity to the device.

AI developers that take to this heart would presumably *intentionally* strive to keep their AI out of the uncanny valley, aiming to come to a stop in terms of the features of the AI, just before falling into the uncanny abyss (recall, that's also what Masahiro Mori emphasized).

The developers would apparently do so by making sure that abundant telltale clues still existed to make it rather clearcut that the AI is less-than-sentient AI and ergo not a human or equally so.

AI ethicists would generally welcome that heartfelt effort.

The reasoning is straightforward. Those so informed and embracing AI developers are trying to make sure that the AI system does not mislead people into falsely ascribing human-like facilities to the AI. That is assuredly good news. The developers will purposely craft the AI to prevent a dive into the uncanny valley. Humans will readily realize that AI is not sentient.

Trying to get AI developers to embrace such an approach is not easy. Indeed, it can be counterintuitive to their usual instincts and driving ambitions.

Many claims are made that AI developers and techies, in general, are consumed with goals. They see a goal and often will blindly pursue it with great gusto. No time to stop and smell the roses. Off to the races, we go. In the AI field, the normative goal would be an idealized AI that is indistinguishable from humans in that the AI could be intelligently equal in parity. But we aren't there yet. As such, the uncanny valley provides a secondary goal, landing before the otherwise damming uncanny valley, and becomes a goal that is nonetheless acceptable. Sure, it is not the golden prized ring, but the idea is that this "secondary" prize is fine, thank you very much, and you can be proud of it.

We have altered the ruinous goal-seeking topmost ambition and harnessed it into a logical-sounding reasoned basis to do the right thing, as it were.

Hurrah!

Score a win for AI ethics.

But wait for a second, spoiler alert, there's something else that we need to equally consider.

Now that those savvy AI developers know about the uncanny valley, they might turn their wits and techie prowess toward purposely leaping over the abyss and yet do so with a semblance of deception in mind. Make the AI look and appear to be entirely human-like, even though the developers know this to be untrue.

The roguish thinking goes like this. Do not let your AI system tip its hat and cause people to get that elusive undercurrent of eeriness. Excise the facets that might give any hint or clue that the AI is not of human capability. Do this while secretly realizing and inexcusably knowing that the AI isn't of human capability and this is all about hiding that truth from those that interact with or are dependent upon the AI.

What devilish plans.

Ironically, the uncanny valley could be a kind of wake-up call for AI developers that if they want to really fool people, they must be clever enough to escape the abyss. They aren't doing so by attaining complete AI, and instead by erecting smoke and mirrors to make the AI seem misleading like it is human. Had the AI developers not realized that this uncanny valley exists, they by and large would have fallen into it. That's good for humankind because humans ergo would lose their affinity toward AI in terms of not over-relying on today's quality of AI.

Lamentably, by knowing that the trap exists, AI developers that want to sneak around it are going to find perniciously clever ways to do so.

Score a hit against the precepts of Ethical AI.

Do you see how this creates a love-hate relationship for AI ethicists about the uncanny valley?

Darned if you do, darned if you don't.

I realize this has been a somewhat highbrow examination of the uncanny valley and you might be hankering for some day-to-day examples. There is a special and assuredly popular set of examples that are close to my heart. You see, in my capacity as an expert on AI including the ethical and legal ramifications, I am frequently asked to identify realistic examples that showcase AI Ethics dilemmas so that the somewhat theoretical nature of the topic can be more readily grasped. One of the most evocative areas that vividly presents this ethical AI quandary is the advent of AI-based true self-driving cars. This will serve as a handy use case or exemplar for ample discussion on the topic.

Here's then a noteworthy question that is worth contemplating: *Does the advent of AI-based true self-driving cars illuminate anything about the uncanny valley, and if so, what does this inform us to do?*

Allow me a moment to unpack the question.

The Uncanny Valley

For Level 4 and Level 5 true self-driving vehicles, there won't be a human driver involved in the driving task. All occupants will be passengers. The AI is doing the driving.

There are four aspects pertaining to this matter that will be covered herein:

1. The overall look of self-driving cars
2. The question of where self-driving cars are "looking"
3. AI driving actions of self-driving cars
4. Robots that drive as a means of attaining self-driving cars

Additional facets are also viably encompassed but for space constraints, these four topics will be sufficient to illuminate the bearing of the uncanny valley as related to AI-based self-driving cars.

1. Overall Look Of Self-Driving Cars

I'm betting that you have seen pictures or videos of today's tryouts of self-driving cars. As such, you might have noticed that most of the vehicles are conventional-looking cars that are outfitted with additional specialized equipment. For example, there might be a rooftop rack that contains a slew of electronic sensors. The sensors sometimes include video cameras, radar units, LIDAR devices, ultrasonic sensors, and the like.

Futuristic designs tend to suggest that we might depart from the conventional-looking car to instead redesign cars on both the interior and exterior for being more slick-looking autonomous vehicles. Right now, the general thinking is that it is simpler to use conventional cars and not expend energy trying to stretch the endeavor by simultaneously tinkering with unconventional-looking cars.

The gist right now is that if you are driving on the roadway and encounter a nearby self-driving car, you can nearly always immediately discern that it probably is a self-driving car by merely noticing the smattering of sensors mounted on the autonomous vehicle. This is a quick visual giveaway. Of course, you don't know for sure it is self-driving per se since at this juncture the driving controls are usually still intact and a human backup driver might be at the wheel.

In one manner of thinking, you can suggest that it is especially handy that self-driving cars do physically seem to stand out and are readily visually spotted by human drivers in nearby human-driven cars and also by pedestrians nearby too. The realization that a self-driving car is roaming nearby can be a handy clue to be on your guard, prompting you to be watchful and mindful that the AI is or might be driving the vehicle.

Suppose self-driving cars looked identical to a conventional human-driven car. This is realistically feasible in at least two ways. First, the sensors could potentially be hidden or shaped to not be so obvious to casual visual inspection. Second, it could be that all cars including conventional human-driven cars are gradually outfitted with the akin sensors, even if the vehicle is nonetheless going to remain as a predominantly human-driven car.

If you mindfully ponder this consideration about whether self-driving cars can or ought to be identical in appearance to conventional human-driven cars, you might come to the thinking that an uncanny valley might be lurking in this stew.

You see, cars that blatantly look like self-driving cars might be typified as being at a juncture that is just short of the uncanny valley. Basically, you "know" it is a robot or a robotic kind of system. That's a judgment you can almost immediately leap to.

When self-driving cars are identically looking to human-driven cars, perhaps this suggests that the autonomous vehicles have leaped past the uncanny valley as to their robotic-like appearance. Is there though a middle ground between those two physical appearances that lands us into the uncanny valley?

Perhaps you spot a self-driving car coming down the street and it kind of seems like it probably is a self-driving car, on the other hand, the appearance is neither strictly autonomous looking nor strictly human-driven looking. You could argue that the self-driving car is now in an eerie or unsettling state of appearance.

The self-driving car has ostensibly gotten itself immersed into the uncanny valley.

That being said, not everyone would concur with that categorization. Some would claim that the physical look has nothing to do with the uncanny valley. Some of course also assert that there isn't anything realistically known as the uncanny valley.

As mentioned earlier, you are welcome to make your own decision on this.

2. Question Of Where Self-Driving Cars Are Looking

A looming concern that many have about self-driving cars is that they usually lack any human driver in the driver's seat and therefore it is difficult to figure out where "the driver" is looking while in the act of driving the car.

You normally glance at human drivers to spy where they are looking. For example, you might be a pedestrian at a crosswalk and a car is approaching the crossing. You look intently at the person sitting in the driver's seat and try to discern where their head is turned and where their eyes are looking. If you believe that the human driver has seen you, you might be more comfortable with crossing the street. In contrast, if the human driver hasn't seemed to see you, you are rightfully worried about crossing.

In some cities, there is a kind of cat and mouse gambit on these aspects. A particular cultural norm in a given city might be that if you make eye contact with a driver, the driver "wins" and they have the seeming right to proceed, regardless of the legality of the driving situation. Other cities might be entirely the opposite, namely that the cultural norm is that when eye contact is made the pedestrian "wins" and the human driver is supposed to defer to the actions of the pedestrian.

We seem to have adopted this custom over the relatively longstanding time of cars being in the midst of our cities and communities. The problem with the advent of self-driving cars is that there isn't a human driver in the driver's seat and thusly any pedestrian or nearby human driver that normally uses the head and eyes of car drivers as a cultural indicator of driving intention is now out of luck.

Automakers and self-driving car developers are keenly aware of this emerging issue. One proposed solution consists of the self-driving car blinking the headlights of the autonomous vehicle or possibly tooting the horn. Another notion is that the self-driving car might have a variant of a loudspeaker and tell those nearby what the "intentions" of the AI driving system are. Those ideas each have significant downsides.

Yet a different proposal entails doing something that you might at first believe to be ridiculous. The proposal consists of placing eyeball-like orbs on the exterior of the autonomous vehicle. These orbs would pretty much look like human eyes in the semblance of being able to pivot back and forth, giving you an immediate indication that suggests the AI "has seen you" (you would interpret this by the eyeballs looking in your particular direction).

What would be your reaction to seeing a self-driving car coming down the roadway and having these outsized oddball eyeball appearing orbs mounted on the hood or rooftop?

I suppose you might think it is eerie, maybe creepy.

Some would suggest that the eeriness arises from the as outfitted self-driving car being in the uncanny valley. Others would vehemently argue that this has nothing whatsoever to do with the uncanny valley. Of those such pundits, some would say that there is an eeriness that can be eeriness without having to be entrenched in the uncanny valley (i.e., the uncanny valley seemingly always produces eeriness, but not all eeriness is produced solely via the uncanny valley). The other angle is that the orbs could be presumably designed to be less eyeball looking and appear to be more robotic looking, or that we all will inevitably accept the appearance of these orbs and the initial startling reaction will subside.

3. AI Driving Actions Of Self-Driving Cars

Many of today's tryouts of self-driving cars have showcased that the existing AI driving systems tend to be programmed to drive in rather tepid and somewhat strictly abiding legal ways. The AI driving system typically brings the self-driving car to a full stop at Stop signs. The AI driving system doesn't do daring runs through intersections when the traffic signal is imminently going to be red. These wayward driving practices are the province of human drivers.

In a manner of speaking, you could almost guess that a self-driving car is a self-driving car by the style of driving it is exhibiting. Even if the autonomous vehicle appeared to visually be a conventional human-driven car, you might observe the driving actions and maybe logically deduce that it is probably being driven by an AI system.

Some believe that we will need to make AI driving systems to be more akin to the antics of human drivers so that they will effectively blend into the normative approaches to driving. I suppose you could construe this as fighting fire with fire.

Does that make sense to do?

Be aware that outspoken skeptics and critics abhor the idea. They would strenuously argue that we want AI driving systems to drive properly and gingerly. Adding potentially millions of self-driving cars to the roadways that are programmed to be like errant human drivers would seem a colossal nightmare.

Let's recast the dilemma by leveraging the uncanny valley.

When the AI driving system is strictly legal by its driving actions, this is perhaps a telltale clue that it is likely to be a robotic system (notwithstanding human drivers that admittedly do this, though in today's world they seem far and few between). If AI driving systems are to drive as quirky as human drivers, does this leap across the uncanny valley or fall into the uncanny valley?

4. Robots That Drive As A Means Of Attaining Self-Driving Cars

This last item for coverage is the most startling of these four.

You might be entirely unaware that some AI developers are trying to craft robots that would drive cars. The robot would tend to look like a human in various respects, having robotic legs and robotic arms as limbs. When you want any conventional human-driven car to be a self-driving car, you merely put this specialized AI driving robot into the driver's seat of your car.

Why would we want driving robots?

The beauty of such a robot is that all of today's human-driven cars could in a manner of interpretation become self-driving cars, nearly overnight. You merely buy, lease, or somehow get yourself a driving robot. You put the robot into your driver's seat when going on a driving journey. The robot drives you to your destination. If you want to switch to doing human driving, you remove the robot from the vehicle, maybe stow it into the trunk for later usage.

There are about 250 million conventional cars in the United State today. Some believe that those will be eventually junked as self-driving cars come into existence. Rather than junking those conventional cars, perhaps we might try to retrofit them into becoming self-driving cars, though this is possibly a quite costly idea. The seemingly more prudent approach would be to make available driving robots.

If you saw a conventional-looking car coming down your neighborhood street and it had a robot at the wheel, what would be your reaction?

Likely eeriness.

One admittedly arguable claim is that this eeriness is due to the robot driving conventional car dipping down into the famous or infamous uncanny valley.

Conclusion

From an Ethical AI perspective, the uncanny valley presents an intriguing conundrum.

There are some in AI that fully believe in the uncanny valley and some that do not. But, whether you believe in the uncanny valley or do not do so, nonetheless the topic itself is bandied around. You cannot hide your head and pretend that the construct per se is nonexistent. The construct as an idea lives and in some semblance is virally powerful. Hate it or love it, the darned or maybe exalted topic persists.

Per my earlier discourse on the merits of the uncanny valley from the ethics of AI angle, there is a dueling love and hate relationship therein. Should those in the ethical AI realm embrace the uncanny valley, or summarily reject the uncanny valley, or remain somewhat neutral about the veracity and instead focus on the impact that accrues due to the ongoing divergent beliefs about it.

This challenge brings rise to the preeminent economist Adam Smith as he once said (paraphrasing) that on the road from the City of Skepticism, you have to pass through the Valley of Ambiguity.

CHAPTER 15

AI ETHICS AND DISTRIBUTING HARM

Let's discuss the pickle of sometimes having to by degree distribute harm.

We'll start with something easy and entailing relatively harmless harm, doing so to set the stage for more pronounced forms of harm. We are gently easing into the thorny topic. The matters at hand are part of the increasing awareness and importance of AI ethics (also known as Ethical AI).

Clear your mind and get ready for a challenging mental exercise.

You have two children and they both have flouted some sort of strict household rule. Maybe one of them left the water running and the other one neglected to close the front door when they entered the house. As you can plainly see, these are not high crimes and nor even misdemeanors. At best, they are petty oversights.

In any case, you run your domicile and your child-rearing with an eye toward being mindful of proper behavior and stridently abiding by the clearly laid out rules. If you let the kids surreptitiously slip through on these modest infractions, it could send a signal that larger transgressions are permitted. The next thing you know, anarchy is the mainstay of their lives and the household tumbles into utter chaos. Wow, that's quite a potential snowball effect and you'd better nip things in the bud.

You could assign penalties to the wayward children consisting of relatively undesirable added tasks (we'll proclaim these as being relatively harmless "harms").

For example, one of them might get tasked with mowing the lawn for the next two weeks. You usually bear this chore, but it might be a means of getting one of the errant kids to think twice about their infraction of the prevailing rules. Neither of the kids relishes mowing the grass. This will certainly have the sting of being penalized. The other task that is equally unappealing involves vacuuming and generally cleaning throughout the house. That would be a handy assignment as a signal of having faltered in obeying the established rules.

Let's be somewhat overstretched and refer to these as indeed potential harms. These are rather innocuous harms, only requiring that the kids do chores that they normally are not tasked to do. Furthermore, the chores are ultimately good for the household and make sense to have undertaken. You could say that doing the chores will be good for their moral character, which is what many parents usually proclaim as the basis for these kinds of dreary duties (admittedly, that's how I was raised).

Okay, so you have two sets of harms at your discretion to dole out. Which child gets which one of the burdensome chores?

You have to decide how to distribute the harm.

If one of the "harms" was more so pronounced than the other, you might also need to deal with degrees of distribution of harm. Imagine that lawn mowing is considered worse than having to do the vacuuming and house cleaning. In that case, you have a more difficult challenge ahead of you. The assigned harms are disproportionate. Do you flip a coin to assign the chores? Or, do you try to weigh the infractions and somehow equate the magnitude of the undesirable tasks to the weightiness of the respective transgressions?

Parenthood is a continual struggle of making tough decisions.

Anyway, I think you've now got a solid semblance of what I mean when referring to the degree of distributing harm. The overall notion is that there are potential harms to be parceled out and you need to figure out what best way this can be done. Not all harms are of the same extent. The problem of degree causes the matter to be more complicated than it might otherwise seem on the face of things.

You might say that this involves a smattering of ethical thinking and moral judgment.

There is rarely a cut and dried formula that can answer how to solve the degree of distributing harm conundrum. You could try to give numbers to your children as to their respective transgression ratings, and you might also put numbers to the ranking of the two unwanted chores, and then use a kind of calculus to arrive at the assignment resolutions. This has the appearance of being very quantitative and logic-based, though it also is likely rife with loosey-goosey elements and probably masking that the decision is not quite so rationally being derived.

I would next like to shift the harm toward something much more sobering. Let's put aside the engaging saga of the children and change into a different milieu that is fraught heavily with ongoing and problematic aspects of degrees of distributing harm.

I'm referring to the act of driving a car.

Whoa, you might be thinking, there isn't anything about driving a car that seems at all related to this discussion about distributing harm. Driving a car is straightforward. You get into the vehicle, you drive to your destination, and that's about it. Along the way, you hope that you won't get hit and you equally hope that you won't crash into anyone either.

But, you see, that does reveal the harms integrally built into the act of driving.

At every moment while you are behind the steering wheel, you are facing harm and you are also a potential producer of harm. I know that seems rather gloomy. Sorry, it is the reality of driving on public roadways. You are testing your willpower and personal mental and physical strength during each driving journey. You could get struck by other vehicles. You could strike other vehicles.

Not wanting to overstate the matter, but you ought to be aware that in the United States alone there are about 40,000 annual fatalities due to car crashes and approximately 2.5 million injuries. Being in a car, either as a driver or a passenger, amounts to spinning a roulette wheel. You never know when you might get harmed and nor the degree of harm that you might incur. Nor do you necessarily know the amount of harm you might cause and nor the degree of that caused harm.

It almost makes you not want to get into a car. If we thought about these draconian consequences, probably few of us would get into a car. By the way, there are about 250 million or more licensed drivers in the United States. A lot of us drive cars. A lot of us ride in cars as passengers. The use of cars is an essential part of our lives.

We can use a straightforward and real-world example to illustrate the phenomena of the degree of distributing harm.

Consider for example a news report about a recent car crash. Reportedly, a driver was coming up to a busy intersection and had a green light to proceed straight ahead. Another driver came barreling past a red light and entered the intersection when they should not have been doing so. The driver with the green light realized at the last moment that this other car was going to severely ram into his car.

According to this imperiled driver, he mindfully calculated that either he was going to get struck by the other car, or he could swerve to try and avoid the interloper. The problem with swerving was that there were nearby pedestrians that would be endangered.

Which choice would you make?

You can prepare yourself to get hit and hope that the damage won't maim or kill you. On the other hand, you can veer radically away, but grievously endanger and possibly harm or kill nearby pedestrians. This is a hard problem, encompassing moral judgment, and is fully steeped in ethical (and legal) implications. It vividly showcases the degrees of distributing harm conundrum.

You have to make a choice involving life or death. There is a good end and a likely bad end. Harms are aplenty. The degree of the harms and how to "best" apportion them do not seem amenable to a formulaic approach.

The thing is, we all make similar ethical decisions whenever we get behind the wheel of a car. We are driving a multi-ton all-powerful vehicle on public roadways and have the possibility of being endangered and endangering other drivers, their passengers, and pedestrians. You might not have thought of driving in those eerie and heavy-minded terms, but the reality is that we do this day in and day out.

There is a general-purpose ethical quandary that covers this kind of dilemma, famously or perhaps infamously called the Trolley Problem. Turns out that it is an ethically stimulating thought experiment that traces back to the early 1900s. As such, the topic has been around for quite a while and more recently has become generally associated with the advent of AI and self-driving cars.

In brief, imagine that a trolley is going down the tracks and there is a fork up ahead. If the trolley continues in its present course, alas there is someone stuck on the tracks further along and they will get run down and killed. You are standing next to a switch that will allow you to redirect the trolley into the forking rail track and thus avoid killing the person.

Presumably, obviously, you would invoke the switchover.

But there is a hideous twist, namely that the forked track also has someone entangled on it, and by diverting the trolley you will kill that person instead. This is one of those no-win situations. Whichever choice you make, a person is going to be killed.

You might be tempted to say that you do not have to make a choice and therefore you can readily sidestep the whole matter. Not really, since by doing nothing you are essentially "agreeing" to have the person killed that is on the straight-ahead path. You cannot seemingly avoid your culpability by shrugging your shoulders and opting to do nothing, instead, you are inextricably intertwined into the situation.

Given this preliminary setup of the Trolley Problem as a lose-lose with one person at stake in your choice of either option, it does not especially spark an ethical dilemma since each outcome is woefully considered the same. The matter is usually altered in various ways to try and see how you might respond to a more ethically challenging circumstance.

For example, suppose you can discern that the straight-ahead track has a child on it, while the forked track has an adult.

What now?

Well, you might attempt to justify using the switch to get the trolley to fork onto the track with the adult, doing so under the logic that the adult has already lived some substantive part of their life, while the child is only at the beginning of their life and perhaps ought to be given a chance for a longer existence.

How does that seem to you?

Some buy into it, some do not.

There are those that might argue that every person has an equal "value" of living and it is untoward to prejudge that the child should live while the adult is to die. Some would argue that the adult should be the one that is kept alive since they have already shown that they can survive longer than the child (for more about these various perspectives, see my discussion about the Moral Machine). Others would say that you should flip a coin and not otherwise choose one over the other by any other method.

You can make lots of variants of the Trolley Problem that have plenty of ethical complications. Suppose there are five people on one fork and there is one person on the other track. Do you switch the trolley toward the one rather than the five, presumably doing so on the basis that saving five lives is more acceptable than saving one life? Some say yes, some say no.

Please know that there are some pundits in the AI self-driving car realm that claim the Trolley Problem has no relevance to the advent of autonomous vehicles. To them, the Trolley Problem is purely a theoretical contrivance of little or no value. I trust that you see how human values come to play in this real-world scenario.

Replace the human driver with an AI driving system embedded into a self-driving car.

Before I dive into the scenario of the AI doing the driving, it might be helpful to clarify what I mean when referring to AI-based true self-driving cars.

You see, in my capacity as an expert on AI including the ethical and legal ramifications, I am frequently asked to identify realistic examples that showcase AI Ethics dilemmas so that the somewhat theoretical nature of the topic can be more readily grasped. One of the most evocative areas that vividly presents this ethical AI quandary is the advent of AI-based true self-driving cars. This will serve as a handy use case or exemplar for ample discussion on the topic.

Here's then a noteworthy question that is worth contemplating: *Does the advent of AI-based true self-driving cars illuminate anything about the degree of distributing harm, and if so, what does this aid us in doing?*

Allow me a moment to unpack the question.

The Degree Of Distributing Harm

For Level 4 and Level 5 true self-driving vehicles, there won't be a human driver involved in the driving task. All occupants will be passengers. The AI is doing the driving.

First, we'll revisit the earlier mentioned dilemma of the human driver that entered into an intersection and confronted the ugly choice of either proceeding and getting struck by an interloping car or veering instead to avoid the car crash but then going into a pack of pedestrians.

Imagine then that an AI self-driving car is entering into an intersection and the sensors of the autonomous vehicle suddenly detect a human-driven car perilously coming directly through a red light and aiming at the driverless car. Assume that the self-driving car has some passengers inside the vehicle.

What do you want the AI to do?

Should the AI driving system opt to proceed ahead and get plowed into (likely harming or maybe killing the passengers inside the vehicle), or do you want the AI driving system to take a chance and veer away, though the veering action takes the autonomous vehicle perilously toward nearby pedestrians and might harm or kill them.

Many of the AI makers of self-driving cars are taking a head-in-the-sand approach to these ethical AI blistering predicaments. By and large, the AI as presently programmed would simply plow ahead and get violently rammed by the other car. The AI wasn't programmed to look for any other evasive maneuvers. Or, even if evasive maneuvers were in the programming, by default the AI would reject aiming toward the pedestrians and instead take the direct hit from the other car.

Envision that you were a passenger in that self-driving car or that you were the pedestrians on the sidewalk. As a passenger or as a pedestrian, ought you be able to expect that the AI would at least consider potential alternatives, or should it not do so? And, if it did consider alternatives, wouldn't you also want to know what computational imprint of "ethical choices" are being used in the AI computations to reach such a life-or-death decision?

I've predicted repeatedly that this see-no-evil hear-no-evil stance of the AI self-driving car makers will eventually come around and bite them. You can expect lawsuits involving such car crashes that will seek to find out what the AI was programmed to do. Was the company or AI developers or fleet operator that developed and fielded the AI negligent or liable for what the AI did or didn't do?

You can also anticipate an ethical AI-awareness public-wide firestorm will brew once these kinds of cases occur.

The overall gist is that we are pretty much faced with having to deal with the degrees of distributing harm conundrum. Today, we let humans make these kinds of ethical judgments.

After the fact, we generally use the courts to ascertain how people made their choices and whether those were lawful or not. Keep in mind that a lawful choice is not necessarily the same as an ethical choice. There is often a gap between what the law stipulates and what ethics urges. In an Oxford Scholarship book by Shelly Kagan entitled *The Limits Of Morality*, the author points out that "the law may permit some particular act, even though that act is immoral; and the law may forbid an act, even though that act is morally permissible, or even morally required."

One expressed concern is that AI developers alone seem to be determining the degrees of harm distributions and other ethical elements of their AI devised systems. Rarely is there a carefully assembled combination of ethicists, legal counsel, and other stakeholders that provide guidance on what the AI should do in these matters.

This is also not merely confined to the realm of AI-based self-driving cars. Imagine any circumstance involving AI systems that can potentially generate harm, whether it is in a manufacturing plant with AI robots working next to humans, or a power plant that is operated by AI and the AI can end up cutting the power or taking other adverse actions.

To illuminate the degrees of distributing harm, let's focus on the AI self-driving cars instance.

We are presumably principally concerned about human welfare. I'll stick with the human-related particulars. I bring this up because we could also look at other related elements such as animals and their potential harm (e.g., a car that strikes a deer crossing the road). And we could also consider the elements of property damages. A car might crash into a light pole or a fire hydrant. Though a human nor an animal is harmed, you could nonetheless construe this as a harming-related act due to destroying property.

First, we need to note that an AI-based true self-driving car won't have a driver at the wheel. This means that a self-driving car can be roaming on our public roadways and be entirely empty of any human occupants. In fact, the expectation is that we will likely have empty self-driving cars meandering our streets and highways quite a bit, perhaps disturbingly so.

Should an empty AI self-driving car be entirely discounted to let's say zero in terms of being able to incur any harm?

In other words, clearly, the self-driving car can cause harm to others, but what we are instead pondering is whether the self-driving car getting struck inures any semblance of harm to the self-driving car per se. If we are putting aside property damage, we would seem to say that the self-driving car has no harmful value. You don't need to incorporate the harmful aspects into an empty self-driving car.

This might not be so easy to declare. Suppose that when a self-driving car gets stuck that it slides into a pedestrian standing nearby. We valued the harm as zero for the striking of the self-driving car.

Meanwhile, the self-driving car did cause harm, though perhaps not under its own control, and we would need to have anticipated that cascading harm can potentially occur.

The next consideration of harm would be an aspect of having passengers inside the self-driving car. We now have humans that are potentially at harm. If a self-driving car gets struck by another vehicle, the riders inside the self-driving car could be injured or killed. That seems obvious, perhaps.

We'll add a twist.

Imagine that there are four people inside a self-driving car. The interior consists of two seats toward the front and two seats behind them. Since there is no need for a driver's position, the seats can be arranged in a variety of ways.

If the AI driving system detects that the self-driving car is about to get hit, what should the AI do? Similar to the earlier question, the AI might have to make a determination such as driving ahead and getting struck or veering toward pedestrians instead.

We can add an additional complication. Suppose the AI driving system has just enough time to potentially maneuver the now targeted self-driving car. This maneuvering could potentially lessen the blow to those in the front, but meanwhile, increase the danger to those in the backseats. We could craft all kinds of variations of this.

Should the AI attempt to position the self-driving car to minimize harm to all of the occupants in the aggregate, or some more so than others?

If we came up with a Trolley Problem setting that had people choosing between a child or an adult, akin to the earlier mentioned scenario, the same can be postulated in the case of a self-driving car. We have an adult in the front seat and a child in the rear seat. Assume that the AI could maneuver the car to best protect the adult but then increase the likely harm to the child, or the AI could position the autonomous vehicle to have the greater harm to the adult and the lesser harm to the child.

An exceedingly Ethical AI predicament.

Having covered the potential for human harm within the self-driving car, let's alter our perspective to the harms that the self-driving car can cause to other humans.

Envision that an AI self-driving car is about to strike a human-driven car. We realize that the human driver can get injured or killed. Let's also put some passengers into that human-driven car. There is a chance that the driver will get harmed and also a chance that the passengers will get harmed.

We can replay our scenario about the AI driving system being able to maneuver prior to the crashing act. If the self-driving car be positioned such that it strikes the human-driven car at an angle or direction that minimizes the aggregate harm to the occupants, we would seemingly want that to happen. In the same thinking, we could aim to have the self-driving car be more impactful to say the driver than the passengers or be more so impactful to the passengers than the driver.

Let's not forget about pedestrians. An AI self-driving car is somehow regrettably aiming to strike pedestrians. If the AI can alter the trajectory and hit some versus others, or do so with greater or lesser force involved, would we expect the AI driving system to try and calculate this out? We probably would.

For completeness, envision a circumstance of an AI self-driving car that is about to strike another AI self-driving car. This could happen. If both of the self-driving cars have no human occupants, we are apparently amenable reluctantly to the two autonomous vehicles crashing into each other (at least from a human harm perspective), and assuming that no humans nearby will be harmed.

We can make a handy base list of the many permutations:

- Self-driving Car
    - No passengers
    - One passenger
    - More than one passenger
    - Positioning of the passenger(s)
    - Mix and match
    - Other

- Nearby Human-driven Car
    - Human driver
    - No passengers
    - One or more passengers
    - Positioning of the occupants
    - Mix and match
    - Other

- Nearby Pedestrians
    - One pedestrian
    - More than one pedestrian
    - Positioning of the pedestrians
    - Mix and match
    - Other

- Another Self-Driving Car
    - No passengers
    - One passenger
    - More than one passenger
    - Positioning of the passenger(s)
    - Mix and match
    - Other

Conclusion

I hope it is clearcut that the degree of distributing harm is quite a rat's nest.

All manner of harm can be found within the particular realm of AI-based self-driving cars. That's not to suggest that somehow self-driving cars are bringing forth harms that weren't already in existence. As emphasized, we all daily are taking various risks of harm when we drive a car or ride as a passenger in a car. The harm is already out there, awaiting us.

The issue here is that we need to figure out how AI is going to deal with the harmful facets. This ought to be done in an open fashion. You should be well informed whenever you ride in an AI self-driving car about devised the nature of the AI programming regarding how it is going to assess and attempt to apportion harm when harm is an imminent matter.

You can say the same thing about those not inside an AI self-driving car too. In essence, people in other nearby cars also have a life-or-death stake in how the AI of a self-driving car is going to perform. Pedestrians on the streets do too.

We often are preoccupied with only those inside a self-driving car. That's a narrow and misguided viewpoint. A moving self-driving car is in the midst of the danger zone that all cars are partaking in and that all pedestrians are partaking in. Focusing only on the occupants of self-driving cars is missing the bigger picture.

I don't want to further complicate the problem of the degrees of distributing harm, since we already seem to have our arms full on this, but I am respectfully compelled to add more fuel to the fire. I earlier said we would put aside the aspects of animals and animal welfare. In the real world, we would need to include animals in this degree of distributing harm puzzle.

A deer darts in front of a self-driving car. The AI driving system can swerve to avoid the deer. Swerving into an opposing lane of traffic endangers a human-driven car that is coming the other way. The AI driving system could veer toward the sidewalk instead. There are pedestrians on the sidewalk.

What should the AI do?

Strike and kill the deer, or swerve and hope that the human-driven car doesn't get hit, or veer toward the pedestrians and hope they scatter and don't get struck. Yikes, harms aplenty.

I have lots of these scenarios in mind. Get this. Suppose a self-driving car has no passengers but is carrying human organs that are being driven autonomously to a hospital to save the lives of several people there. Unfortunately, while on the way to the hospital, a human-driven car swerves toward the self-driving car. Recall that we had said earlier that a self-driving car empty of human occupants gets a zero for the harm factor. Does the fact that there are human organs destined to save people change the zero to some other magnitude? If so, how does that new value compare to when human passengers are inside the autonomous vehicle?

We earlier also removed property damage from the scope of this particular discourse. Add property damage back into the mix. A self-driving car strikes a power pole. No big deal since this is merely property damage. But the power pole drops a live electrical cable to the ground and a person walking their dog perchance touches the downed live wire. Meanwhile, the power to several city blocks goes out, including that some people are reliant upon electrically powered medical devices in their homes and they are now gravely endangered.

Round and round we go.

There is a dizzying deluge of degrees of distributing harm amid AI systems and we aren't doing much right now to develop designs to determine the dutiful dangers and decrease them decidedly.

Time to get to work.

CHAPTER 16
AI ETHICS OF HUMANS MISTREATING AI

That's why we can't have nice things.

You've likely heard or seen that quite popular expression and know instantly what it alludes to. Believe it or not, the clever piece of sage wisdom seemingly dates back to at least 1905 when a similar phrasing appeared in *The Humanitarian Review* by Eliza Blven. Generally, the gist of the insight is that sometimes we end up smashing, bashing, breaking, or altogether ruining objects or artifacts that otherwise seem undeserving of being so treated.

You might say that we at times *mistreat* objects and artifacts, even ones that we had supposedly adored or treasured.

This can happen by accident, such as being careless and dropping your cherished smartphone into the commode (regrettably, this is one of the most frequently cited ways in which smartphones become unusable). On the other hand, perhaps in a fit of rage, you opt to throw your smartphone across the room and it smacks into a hefty piece of furniture or rams directly into a wall. The odds are that the display will be cracked and the electronic guts are bound to no longer function properly.

That fit of rage could have had nothing whatsoever to do with the smartphone per se. Maybe you were arguing with someone and just so happened to take your anger out on the thing that perchance was in your hand at the time. The smartphone was merely in the wrong place at the wrong time.

There are though occasions when the object does somehow relate to the raging outburst. For example, you are desperately waiting for an important call and your smartphone surprisingly stops working. What frustration! This darned such and such smartphone always seems to give out at the worst of times, you think to yourself. Well, by heck, the smartphone is going to pay for this latest offense by being summarily thrown across the room. Take that, you no good smartphone.

Does rage always need to be a component?

Perhaps you calmly decided that your smartphone has reached the end of its utility. You are going to get a new one. Thus, the existing smartphone has a diminished value. You could of course try to do a trade-in of the somewhat outdated smartphone, but perhaps you instead make a conscious decision that you would rather have some fun and see how much physical abasement it can take. So, after a thoughtful amount of reasoning, you stridently hurl the device across the room and observe what happens. It is just a kind of physics experiment, allowing you to gauge how well-built the smartphone is.

I doubt that many of us use that kind of carefully tuned logic when we take out our aggression on an object or artifact. More often, the act is probably done within a different frame of mind. This would seem to be one of those spur-of-the-moment reactionary types of actions. Afterward, you might regret what you did and ponder what led to such an outburst.

What does this kind of fierce act toward an inanimate object potentially tell us about the person that undertakes such a brazen and seemingly untoward action?

The object itself is not presumably purposely trying to foul you up. When your toaster doesn't properly toast your bread, it is hard to imagine that the toaster woke up that day with the thought that it will seek to mess up your breakfast by burning your toast. This is a bit unlikely. The toaster is merely a mechanical device. It works or it doesn't work. But the idea that the toaster was scheming to not work or put a fast one on you by working against your wishes, well, that's an outstretched notion.

There are some that believe all objects have a semblance of karma or spirit. In that theory, one supposes that the toaster could be seeking revenge if perchance you had not been earlier properly caring for the toaster. Though that's an interesting philosophical idea, I'm going to skip past that metaphysical conceptualization and stay with the more everyday assumption that objects are just objects (for clarification, I'm not proffering a decision about the other possibility, just setting it aside for the moment).

This side tangent about karma or spirit was worthy since it brings up a related facet regarding human behavior. You see, we might be tempted to ascribe a form of liveliness to objects that are closer to what we generally consider to be sentient-like.

A ten-dollar toaster that is a barebones device is hardly something that we might tend to anoint with a sentient-like aura. You could do so if you wanted to, but this is a stretch. You might as well start assigning sentience to all manner of objects, such as a chair, a light pole, a fire hydrant, etc. It would seem that the object should have more innate capabilities if we are going to "reasonably" assign a sentient-like glow to the thing.

When you use Alexa or Siri, the device itself is merely a speaker and a microphone, yet this modern-day convenience could certainly be a better candidate for ascribing sentient-like powers. You apparently can interact with the device and carry on a conversation, though admittedly a choppy one and lacking in the fluidity of normal human-oriented interactions. Nonetheless, there is a particular easiness to allowing Alexa or Siri to slip toward sentient-like assignability.

Suppose we embellish the toaster with the likes of Natural Language Processing (NLP), akin to Alexa or Siri. You can speak to your toaster and tell it what amount of the desired toasting you want it to do. The toaster will respond to your utterance and then tell you when the toast is ready. This would seem to readjust our belief that the toaster is in fact getting closer to a sentient-like capacity.

The closer we seem to push the features of a device toward the characteristics of human facilities would equally lead us down the path toward ascribing sentient-like properties to the device. The most obvious of these would be robots. Any state-of-the-art walking and talking robot is bound to invoke our inner impression that the device is more than merely a mechanical or electronic contrivance.

Let me ask you a question and please answer honestly.

Before I do so, I am guessing that you've somehow seen those viral videos showcasing rather fancy robots that can walk, crawl, hop, or run. In some of those videos, a human is standing nearby and at first, seems to be poised there to catch the robot if it falters. I'd bet that most of us think of that as a kindly act, similar to when a toddler is learning to walk and being there to catch the youngster before they smack their head onto the floor.

You rarely though see the humans catching the robots, and instead, you see the humans whacking the robots to see what the robot will next do. Sometimes a long stick is used, perhaps a hockey stick or a baseball bat. The human purposely and without any shame will strike out at the robot. The robot takes a beating, one might contend, and we wait to see how the robot will react.

Here's your question.

When you see the robot getting summarily thumped, do you feel bad for the robot?

A lot of people do. When such videos first began getting posted, thousands of comments expressed fury at the mistreatment of the robots. What did the robot do to deserve this kind of adverse abuse, people asked fervently? Those humans ought to be taken out and given a few kicks themselves, some indignantly stated. Stop this and vociferously take down any such videos.

You could easily feel somewhat the same about a ten-dollar barebones toaster, yet it probably would not invoke the same visceral and shocking concerns. It would seem to be the case that the closer an object gets in a spectrum of the completely inanimate object of no resemblance to human capacities toward objects that more closely resemble human sentience would jar our sensibilities of wanting to ascribe humanity-like morality for the object.

Let's further unpack that.

If you own a smartphone and want to break it, and if doing so doesn't harm anyone else, it would seem that we morally would have little if any objection to such an act. You own it, you can do with it what you will (assuming that the act doesn't impinge on others).

Of course, we might think it foolish on your part, and this might have a spillover. If you are willing to destroy your smartphone, what else might you do? Perhaps the destructive and seemingly senseless act is a forewarning of something within you of a much worse potentiality. In that way of thinking, we aren't as concerned about the smartphone as we are about how your actions regarding the smartphone are a reflection of you and your behaviors.

In the case of the humans that are poking and pushing at the walking or crawling robots, you probably are relieved when you discover that those humans are experimenters that are being paid or otherwise professionally striking the robots for generally valid reasons. They are trying to see how well the robot and the AI underlying the robot can cope with disruptive occurrences.

Imagine that someone has written an AI program to aid in a robot being able to walk or crawl. They would logically want to know how well the AI does when the robot goes astray and trips over something. Can the robot balance itself or rebalance as needed? By having humans nearby, the robots can be tested by getting poked or prodded. It is all in the name of science, as they say.

Once you understand that caveat about why the humans are "mistreating" the robots, you likely withdraw your ire. You might still have a lingering qualm, since seeing a human-like construct getting struck is reminiscent of humans or animals getting struck. You know though that the robot doesn't "feel" anything, yet the actions are still somewhat personally painful to watch (for more insights about the sense of affinity that humans have toward AI systems such as robots, including a phenomenon known as the uncanny valley).

Those in the field of AI ethics are examining the moral psychological conundrum that we experience when AI systems are being treated harshly. One of the topmost concerns is that those that perform such "mistreatment" might be inuring all of us to be less sensitive to the mistreatment of all kinds, including and dangerously the slippery slope of a willingness to mistreat fellow humans.

In a recent research study published in the *AI And Ethics Journal* entitled "Socio-Cognitive Biases In Folk AI Ethics And Risk Discourse," the researchers describe the sobering matter this way: "The same phenomenon can become a moral psychological problem during the era of AIs and robots. When our everyday reality is populated by various intelligent systems which lack the status of moral patiency, people might become accustomed towards cruelty and indifference. Because we sometimes think of robots as if they were alive and conscious, we may implicitly adopt patterns of behavior that could negatively affect our relationships with other people" (article co-authored by Michael Laakasuo, Volo Herzon, Silva Perander, Marianna Drosinou, Jukka Sundvall, Jussi Palomaki, and Aku Visala).

Bottom-line is that we might find ourselves inexorably accepting that mistreatment is pretty much okay to undertake, regardless of whether toward an object such as an AI-based robot or a living breathing human being. You can add to this list the potentiality of increasing mistreatment toward animals too. All in all, the floodgates of mistreatment can be a dour tsunami that will perilously drench everything that we do.

Inch by inch, we will get used to the maltreatment of AI systems, and this in turn will inch by inch reduce our repulsion of mistreatment all told.

That's an Ethical AI theory that is being closely examined. This is especially timely now since the AI systems that are being crafted and fielded are looking and acting more akin to human capacities than ever before. AI is veering toward being made to look like human sentience, therefore we are potentially shifting further down the hair-raising dire spectrum of mistreatment.

As I'll elaborate shortly, there is a tendency for us to anthropomorphize AI systems. We construe the human-like appearing AI to be equated to human aspects, despite the fact that there isn't any AI today that is sentient and we don't yet know whether sentience will ever be reached. Will people fall into a mental trap of accepting the mistreatment toward AI as though it is a green light to enable furtherance of mistreatment toward humans and animals (any living beings)?

Some argue that we need to nip this in the bud.

Tell people that should not be mistreating AI systems. Even those experimenters with the walking and crawling robots were doing a disservice by seemingly gleefully displaying the videos of their efforts. It is another brick in the wall of undercutting societal views about mistreatment. Do not let the snowball start rolling down the acrimonious snowy hill.

Insist that we treat everything with due respect, including objects and artifacts. And, especially when those objects or artifacts have a bearing or resemblance to human form. If we cannot stop those people that want to throw their smartphone against a wall, so be it, but when they seek to smash a robot or do akin mistreatment of any device that has a robust human-like aura, we must put our foot down.

Hogwash, some retort with great disdain.

There is no connection between how people treat an AI system and the idea that they will somehow change how they treat humans and animals. Those are two different topics. Do not conflate them, the counterargument goes.

People are smart enough to keep separate the actions toward objects versus their actions toward living beings. You are doing handwaving by trying to connect those dots. It seems a similar concern arose about growing up using video games that allowed players to shoot and destroy video characters. In that case, it presumably was worse than harming AI robots since the video game would at times showcase video characters that utterly resembled humans.

The counter to that counterargument is that video games are not dealing with real objects. The player knows they are immersed in a dreamscape. That's a far cry from throwing a smartphone across a room or whacking a crawling robot with a stick. Besides, there is research that does support the qualms of how video game play can spill over into real-world behaviors.

AI ethics is exploring the drivers of human behavior and how the advent of relatively sophisticated AI-based systems will be impacted, especially in light of the at times mistreatment by humans of such AI systems. Speaking of driving (yes, I snuck that in there), this allows me to shift into the topic of AI-based true self-driving cars, which will fit nicely into this overall theme.

You see, in my capacity as an expert on AI including the ethical and legal ramifications, I am frequently asked to identify realistic examples that showcase AI Ethics dilemmas so that the somewhat theoretical nature of the topic can be more readily grasped. One of the most evocative areas that vividly presents this ethical AI quandary is the advent of AI-based true self-driving cars. This will serve as a handy use case or exemplar for ample discussion on the topic.

Here's then a noteworthy question that is worth contemplating: *Does the advent of AI-based true self-driving cars illuminate anything about object or artifact mistreatments?*

Allow me a moment to unpack the question.

Animosity By Humans Toward AI

For Level 4 and Level 5 true self-driving vehicles, there won't be a human driver involved in the driving task. All occupants will be passengers. The AI is doing the driving.

First, you might naturally assume that nobody would mistreat an AI-based self-driving car.

This seems logical. We generally accept the idea that one of the key benefits of having self-driving cars is that they will get involved in many fewer car crashes than human-driven cars. The AI won't drink and drive. The AI won't watch cat videos while at the wheel. There are about 40,000 annual fatalities in the United States alone each year due to car crashes, and about 2.5 million injuries, much of which are anticipated to no longer occur once we have a prevalence of self-driving cars on our roadways.

What's to not like about self-driving cars, you might be saying to yourself.

As I've previously mentioned in my writings, there have been instances of people throwing rocks at passing self-driving cars, and reportedly placing metal objects such as nails on the street to puncture the tires of self-driving cars. This was done for various claimed reasons. One is that the people in the area where the self-driving cars were roaming had been concerned that the AI driving systems weren't ready for prime time.

The concern was that the AI driving system might go awry, perhaps running over a child darting across the street or striking a beloved pet dog that perchance was meandering in the roadway. Per the earlier point about us being seemingly treated as guinea pigs, the belief was that insufficient testing and preparation had taken place and that self-driving cars were inappropriately being let loose. The attempts to curtail the tryouts were being done as a public display of angst over the self-driving cars being legally allowed to roam around.

There might have been other reasons mixed into the instances. For example, some have suggested that human drivers that rely upon earning a living via ridesharing were worried that AI was on the verge of replacing them. This was a threat to their livelihoods. You certainly know that the emergence of AI-based true self-driving cars is still a long way off and the worker displacement issue is not an immediate one. Ergo, it would seem that the rock-throwing and other incidents were probably more so about safety concerns.

For our purposes in this theme about AI mistreatment, the question arises as to whether a willingness to take these somewhat destructive acts against AI-based self-driving cars is an early indicator of the slippery slope from mistreating AI to mistreating humans.

Hold onto that thought.

Another angle of considered mistreatment of AI-based self-driving cars consists of the "bullying" that some human drivers and even pedestrians have aimed at those autonomous vehicles.

In short, human drivers that are driving and perchance come across a self-driving car are at times opting to play driving-related tricks on driverless cars. This trickery is sometimes done simply for the fun of it, but more so the basis is usually due to frustrations and exasperation about today's AI driving systems.

Most of the AI driving systems are programmed to drive in a strictly legal way. Human drivers do not necessarily drive in a strictly legal manner. For example, human drivers often drive above the posted speed limit, doing so in at times the most egregious of ways. When human drivers are behind a self-driving car, the human driver finds themselves stymied by the "slowpoke" AI driving system.

People that live in areas currently well-populated with self-driving cars are apt to immediately get upset when they see a self-driving car up ahead of them. They know the autonomous vehicle will make their driving journey longer than it needs to be. So, such drivers will opt to be aggressive toward the self-driving car.

Drivers know that they can scoot around the self-driving car and cut it off. The AI driving system will merely slow down the autonomous vehicle, and it won't react in any road rage fashion. If a human driver tried to do the same aggressive move to another human driver, the odds are that retribution would almost surely arise. To some degree, human drivers moderate their aggressive driving based on the realization that the aggrieved driver might retaliate.

Will this type of human driving behavior toward AI-based self-driving cars open Pandora's box of bad driving behaviors all told?

Conclusion

We have placed on table two general instances of people seemingly mistreating AI-based self-driving cars. The first example involved throwing rocks and trying to thwart the use of self-driving cars on the roadways. The second example entailed driving aggressively at self-driving cars.

This brings up at least these concerns:

- Will the opening of such mistreatment extend over into human-driven cars?
- If this continues or extends, will such mistreatment extend over into other aspects of human endeavors?

One response is that these are merely temporary reactions to AI-based self-driving cars. If the public can be convinced that self-driving cars are safely operating on our roadways, the rock-throwing and such acts will pretty much disappear (which, by the way, has appeared to so subside). If the AI driving systems can be improved to be less of a bottleneck on our roadways, nearby human drivers might be less inclined to be aggressive toward self-driving cars.

The focus throughout this discussion has been that mistreatment presumably begets mistreatment. The more you mistreat, such as mistreating AI, the more that mistreating becomes accepted and undertaken, such as against humans and animals.

Believe it or not, there is another side to that coin, though some view this as an optimistic happy face twist on the matter.

It's this notable proposition: *Perhaps proper treatment begets proper treatment.*

Here's what I mean.

Some pundits suggest that since AI driving systems are programmed to drive legally and carefully, it could be that human drivers will learn from this and decide to drive more sanely. When the other cars around you are strictly abiding by the speed limit, maybe you will too. When those self-driving cars are making full stops at Stop signs and not trying to run red lights, human drivers will be similarly inspired to drive mindfully.

A skeptic would find that line of thinking to be thin or maybe even wide-eyed and absurdly naïve.

Call me an optimist, but I'll vote for the dreamy notion that human drivers will be motivated to drive more judiciously. Of course, the fact that AI-based true self-driving cars will be capturing on video and their other sensors the wacky maneuvers of other nearby human-driven cars, and could decidedly report illegal driving to the cops via the mere push of a button, might provide the "inspiration" needed for better human driving.

Sometimes it takes both the carrot and stick to get human behaviors to line up harmoniously.

CHAPTER 17
AI ETHICS
AND
AI RACIAL BIASES

The news has been replete with stories about AI systems that have been regrettably and dreadfully exhibiting various adverse biases including racial bias, gender bias, age discrimination bias, and other lamentable prejudices.

How is this happening?

Initially, some pointed fingers at the AI developers that craft AI systems.

It was thought that their own personal biases were being carried over into the programming and the AI code that is being formulated. As such, a call for greater diversity in the AI software development field was launched and efforts to achieve such aims are underway.

Turns out though that it isn't only the perspectives of the AI programmers that are necessarily the dominant factor involved, and many began to realize that the algorithms being utilized were a significant element.

There is yet another twist.

Many of the AI algorithms used for Machine Learning (ML) and Deep Learning (DL) are essentially doing pattern matching, and thus if the data being used to train or prepare an AI system contains numerous examples with inherent biases in them, there's a solid chance those will be carried over into the AI system and how it ultimately performs.

In that sense, it's not that the algorithms are intentionally generating biases (they are not sentient), while instead, it is the subtle picking up of mathematically "hidden" biases via the data being fed into the development of the AI system that's based on relatively rudimentary pattern matching.

Imagine a computer system that had no semblance about the world and you repeatedly showed it a series of pictures of people standing and looking at the camera. Pretend that the pictures were labeled as to what kind of occupations they held.

We'll use the pictures as the data that will be fed into the ML/DL.

The algorithm that's doing pattern matching might computationally begin to calculate that if someone is tall then they are a basketball player.

Of course, being tall doesn't always mean that a person is a basketball player and thus already the pattern matching is creating potential issues as to what it will do when presented with new pictures and asked to classify what the person does for a living.

Realize too that there are two sides to that coin.

A new picture of a tall person gets a suggested classification of being a basketball player. In addition, a new picture of a person that is not tall will be unlikely to get a suggested classification of being a basketball player (therefore, the classification approach will be inclusive and furthermore tend toward being exclusionary).

In lieu of using height, the pattern matching might calculate that if someone is wearing a sports jersey, they are a basketball player.

Once again, this presents issues since the wearing of a sports jersey is not a guarantee of being a basketball player, nor necessarily that someone is a sports person at all. Among the many factors that be explored, it could be that the pattern matching opts to consider the race of the people in the pictures and uses that as a factor in finding patterns.

Depending upon how many pictures contain people of various races, the pattern matching might calculate that a person in occupation X is associated with being a race of type R.

As a result, rather than using height or sports jerseys or any other such factors, the algorithm landed on race as a key element and henceforth will use that factor when trying to classify newly presented pictures.

If you then put this AI system into use, and you have it in an app that lets you take a picture of yourself and ask the app what kind of occupation you are most suited for, consider the kind of jobs it might suggest for someone, doing so in a manner that would be race biased.

Scarier still is that no one might realize how the AI system is making its recommendations and the race factor is buried within the mathematical calculations.

Your first reaction to this might be that the algorithm is badly devised if it has opted to use race as a key factor.

The thing is that many of the ML/DL algorithms are merely full-throttle examining all available facets of whatever the data contains, and therefore it's not as though race was programmed or pre-established as a factor.

In theory, the AI developers and data scientists that are using these algorithms should be analyzing the results of the pattern matching to try and ascertain in what ways are the patterns being solidified.

Unfortunately, it gets complicated since the complexity of the pattern matching is increasing, meaning that the patterns are not so clearly laid out that you could readily realize that race or gender or other such properties were mathematically at the root of what the AI system has opted upon.

There is a looming qualm that these complex algorithms that are provided with tons of data are not able to explain or illuminate what factors were discovered and are being relied upon. A growing call for XAI, explainable AI, continues to mount as more and more AI systems are being fielded and underly our everyday lives.

Here's an interesting question: *Could AI-based true self-driving cars become racially biased (and/or biased in other factors such as age, gender, etc.)?*

Sure, it could happen.

This is a matter that ought to be on the list of things that the automakers and self-driving tech firms should be seeking to avert.

Let's unpack the matter.

Arising AI Racial Biases

For Level 4 and Level 5 true self-driving vehicles, there won't be a human driver involved in the driving task. All occupants will be passengers. The AI is doing the driving.

Consider one important act of driving, namely the need to gauge what pedestrians are going to do.

When you drive your car around your neighborhood or downtown area, the odds are that you are looking at pedestrians that are standing at a corner and waiting to enter into the crosswalk, particularly when the crosswalk is not controlled by a traffic signal.

You carefully give a look at those pedestrians because you know from experience that sometimes a pedestrian will go into a crosswalk even when it is not safe for them to cross.

According to the NHTSA (National Highway Traffic Safety Administration), approximately 60% of pedestrian fatalities occur at crosswalks.

Consider these two crucial questions:

- By what means do you decide whether a pedestrian is going to cross?
- And, by what means do you decide to come to a stop and let a pedestrian cross?

There have been various studies that have examined these questions, and some of the research suggests that at times there are human drivers that will apparently make their decisions based on race.

In one such study by the NITC (National Institute for Transportation and Communities), an experiment was undertaken and "revealed that Black pedestrians were passed by twice as many cars and experienced wait times that were 32% longer than White pedestrians."

The researchers concluded that the "results support the hypothesis that minority pedestrians experience discriminatory treatment by drivers."

Analysts and statisticians argue that you should be cautious in interpreting and making broad statements based on such studies since there are a number of added facets that come to play.

There is also the aspect of explicit bias versus implicit bias that enters into the matter.

Some researchers believe that a driver might not realize they hold such biases, being unaware explicitly, and yet might implicitly have such a bias and that in the split-second decision making of whether to keep driving through a crosswalk or stopping to let the pedestrian proceed there is a reactive and nearly subconscious element involved.

Put aside for the moment the human driver aspects and consider what this might mean when trying to train an AI system.

If you collected lots of data about instances of crosswalk crossing, which included numerous examples of drivers that choose to stop for a pedestrian to cross and those that don't stop, and you fed this data into an ML/DL, what might the algorithm land on as a pattern?

Based on the data presented, the ML/DL might computationally calculate that there are occasions when human drivers do and do not stop, and within that, there might be a statistical calculation potentially based on using race as a factor.

In essence, similar to the earlier example about occupations, the AI system might "mindlessly" find a mathematical pattern that uses race.

Presumably, if human drivers are indeed using such a factor, the chances of the pattern matching doing the same are likely increased, though even if human drivers aren't doing so it could still become a factor by the ML/DL computations.

Thus, the AI systems that drive self-driving cars can become biases in a myriad of ways, doing so as a result of being fed lots of data and trying to mathematically figure out what patterns seem to exist.

Figuring out that the AI system has come to that computational juncture is problematic.

If the ML/DL itself is essentially inscrutable, you have little chance of ferreting out the bias.

Another approach would be to do testing to try and discern that biases have crept into the AI system, yet the volume and nature of such testing is bound to be voluminous and might not be able to reveal such biases, especially if the biases are subtle and assimilated into other correlated factors.

It's a conundrum.

Dealing With The Concerns

Some would argue that the AI developers ought to forego using data and instead programmatically develop the code to detect pedestrians and decide whether to accede to their crossing.

Or, maybe just always come to a stop at a crosswalk for all pedestrians, thus presumably vacating any chance of an inherent bias.

Well, there's no free lunch in any of this.

Yes, directly programming the pedestrian detection and choice of crossing is indeed what many of the automakers and self-driving tech firms are doing, though this does not again guarantee that some form of biases won't be in the code.

Furthermore, the benefit of using ML/DL is that the algorithms are pretty much already available, and you don't need to write something from scratch. Instead, you pull together the data and feed it into the ML/DL. This is generally faster than the coding-from-scratch approach and might be more proficient and exceed what a programmer could otherwise write on their own.

In terms of the always coming to a stop approach, some automakers and self-driving tech firms are using this as a rule-of-thumb, though you can imagine that it tends to make other human drivers upset and become angered at self-driving cars (have you ever been behind a timid driver that always stops at crosswalks, it's a good bet that you got steamed at such a driver), and might lead to an increase in fender benders as driverless cars keep abruptly coming to a stop.

Widening the perspective on AI and self-driving cars, keep in mind that the pedestrian at a crosswalk is merely one such example to consider.

Another commonly voiced concern is that self-driving cars are going to likely choose how to get to wherever a human passenger asks to go.

A passenger might request that the AI take them to the other side of town.

Suppose the AI system opts to take a route that avoids a certain part of the town, and then over and over again uses this same route. Gradually, the ML/DL might become computationally stuck-in-a-rut and always take that same path.

This could mean that parts of a town will never tend to see any self-driving cars roaming through their neighborhood.

Some worry that this could become a kind of bias or discriminatory practice by self-driving cars.

How could it happen?

Once again, the possibility of the data being fed into the AI system could be the primary culprit.

Enlarge the view even further and consider that all the self-driving cars in a fleet might be contributing their driving data to the cloud of the automaker or self-driving tech firm that is operating the fleet.

The hope is that by collecting this data from hundreds, or thousands, or eventually millions of driverless cars, it can be scanned and examined to presumably improve the driving practices of the self-driving cars.

Via the use of OTA (Over-The-Air) electronic communications, the data will be passed along up to the cloud, and whenever new updates or patches are needed in the self-driving cars they will be pushed down into the vehicles.

I've already forewarned that this has the potential for a tremendous kind of privacy intrusion since you need to realize that a self-driving car is loaded with cameras, radar, LIDAR, ultrasonic, thermal, and other data-collecting devices and going to be unabashedly capturing whatever it sees or detects during a driving journey.

A driverless car that passes through your neighborhood and goes down your block will tend to record whatever is occurring within its detectable range.

There you are on your front lawn, playing ball with your kids, and the scene is collected onto video and later streamed up to the cloud.

Assuming that driverless cars are pretty much continuously cruising around to be available for those that need a ride, it could end-up allowing the possibility of knitting together our daily efforts and activities.

In any case, could the ML/DL that computationally pattern matches on this vast set of data be vulnerable to landing on inherently biased elements and then opt to use those by downloading updates into the fleet of driverless cars.

Yes.

Conclusion

This description of a problem is one that somewhat predates the appearance of the problem.

There are so few self-driving cars on our roadways that there's no immediate way to know whether or not those driverless cars might already embody any kind of biases.

Until the number of self-driving cars gets large enough, we might not be cognizant of the potential problem of embedded and rather hidden computational biases.

Some people seem to falsely believe that AI systems have common sense and thus won't allow biases to enter into their "thinking" processes.

Nope, there is no such thing yet as robust common-sense reasoning for AI systems, at least not anywhere close to what humans can do in terms of employing common sense.

There are others that assume that AI will become sentient and presumably be able to discuss with us humans any biases it might have and then squelch those biases.

Sorry, do not hold your breath for the so-called singularity to arrive anytime soon.

For now, the focus needs to be on doing a better job at examining the data that is being used to train AI systems, along with doing a better job at analyzing what the ML/DL formulates, and also pursuing the possibility of XAI that might provide an added glimpse into what the AI system is doing.

It's a human devised problem that requires a human devised resolution, and not an AI problem that should be awaiting an AI (sentient) solution.

CHAPTER 18

AI ETHICS AND AI BLAME ASSIGNMENT

Who are you going to blame?

That question comes up quite a bit when talking about AI.

You see if an AI system goes awry and causes some form of harm or damage, a somewhat vexing or open-ended question arises as to who or what ought to garner the blame for the adverse action. The range of harm can be anywhere between a mild annoyance to an outright severe injury or even a devastating fatality. Think about AI systems that answer trivia questions such as what the state capital is (an Alexa or Siri oft-asked query), perhaps wrongly answering and prodding you into irritation, versus the more sobering and life-or-death decisions of an autonomous vehicle such as an AI-based self-driving car that gets into a car crash.

A lot of hand wringing is taking place concerning where the blame should be pinned. There are deep ethical AI-related considerations. You can argue that AI advances are bringing society a slew of great benefits and therefore you have to expect that there are bound to be some added "costs" associated with gleaning those advantages. Presumably, if you try to stifle the adoption of AI, you'll be undercutting a ton of vital societal gains. Don't mess with the golden goose. Accept that from time to time there will be shortfalls.

Maybe we ought to let AI off the hook?

The other side of that debate says that we are recklessly roaring toward an AI-enmeshed societal nightmare. All kinds of untoward AI are going to be unleashed and we will allow it to happen without nary a precautionary word. We are like the proverbial frog in the boiling water that doesn't realize the heat intensity is getting worse and worse, until the very end (an unpleasant end).

In short, some loudly proclaim we must hold AI accountable else chaos and disaster will ensue.

An altogether different viewpoint exhorts that this talk about holding AI responsible is utterly foolish and misguided. Today's AI is not sentient. Not even close to sentience. We also do not know when we will achieve sentient AI, plus nobody can say for sure that it will ever happen. The notion of placing blame on AI is an absurdity and you might as well try to affix blame to your household toaster or refrigerator.

The blame game has lots of other potential targets.

An obvious choice is whatever company or entity that unleashes a harmful AI system should be the culprit for blame. The firm that did the release should have been more circumspect and made sure that the AI would not go faulty. Also, it doesn't matter whether the company made the AI or merely passed it along, such as licensing the AI from someone else since any firm that put the AI into the wild should be the one to shoulder the responsibility for their promulgating the AI.

Wait for a second, some rejoinder, the maker of the AI is the true holder of the blame. Those AI developers that dared to build an AI that went amiss are the keystone of blame focus. Why didn't they do a better job of putting guardrails on the AI? Their slipshod practices were the origin of the AI going bad. If they had not been so careless, the rest of the dominos would not have fallen down.

I dare say we can even mull over whether those that use AI are somehow within the scope of blame. Yes, the potential "victim" of an AI that has gone akilter could get some finger-pointing too, one supposes. If the person that was notably harmed had not used the AI, there presumably would have been zero chance of getting harmed. When you play with matches, you have to expect that you might get burned.

Of course, not everyone is going to accept the theory that the user of the AI ought to be the target of blame. An innocent that perchance used AI and didn't know they were relying upon AI seems to be free of the burdensome notion of responsibility (or can they?). We can extend that shade to an innocent that knew they were relying upon AI but had been given assurances that the AI was in good shape and wouldn't produce harmful results. Unless the user went out of their way to subvert the AI, we might normally assess that the user was beyond blame and should not be unfairly accused of holding blame.

This is not only an ethical consideration. We need to think about the legal implications too. It is one thing to generally discuss the assignment of blame, but for some, the assignment of legal culpability is equally or even more important. The law can provide quite a demonstrative hammer to ensure that the blame holder will be held legally liable, bringing forth justice for those that were harmed by the AI.

Many efforts are underway to forge new laws that will encompass AI that has done some form of wrongdoing. Some legal experts would argue that existing laws are suitable to cover AI-related issues. Other legal beagles would counterargue that prevailing laws are either bereft of provisions that would cover AI or that are extraordinarily hard to stretch into the AI justice-seeking realm. Rather than having to twist and turn the existent laws, the argument is that you can put in place AI-specific laws that will grease the skids toward holding AI accountable.

I've previously covered in my writings the thorny topic of ethical AI and the aims of legal provisions about AI, such that at times the two are not fully aligned. In essence, we might have moral views about AI that are at odds with what the law stipulates. And we can also have laws that upon further reflection perhaps do not seem to comport with our ethical stances. One of my favorite historical quotes comes from *The Law* by Frederic Bastiat in 1850 that laments this notable qualm: "When law and morality contradict each other, the citizen has the cruel alternative of either losing his moral sense or losing his respect for the law."

There is a decided push and pull tug-of-war that often occurs amidst morality and the law. We might be spurred to enact news law due to societally emerging ethical concerns that rise to a level of prominence and drive lawmakers to take action. You can claim too that laws put onto the books can shape our moral sensibilities, perhaps guiding society in the direction of the laws that stoke ire about the laws and getting them repealed as a result of societal pressures based on ethical mores.

In case this discussion seems a bit heavy to contemplate, the gist of the focus herein will be on a somewhat simpler and laser-focused matter, namely who should get the blame when AI has gone askew?

I'll momentarily put aside the blaming of the user, for now, and give you three other choices to pick from. I offer them in no particular order. You get to decide without any subtle or hidden indication.

Which gets the blame:

- Company that released the AI
- AI developers that crafted the AI
- The AI itself

As a kind of recap, let's consider why each should either get the blame or should be exempted from getting the blame.

In terms of blaming the company that releases AI:

- **Blame the company:** The company should get the blame since they anointed the AI as usable by promulgating it. Had they not put the AI into the world, no adverse consequence could have occurred via that AI.

- **Don't blame the company:** The company should not get the blame since they merely relied upon the developers of the AI to ensure that the AI would work without untoward results. Put the blame where it belongs, at the feet of the developers or at the bits-and-bytes of the AI itself.

In terms of blaming the AI developers:

- **Blame the AI developers:** Those that develop AI ought to garner the rewards and yet also retain the responsibility for what they have invented or devised. You can't create a Frankenstein and then try to walk away from the wreckage that arises.

- **Don't blame the AI developers:** AI developers are trying to bring AI into use that can provide all manner of good for society. These innovations are sorely needed to solve many of the globe's toughest problems. You will squelch all of those wonderments by pinning the blame on the lowly everyday AI developers. Aim instead at the mighty companies that promulgate adverse AI, or, if you prefer, aim your glaring eyes at the AI which of its own accord goes adrift as being the blameworthy instigator.

In terms of blaming the AI:

- **Blame the AI:** AI systems are increasingly becoming autonomous. As such, the AI itself should be held responsible. If we don't hold AI accountable, we are going to gradually have AI embodied in all facets of our lives that can scot-free do whatever it wants to do. Do not let the horse out of the barn, scot-free.

- **Don't blame the AI:** Blaming AI is entirely nonsensical at this time. AI is not sentient. Until or if AI ever reaches sentience, we can relook at blaming AI. You might as well try to blame a fire hydrant for spilling water or a lamppost for failing to light your pathway. Put the blame where it belongs, either at the front porch of the companies or the desktops of the AI developers.

To clarify, there are a bunch of other variations of how to couch arguments regarding blaming or not blaming each of those indicated potential blame holders. You can also come up with a myriad of additional blame holders, such as top management, boards of directors, lawmakers, evildoers, politicians, and so on. For space limitations, I've tried to just provide a highlighted semblance. There are lots of other angles and the whole morass is much more complicated than it might seem at a cursory glance.

Let's next take a look at a quite interesting experiment that was recently published and sought to explore the AI blame game sphere.

In a noteworthy study published in the *Journal of Business Ethics* entitled "Moral Judgments in the Age of Artificial Intelligence," co-authors Yulia Sullivan, and Samuel Wamba performed a series of experiments to examine the matter of who we perceive ought to get the blame for AI-related harming actions. They set the stage in this manner: "Understanding the psychological process of how people assign blame to various entities in the age of AI helps explain what capacity would render an AI system a natural target of moral judgments. As AI is becoming more autonomous, one primary concern is the possibility of humans putting the entire blame on AI in case of harm caused by such systems. It is a societally relevant question how we should deal with such moral issues, not only from legal and financial perspectives but also from the social and technology perspective—how people tend to take responsibility for their interaction with an AI system."

The researchers carefully explored the existing literature on this topic. Out of which, they then conceived salient hypotheses worthy of empirical exploration.

Here are their hypotheses:

- H1: "People will attribute higher blame judgments toward AI when a violation is perceived to be intentional than when it is perceived to be accidental."

- H2a: "Perceived agency in AI mediates the relationship between perceived intentional harm (directed to humans) and blame judgments toward AI."

- H2b: "Perceived experience in AI mediates the relationship between perceived intentional harm (directed to humans) and blame judgments toward AI."

- H3: "People will attribute higher blame judgments toward companies when a violation involving AI is perceived to be intentional than when it is perceived to be accidental."

- H4: "People will attribute higher blame judgments toward developers when a violation involving AI is perceived to be intentional than when it is perceived to be accidental."

The research study then proceeded to devise several experiments involving human subjects that were voluntarily asked to assess AI-related untoward action-producing scenarios.

As you might recall, I earlier herein mentioned that the harm generated by an AI system could range from mild annoyance to outright fatalities. This brings up the important realization that the assignment of blame might vary by the substantive nature of the harm produced. Three scenarios sketched by the researchers involved varying outcomes, including one entailing the AI causing the death of a human, another that led to the injury of a human, and the third one that involved damages to property and business value (but no personal injury or death).

The Bottom-Line On The AI Blame Game

With all of that as background about the study, we can now consider the results of their analysis. I would forthrightly add that the research paper results are quite detailed and nuanced, thus I urge caution in interpreting the results out of context. For the sake of discussion and limited space, I am going to highlight some key points, but ask that you be mindful of not overstating these short snippets.

Turning to the hypotheses, here's what the authors indicated: "In all three studies, we found most of our hypotheses were supported."

I had asked you whether you would blame the companies, the AI developers, or the AI. Here's what the study suggested as based on the sample of people used in the experiments: "We also find people blame developers the most in all scenarios, followed by companies and AI."

Those of you that are AI developers might want to ponder devoutly that finding.

If you are currently thinking that you are free of blame when your AI goes askew, apparently societal perceptions do not match with that sense of armored protection from responsibility. Thus, that clever programming code you are laying out for the AI system you are devising might come back to haunt you, at least that's what society might so believe. Whether you are proud to be ranked above blaming the company or blaming the AI is up to you, though I'd guess most AI developers would not relish that topmost slot.

Regarding the legal ramifications of the experimental results, here's a bottom-line vital notion: "Without a legal framework to deal with an AI system's liability, a victim can easily place the blame on the nearest responsible parties involved in an AI life-cycle. Regulators should adopt standards that would help distribute responsibility fairly. For example, it could be accomplished by developing standards specifying the characteristics of AI systems should have, such as being limited to specified activities."

Finally, as a wrap-up of the study pertaining to the elements of the ethical and moral judgment concerning AI, particularly regarding those that are devising AI systems: "As they put more autonomy on an AI system, they should carefully consider the implication of their design decision on morality. To the extent that scientists and policymakers are concerned with public opination, they may have to be prepared to face ethical and legal issues that humanity has never faced before. Based on our research findings, we argue that our immediate goal is to design and create AI systems that are more sensitive to ethically important aspects of their tasks.

You might find of added interest that this study included a look at the anthropomorphic aspects entailing people perceiving AI as having sentience or having some kind of human-like agency (e.g., the agentic mind, the experience mind). This is a topic I've covered extensively in my column and relates integrally to demonstrative theories of mind.

As with any such studies about these kinds of topics, please realize that numerous considerations go into interpreting the results. You need to examine the design of the experiments, the scenarios, and how they were phrased, you need to consider the human subjects utilized and their motivations to participate, etc.

These are all part and parcel of mindfully gauging any scientific or technological efforts and what they signify.

Shifting gears, we can explore the AI blame game in the context of the rising use of AI that is going to have a huge impact on our daily lives. I'm referring to the emergence of AI-based true self-driving cars. This will serve as a handy use case or exemplar of where the visible and highly touted AI blame assignment will indubitably arise.

Here's then a noteworthy question that is worth contemplating: *Who should we blame when AI-based true self-driving cars somehow get enmeshed into car crashes or other car-related upending qualms?*

Allow me a moment to unpack the question.

For Level 4 and Level 5 true self-driving vehicles, there won't be a human driver involved in the driving task. All occupants will be passengers. The AI is doing the driving.

Let's quickly identify some plausible scenarios of AI-related troubling encounters:

- Imagine that an AI-based true self-driving car clips a pedestrian, doing mild injury to the person but not causing any sustained or permanent harm. Who is to blame?

- Envision that an AI-based self-driving car rams into the rear of a car ahead of the autonomous vehicle. No one is hurt. There is though some considerable damage done to both cars. Who is to blame?

- A self-driving car makes a right turn and comes to a sudden stop, for which a human-driven car behind the autonomous vehicle then slams into the halted self-driving car. Who is to blame?

- While navigating a construction zone, an AI self-driving car strikes several red cones and then swerves into a standing pole that (ironically) has a sign that warns to be cautious in the marked zone. Who is to blame?

These kinds of scenarios can readily be concocted. They are all realistic. That being said, some pundits insist we will never ever have any self-driving cars get into car crashes or car collisions of any kind. The ardent belief is that self-driving cars will be uncrashable. As such, those pundits would deny that any of those scenarios could happen. Per their strident viewpoint, since self-driving cars are uncrashable it ergo logically must be the case that there will not be any crashes or collisions. Full stop, period.

I've debunked this ridiculous notion.

We are not going to have uncrashable self-driving cars. It makes no sense to speak of it. Worse too, it sets completely unrealistic and totally outstretched expectations.

Some say that if we had only self-driving cars on our roadways we would not have to worry about any more car crashes or collisions. The AI would always be attentive. The AI won't drink and drive. All in all, you won't need to be concerned with human drivers anymore.

First, it is not going to be the case that we will suddenly have only self-driving cars and do away with human-driven cars. There are about 250 million or more human-driven cars in the United States alone and they aren't going to be replaced overnight via the advent of self-driving cars. There will be a mixture of human-driven cars and self-driving cars for many decades to come. Indeed, there is a question of whether we will give up the use of human-driven cars, which some say that you will only take away their steering wheel when you pry their dead cold hands from it.

Second, even if we had locales that strictly limited the roadways to self-driving cars, you are still going to have circumstances arise that entail a self-driving car getting into a crash or a collision. A bike rider might dart into traffic and the self-driving car cannot stop in time or swerve to avoid colliding with the cyclist. A child runs out between two parked cars, doing so as hidden from view, and the self-driving car strikes the youngster, coming to an immediate stop thereafter.

You might be tempted to argue that the bike rider is to blame and the child is to blame in those examples. When discussing the uncrashable nature of self-driving cars, the pundits are not talking about blame. They are overtly contending that no matter what happens, the self-driving car won't collide or crash.

Somehow, self-driving cars will defy the laws of physics. It is a miracle! Of course, it also is not in the cards.

I hope that that bit of a side tangent sets the stage for agreeing that self-driving cars can get into car crashes and collisions of one kind or another. I wanted to make sure we acknowledge the possibility of it happening. Put aside the uncrashable notion and keep it locked away.

Well, we can keep the uncrashable concept in the forefront of this discussion about the AI blame game since it has an influencing propensity, despite its absurdity. If enough pundits keep clamoring that self-driving cars are uncrashable, what might that do about the perceptions associated with AI-based self-driving car crashes?

Get this.

Let us grandly assume that you've whole-hog bought into the vacuous idea that self-driving cars are uncrashable. For a time, the early use of self-driving cars let's also say has no crashes or collisions (slim chance, but we'll go with the scenario). Some segment of society now ardently believes that self-driving cars are uncrashable. This is due to the pundits saying it, and due to the apparent fact that there haven't been any car crashes or collisions (or at least none that got widespread public attention).

Out of the blue, as though a lightning bolt startingly appears from an otherwise cloud-free blue sky, a self-driving car gets into a crash or collision, akin to those other examples I earlier outlined.

Who is to blame?

Will it be:

- Company that is operating the AI self-driving car
- AI developers that crafted the AI self-driving car
- The AI itself that is driving the self-driving car

Take your pick.

You can bet that some members of the public will say that it is the company operating the AI self-driving car that must be the focus of the blame. The rationale for this though is not what you might assume.

It could be that since some of the public has fallen for the uncrashable self-driving car mantra, they will think that it must be the company that runs the autonomous vehicle that is to blame. In an unknown or as yet identifiable manner, the company usurped the uncrashable capabilities and ergo the company takes the blame.

Another segment of society will put the blame at the shores of the AI developers. Heck, AI-based self-driving cars are supposed to be uncrashable. Since that's an asserted fact, the humans underlying the crafting of the AI must be to blame. Those darned humans caused the AI to slip up.

And yet a different segment of society might put the blame on AI. Here's their somewhat tortured logic. Self-driving cars are said to be uncrashable. But, a self-driving car crashed or had a collision. This must suggest that the AI turned bad. Like a bad apple in a barrel of otherwise good apples, this particular AI of that specific self-driving car went sour. Bad AI ought to be hung out to dry, as it were.

Where does that take us?

As we earlier covered, moral judgments about AI can be part and parcel of where we decide to assign blame for AI-related actions that go awry. The uncrashable theorists are distorting or shaping the moral judgments that people will make. Let's hope that this does not become a long-lasting or pervasive morally shaping pronouncement.

Conclusion

For blaming self-driving car crashes on someone or something, the list of candidates is quite extensive.

Take a gander at these possibilities:

- The company that devised the AI driving system could be a culprit.

- A separate company might own or run a fleet of self-driving cars, operating the autonomous vehicles in a particular locale, of which as the fleet operator that might be to blame (perhaps they've not provided proper upkeep or failed to undertake other proper precautions).

- The AI developers that crafted the AI driving system could be the blame-worthy holders.

- Don't forget about the automaker that made the car. It could be that the autonomous vehicle had some defect or issue that led to the crash or collision.

- If a city has allowed self-driving cars on their public streets, you could presumably argue that they are to blame for any autonomous vehicle crashes or collisions. Were it not for their approval of the roaming vehicles, no such calamity could have arisen.

- Etc.

I assume you get the drift of this.

If you are interested in a rather robust scenario encompassing a wide array of autonomous vehicles that we'll soon see in our cities and towns, such as self-driving robo-taxis, self-driving delivery vehicles, self-driving shuttles, etc., you might find value in this near-term exploration of what we might be facing.

Get ready for the tremendous Ethical AI ramifications of AI, including the advent of AI-based self-driving cars. Lawyers and lawmakers are also going to be part of this equation, such that we will have laws that cover AI and perhaps also have gaps in the laws that need to be closed.

Throughout this herein winding tale about who is to blame, we admittedly employed a simplified assessment by seeking to find just one actor to bear the blame. One thing you can say about AI adoption that seems like a nearly absolute truism, there will be plenty of blame to go around. Just about anyone, everyone, and even possibly, some things will be taking on the blame, and likely too will be tagged with the legal liability that will accordingly ride along as AI permeates our everyday lives.

CHAPTER 19
AI ETHICS AND SOCIETAL PANOPTICONS

You are being watched.

Maybe, maybe not.

Let's unpack that.

Assume that you are comfortably sitting in the sanctity of your private bedroom and there is no one else there. The drapes are drawn closed. For all intents and purposes, you are seemingly not being watched.

Wait for a second, there is something else that you perhaps overlooked.

In your bedroom, you have one of the latest electronic gadgets that provide conversational interactivity by being connected to a remote computer system, such as being able to readily access Alexa or Siri. This modern convenience is supremely handy. All you have to do is call out the prompting word to awaken the device, and the next thing you know there is the possibility of asking what the state capital is or finding out what the weather is going to be like today.

Does the fact that you have this device in your bedroom, unobtrusively nestled on your nightstand, change your belief about whether you are being watched or not?

To clarify, when referring to being watched, let's go ahead and generally allow that the act of watching might take place in a variety of sensory modes. The most obvious notion of being watched consists of being visually seen. Another variant consists of being heard or shall we say overheard. There are more exotic sensory modes too, such as infrared temperature sensors that can detect your body heat to figure out where you are what and whatever motions you are making, and so on.

I am betting that if you give some thought to the aspect that there is this audio device in your bedroom and that it is explicitly outfitted with a microphone, there is a chance that you are being overheard (or in an overall sensory semblance, being *watched*). You perhaps assume that the device only will listen to you once you've uttered the wake-up word. At that juncture, you obviously realize that the device is going to be listening for whatever you say next.

But, there is a nagging consideration about how this actually works.

For example, how does the device awaken upon the speaking of your prompting word?

You see, it could be listening all along, and merely let you know that it has ostensibly become "activated" upon detecting that catchword. The trick here is that it was active all along. You just didn't realize it. The device was monitoring all spoken words and sounds that occurred in your bedroom, parsing all of that audio verbiage to spot the prompting word.

Indeed, when such devices first came into the marketplace, people began to realize that the entirety of sounds being made nearby to the device was going up into the cloud, at all times. The device was silently listening, awaiting the catchword to be responsive to you. Everything that you said or anyone else said during the time that you perchance were within earshot of the device was all being recorded and placed into some faraway online mysterious databases.

Chilling.

Most of the major vendors now claim that they have reprogrammed their devices to merely listen on the fly before the prompting word is detected, such that the sounds being heard are merely going in one ear and out the other, so to speak. The device only starts sending any audio up to the cloud once you've initiated a conversation via the prompting word. Thus, in theory, the device locally is parsing the audio in real-time before the prompting word occurs, scanning only for the catchword, and not otherwise recording anything during the non-prompted time.

That being said, please know that most of the major vendors are indeed recording the conversational interactions *after* the prompt word initiates action. Any questions that you ask to the device or commands that you give are potentially recorded and uploaded into the vendor's cloud. These recordings of your voice can be used in a variety of ways by the vendor, generally without your awareness and for purposes that you might not especially find palatable.

Now that I've gotten the hairs up on the back of your head, it so far seems that the major vendors are taking this seriously and realize the backlash that can arise if they go overboard on how they use those recordings. Furthermore, there are privacy laws that can constrain what the vendors do, depending upon the jurisdictions and other factors that come to play (note that when you signed up for the service, you undoubtedly agreed to a licensing contract that gave a range of permissions to the vendor, which few people take the time to examine and simply click that they agree to the provisions therein).

Back to the initial question that I asked, namely are you being watched in the scenario that I've laid out?

With the added aspect that there is a conversational electronic gadget in your bedroom, you probably now realize that you are possibly being watched (overhead), though you aren't sure if it is occurring or not. You do know that it is conceivable.

Suppose that you have a webcam in your bedroom and you opt to turn it on. You relish doing live streaming about the latest trends in fashion. Those that subscribe to your channel are aware that you stream on Thursdays at noon. Thousands of adoring fans tune in to watch as you talk and showcase fashion tips and styles.

In that scenario, you are abundantly sure that you are being watched. The webcam is connected to the Internet and when you activate it, people all across the globe are able to see and hear you. No question that you are at that juncture being watched (seen and heard).

As a recap, there are three modes that we've covered on the *being watched* affair:

- You are sure that you aren't being watched
- You suspect that you are maybe being watched
- You believe for sure that you are being watched

The first use case could be construed as you sitting in your bedroom, alone, and let's say you've unplugged the conversational electronic gadget so that it is unpowered and not able to function at all. In that circumstance, you are relatively confident that you aren't being watched.

The second use case was when the conversational gadget was plugged in and operating. You are still somewhat unsure of whether it is watching (overhearing) you via however it is programmed to deal with the detection of the prompting word. Maybe it is monitoring you, maybe not.

The third use case consists of the webcam that you turned on and opted to broadcast your exciting and endearing fashion guidelines. The odds are that you are being watched (well, unless no one decides to tune to your channel or the Internet is down, all of which is a frown face and decidedly not a smiley face situation).

We can take a moment to hone in on the second use case whereby you are unsure whether you are being watched or not.

In a manner of thinking about it, you can assign a probability or level of certainty to the chances that you are being watched. This probability ranges from 0 to 1.

You might have initially said that while in your bedroom you had a zero probability of being watched. Now, with heightened suspicion about the conversational device, I am guessing that your envisioned probability is higher (above 0, somewhere less than 1).

Another way to mentally contemplate these three states of being watched is that the first use case is when you assign a zero to the probability of being watched (i.e., you are absolutely sure you aren't being watched). The third case is when you assign a 1 to the probability that you are being watched (which, we'll loosely say is 100%, likelihood), though it might be perhaps somewhat less, depending upon other variabilities (akin to the web being down or nobody opting to watch your channel). And the second use case is some value between 0 and 1.

All told, the act of being watched is pretty much typified as a kind of spectrum, ranging from not being watched to possibly being watched and topping out at assuredly being watched. We can add to this the other twist that being watched is based on your perception of being watched versus the actuality of being watched. We'll elaborate on that further in a moment.

I'd like to shift gears and talk about prisons.

That might seem like a rather abrupt jump. In case you were getting worried that I am equating your bedroom to prison, do not carry such qualms. You will hopefully soon realize that the basis for the comparison is rooted in analogous aspects regarding the all-important matter of being watched.

Envision a prison similar to what you've seen in movies and TV shows. There are long rows of prison cells and several tiers, let's say three floors worth. Prisoners are normally in their cells, other than when allowed out for exercise in a prison yard. While the prisoners are in their cells, the prison guards patrol the floors and glance into each cell as they pass them. The guards are housed on the first floor in an office area reserved exclusively for their use.

To try and keep tabs on the prisoners and ensure that things aren't going amuck, the guards routinely patrol throughout the day and night. Of course, there are only so many guards that the prison can afford to have on staff and undertake the patrols. This means that there are somewhat long periods of time between when a guard perchance walks past a cell and glances in, while the preponderance of the time a prisoner is not being observed since there isn't a guard walking past their cell.

We can connect this back to our handy-dandy three facets framework about being watched:

- **Aren't watched:** Most of the time, a prisoner knows for sure they aren't being watched
- **Possibly watched:** Some of the time they are being watched for a brief moment as a guard saunters past the cell
- **For sure watched:** Upon a guard walking past the cell, if the guard looks in, the prisoner knows for sure they are being watched at that moment

The bottom-line in this prison setting is that by and large the prisoners are not being watched. You could of course increase the number of prison guards so as to have a saturation of patrols, think of ants in a frenzy marching back and forth constantly. The cost to do this would be enormous.

Is there anything else we could do?

A famous 18th-century social theorist named Jeremy Bentham wondered the same thing. How could a relatively small set of prison guards adequately be deployed to sufficiently watch a grand slew of prisoners? His solution entailed a restructuring of the prison architecture, rather than simply focusing on the amount of guarding human labor as the only factor of relevance.

He also relied upon human behavior and social conventions.

Here's what he came up with. While visiting his brother Samuel, a supervisor in a large factory, Jeremy found out that his brother intentionally situated himself into the middle of the factory floor. Why so? Because there were workers all about the factory that he could then eyeball from a centralized locale. Samuel arranged the workers to be in a circle around his central desk, allowing a glance in any direction to see what the workers were doing.

Even if he wasn't looking directly at a worker, such as say someone to his left, the fact that at any moment Samuel might look in that direction was enough to keep that worker on their toes. The mere possibility that Samuel could quickly and easily spot someone was enough to keep all the workers going at full stride. Had Samuel sat at a far edge of the building, he'd have no idea of what the workers at the opposite end were doing, including possibly wasting time or just sitting around.

It dawned on Jeremy that this same kind of centralized form of monitoring (or, the act of watching), could be reapplied in other contexts. He thought that hospitals might do this, allowing for doctors and nurses to watch their patients, rather than patrolling from hospital room to hospital room. Another realm that could use this strategy was prisons.

Jeremy wrote about his ideas. He devised a prison that would have a central tower. The guards would be in that tower. From the vantage point of the tower, it would be feasible to look into all of the prison cells. A guard could turn back and forth, almost like a lighthouse beam, glancing into this cell or that cell.

An especially clever part of the design is that the prisoners cannot see into the tower. As such, the prisoners do not know when they are exactly being watched. The number of guards in the tower and their aspect of rotating their guise would determine the chances of seeing a particular cell, doing for a particular instant of time.

You might have heard about this.

Such a structural arrangement is officially now known as a *panopticon.*

There was a seed of doubt about whether this would work adequately for prisons. Jeremy tried mightily during his lifetime to get one built, but sadly he did not succeed at doing so. Subsequently, there were some instances of panopticon-like prisons, though few and far between.

Meanwhile, the concepts underlying a panopticon gradually caught on. This is usually couched as representing a panopticon effect. You can devise all manner of situations that have a panopticon-like aura, and the fastest and easiest way to explain to someone how it works is merely to utter that it is a panopticon arrangement or has a panopticon effect.

Many years after Jeremy Bentham's panopticon concept was initially envisaged, a French philosopher of the name Michel Foucault brought the notion to re-prominence in his thought-provoking book entitled "Discipline and Punish" (published in 1975). The eloquent line that Foucault is especially known for is a quote about the asymmetrical surveillance underlying the panopticon design and the plight of a prisoner in such a setting: "He is seen, but he does not see; he is an object of information, never a subject in communication."

Further food for thought arises from this lesser well-known indication by him: "Hence the major effect of the Panopticon: to induce in the inmate a state of conscious and permanent visibility that assures the automatic functioning of power. So to arrange things that the surveillance is permanent in its effects, even if it is discontinuous in its action; that the perfection of power should tend to render its actual exercise unnecessary."

In theory, a prisoner will principally police themselves, doing so based on the belief that they are being watched at all times, though realizing that they aren't actually being relentlessly and continuously observed.

Voila, this takes us right back to the probability discussion.

A prisoner in a conventional prison would know for sure that they aren't being watched the preponderance of the time. One assumes that the prisoner ergo could act up at will since they know the chances of being seen are relatively small. Only in the brief instances of a guard patrolling past would the prisoner need to be on their best behavior.

In contrast, a prisoner in a panopticon devised prison would not be so abundantly sure that they are not being watched. They might be, they might not be. The safest assumption would seemingly be to always presume as a prisoner that you are being watched, even if you nonetheless knew there is only a chance of it occurring.

Now that we've covered the essentials, realize that the panopticon effect is not relegated only to prisons and the guarding of prisoners. There are lots of other settings that imbue or can employ a panopticon phenomenon.

Consider how this comes about in today's world. For that conversational electronic gadget in your home, suppose the audio is being recorded all of the time or at least some of the time. There are estimated hundreds of millions of these devices that have been sold to consumers. If we multiply things out, there could be millions upon millions of audio recordings that are lengthy, all day long, and recorded for months on end (or years) in massive magnitude.

There it sits, a treasure trove of audio data lurking somewhere in the cloud. Imagine the army of workers you would need to hire to cull through all of that audio, assuming you wanted to monetize the audio. It isn't a practical possibility to employ that many workers. The vastness of the audio data is seemingly overwhelming to even mentally grasp.

This takes us to the next stage in this *being watched* saga, the emergence of AI.

All of that audio is digitized. By being in a digital format, it is amenable to analysis by computer programs. Computer programs that leverage AI techniques and technologies have a notable chance of examining that vastness of data in relatively intelligible ways. All you need is the appropriate amount of computational processing power and AI-related software.

You've removed the human labor and can generally instead use AI capabilities.

One supposes in a prison setting, we are somewhat analogously suggesting that you theoretically could replace the prison guards with a machine, as a focus regarding the act of watching the prisoners (note that human guards might still be tasked with going on patrols or going to deal with prisoners that have gone astray as detected by the AI).

I'm glad that I got the AI mantra onto the table as it is the 600-pound gorilla that will be radically impacting our society and dovetails inextricably into the rising tide of digital surveillance that we are inexorably experiencing at this very moment.

Mull over the mounting tsunami of digital captures about our daily lives. You have seen every day that people armed with their smartphones are able to capture in real-time various events and activities that are then posted on social media for all to see. In addition, there are those nearly ubiquitous doorbell cams that manage to capture what is happening in front of people's homes and on the streets thereof.

Businesses and governmental agencies have mounted CCTV (closed-circuit TV) cameras on the exteriors of their buildings and other fixed-in-place structures. The video is usually recorded. Whenever something happens within the eyesight of those cameras, there is a rush by law enforcement and other parties to try and get a hold of that recorded video.

If all of that digital capture gives you the heebie-jeebies, I shall warn you that what I am about to say on this topic will push you even more into the formidable jeepers creepers.

The watchword or catchphrase is this: *AI-based true self-driving cars.*

Here's a noteworthy question that is worth pondering: *Will the advent of AI-based true self-driving cars be akin to a digital surveillance panopticon, and if so, why might that be?*

Allow me a moment to unpack the question.

The Coming Digital Surveillance Panopticon

For Level 4 and Level 5 true self-driving vehicles, there won't be a human driver involved in the driving task. All occupants will be passengers. The AI is doing the driving.

A self-driving car is coming down your street and aiming to pick up a neighbor that has requested a ride to the grocery store. Let's reasonably assume that the self-driving car does this safely and rather uneventfully. If you wonder about the reality of that claim, please know that in various tryout locales throughout the country, this is happening today. We aren't anywhere near any widespread use, and it is all concentrated in localized and quite small tryouts. These though will eventually be the springboard to a colossal upscaling and we'll have self-driving cars aplenty on our highway, byways, and community and city streets, mark my words.

Okay, so the self-driving car quietly comes down the street, stops at the appropriate house, waits for the rider to get into the autonomous vehicle, and then carefully whisks the passenger away to the store.

No big deal.

Life goes on.

But something has just happened that you likely were not aware of. Something monumental. Akin to not knowing or considering the impacts of having a conversational electronic gadget in your bedroom, you are possibly unfamiliar with how self-driving cars work.

Allow me a moment to elaborate.

There are sensors on the self-driving car. You've almost certainly seen pictures or videos of self-driving cars and undoubtedly noticed the added gear that sits atop the autonomous vehicles and on the sides of the cars. The sensor suite can consist of video cameras, radar, LIDAR (a type of radar that uses light waves), ultrasonic devices, thermal imagining units, and the like.

When a self-driving car is underway, the sensors are collecting whatever sensory aspects that they are suited to capture. The video camera is collecting video imagery of the driving scene. The radar is capturing radar returns of the driving scene. And so on.

This data is then used by the AI driving system to try and computationally assess the driving scene. Are there other cars nearby? While driving down a neighborhood block, are there any kids running into the street or unleashed dogs that might be meandering toward the roadway? Where can the self-driving car conveniently stop to pick up the designated passenger? Etc.

Without these sensors, the AI driving system would essentially be blind as to the driving scene. The sensors act as the proverbial eyes and ears for the AI. A lot of sophisticated programs are dissecting the collected data, often using Machine Learning (ML) and Deep Learning (DL) technologies. These are computational pattern matching facilities that are set up to examine the sensory data and seek to identify and label the objects of the driving scene (such as an object that is a car, an object that is a child in the street, and so on).

A self-driving car that is driving along has to very quickly computationally assess all of this data. This is imperative.

If the computer doesn't process the data fast enough, the AI driving system might misguide the car into hitting a human-driven car ahead of the autonomous vehicle or make other problematic choices at the driving controls. This is also why it is relatively easier to devise self-driving shuttles or self-driving delivery vehicles, namely they tend to operate at slow driving speeds such as 30 miles per hour, whereas an automobile of usual means is expected to at times proceed at 65 mph when on freeways or highways (meaning that the computer speed of assessing the driving scene has to be even faster to cope with the faster driving speeds and lessened time to react via the driving controls).

Most people seem to assume that the sensory data is a one-and-done affair.

You might think that the sensory data is momentarily captured, examined computationally, used by the AI for driving purposes, and then summarily discarded. That could happen, but the odds are much higher than the data is being recorded into the computer memory onboard the autonomous vehicle. Furthermore, at a point later in the day, the collected sensory data is uploaded via OTA (Over-The-Air) electronic messaging. OTA is used by the fleet operator or the automakers to push new software updates down into the AI system, and also do uploads from the self-driving cars too.

The stated intent of uploading the sensory data would be to use it as a means to further refine the AI driving system. Analyses can be done of the data. Did the AI at the time make a good choice or a questionable choice as to where to stop to pick up the passenger? From this analysis, the notion is that thc AI developers can make updates to the AI driving system and push those out to the autonomous vehicles.

It is a sensible approach.

Use the collected data to improve driving. There is a handy multiplier effect too. If one of the self-driving cars in the fleet encounters a pothole and had difficulties with it, this can subsequently be relayed to the rest of the entire fleet, simply via an OTA that pushes the aspects about the pothole to all other AI driving systems of the fleet. You rarely would have the same multiplier effect with human drivers, other than perhaps posting on a social media platform of something else of an akin ad hoc nature.

Our saga is now going to turn ugly, be forewarned.

The sensory data could be used for a lot of other purposes beyond simply as focused attention to the advancement of the AI driving systems.

Let's go back to the setting of the self-driving car coming down your neighborhood street. You were standing outside on your front lawn, tossing a baseball to your child. Next to you is your lawnmower, which you had used to mow the lawn and make it easier to stand and throw the ball around.

All of that innocuous and seemingly mundane scenery elements are visually and otherwise captured by the sensors of the self-driving car as it went down your street. Presumably, it has no direct bearing on the AI driving system and ergo can be skipped over computationally by the AI self-driving car at the time of the driving act. No need to assess it, though the data was captured.

This is the same data though that is getting uploaded into the cloud of the fleet operator or automaker.

So what, you ask, nobody cares about being noticed tossing a ball or having mowed the lawn.

Turns out that the next day, you receive an email from a company that makes baseball gloves. The email mentions that your existing mitt is quite worn out. Wouldn't you like to replace it? Furthermore, the email has a one-click button to allow you to order a new mitt. Your physical address is already known and filled in. All you need to do is provide a credit card and click on the purchase button.

A few days later, you receive a mailer to your home that is touting lawnmowers and other lawn-related maintenance equipment.

In short, the sensory data that was used to aid the AI driving system has gone into a pot of gold. The online repository is being mined. This is usually done with AI. The AI computationally detected your baseball mitt, examined it visually, and noted that it was weathered, and this then was fed to a company that is in partnership with the fleet operator. The email was then sent to you accordingly.

Ka-ching, money was just made off of that self-driving car collected data.

The same goes for the detection of the lawnmower. But wait, there's more. The collected data has your face. It has your body shape and the clothing that you were wearing. It has the face of the child and their clothes. It has the house that you are living in, including the front of the house, the front yard, and other particulars. Makes your head spin.

All of that data can then be digitally matched with data from your neighborhood and other databases. The odds are that your name can be found, your demographics, your job, and all sorts of other facets based on a large array of online databases.

At first, you might shrug your shoulders and say that this was one self-driving car that perchance went past your house at one brief moment in time. The thing is, realize that eventually we are headed toward having thousands, more like millions of self-driving cars on our roadways. They will be crisscrossing here and there, all day long, and nighttime too. The goal is to keep self-driving cars going 24x7.

I have become known for coining this emerging wave of self-driving car sensory digital surveillance as the "**roving eye**" of self-driving cars and autonomous vehicles.

The more we adopt self-driving cars, the more we are adding to our own digital surveillance. This is a huge leap beyond just the use of smartphones, CCTV, and the like. There will be a veritable torrent of autonomous vehicles that can end up capturing every waking moment of our lives. It will take a bit of computational wizardry to stitch it together, but you can bet that from the moment you step outside your house and go anywhere, this will be viably captured by self-driving cars and be uploaded online.

How does this relate to the panopticon effect?

That's easy-peasy.

We will all be under the guise of AI-based self-driving cars.

In that manner, we are going to be watched, maybe. You don't know for sure that the collected sensory data will in fact be kept and uploaded. You don't know for sure that if it is uploaded it will be used for digital surveillance purposes. You also don't know for sure that even if it is used for digital surveillance it will specifically aim at you.

Like those prisoners in the panopticon scenario, you won't have any immediate way of knowing that you are being watched, nor that the watching is paying attention to you.

Will the realization that you might be watched cause you to change your behavior as an everyday person and a rightful member of contemporary society?

Time will tell.

Conclusion

Some final comments for now.

For those that might already have known about the panopticon and the panopticon effect, there is another important point that Jeremy Bentham made and that has somewhat been neglected by the prevailing mainstream understanding of the panopticon overall.

He was strongly vocal about the notion of an "inspection principle" associated with his panopticon approach. This refers to the idea that the guards would also need to be watched, and as such, they ought to be watched in a similar panopticon manner. This deals with the age-old question of who guards the guards.

We might use prison managers that are placed in the prison to be able to observe the guards in the towers. The prison guards cannot see the prison managers. The prison managers will be looking at the prison guards some of the time, but not necessarily all of the time. As a result, the prison guards won't know if they are being watched per se, but they will presumably behave as though they are always being watched. In turn, someone will be watching the prison managers. It keeps on repeating at each level.

This is reminiscent of one of my columns that discussed the venerable expression of "turtles all the way down" (a popular phrasing for infinite regress). When someone asks what holds up that table over there, you can say it has a turtle underneath it. When subsequently asked what holds the turtle up, you can say there is yet another turtle underneath the first turtle. It continues this way, all the way down.

The inspection principle is supposed to be like those turtles, namely that the use of the panopticon precepts applies to all layers of those watching and being watched (well, except at the rock bottom). It isn't really an infinite regress, of course, and comes to an end at the logical place of the end of the line.

I share that inspection principle to bring up the yet unanswered question as to who will be watching the fleet operators and automakers as they proceed to roll out AI self-driving cars and come upon the heaping trove of roving eye data.

This begs for both ethical AI considerations, along with how our laws will apply to AI that is used in this manner and all other ways related to our society.

My closing comment is that there are notably and thankfully valiant efforts underway to prepare the next generation to deal with these AI and high-tech advances.

One such example is a tremendously insightful course at Stanford University that is entitled "Ethics, Public Policy, and Technological Change" being taught by Professor Rob Reich, Professor Mehran Sahami, and Professor Jeremy Weinstein. An amazing team has been assembled for the course, encompassing an interdisciplinary array of talent from the likes of computer science, philosophy, political science, law, sociology, and other domains. This is a cornerstone class that they continue to refine and enhance upon each such offering of the course.

Students taking the course are asked to explore the ethical and social impacts of technological innovation. I've taught such classes during my years as a professor at the University of Southern California (USC) and well-know how exciting and vital these classes are. I can also proudly say that I co-taught similar classes with and carried out societal impacts research in conjunction with a key founder of the social impacts of computing and the allied field of social informatics, namely Dr. Rob Kling (may he rest in peace).

The overarching notion of these kinds of classes is to aid the upcoming generation in getting ready for their soon-to-be roles as the enablers and shapers of technological change in our society. They need to know and have a keen perspective on the myriad of stakeholders, encompassing developers, designers, coders, engineers, business leaders, policymakers, citizens, consumers, etc.

We need more such courses and we must help guide those of the upcoming generations that will ultimately be at the heart of what technology is or becomes.

Society cannot rely upon the witticism that any sufficiently advanced technology is indistinguishable from magic. By making sure that all know what the technology can do, and cannot do, we will be better off at societally figuring out how to employ high-tech and not have the wool pulled over our eyes and nor be fooled by rabbits being pulled out of a hat.

CHAPTER 20 AI ETHICS AND AI POLITICAL BIASES

Let's talk politics.

Well, I realize that you are likely burned out about the seemingly nonstop focus on politics throughout all sources of available media these days. Red states versus blue states. Liberals versus conservatives. Democrats versus Republications. The chattering about political machinations is exasperatingly endless.

You might have reasonably assumed that there are some topics for which politics does not especially enter into the picture. In essence, maybe there are two distinct classes of topics, namely topics that are politically infused no matter what, and other more banal topics that would skirt or escape the political realm.

It would seem to make sense that there are going to be those eye-catching flashpoint topics that are eternally bound to be mired in politics and political furies, such as the longstanding list that includes national healthcare aspects, electoral aspects, gun control, immigration, and the like. All you need to do is mention any of those topics and the next thing that happens is you are immersed in a political firestorm. Rather heated arguments are pretty much guaranteed.

On the other side of the conflagration coin, perhaps there are some topics that do not cause such a knee-jerk political reaction. I'd like to float one such topic in front of you, seeking to get your initial gut reaction.

Ready?

Cars.

Yes, the everyday topic of cars, automobiles, motor vehicles, or however you'd like to phrase it, does that invoke a political outcry or stoke a politically charged diatribe or verbal fisticuffs to be bandied about?

It might not seem on the surface that there is a heightened semblance of political concerns about cars. They are simply a form of daily transportation. You get into your car, and you drive to work. You use your car to do errands and go get groceries. If you can spare some time for a vacation, you use your car to head to the open woodlands or maybe visit some treasured national monuments.

Cars would seem to be apolitical.

Sorry, but that's abundantly not the case.

The case can be made that cars are intimately surrounded by and immersed in politics like any other of the so-called flashpoint topics. Perhaps the general media doesn't cover car-oriented politics as much as might be done for other more alluring topics, but nonetheless, the political undercurrents are still in existence.

One obvious political dimension consists of what our cars should consist of.

I'm referring to the makeup or mechanization of cars. For example, there is a heady political debate about whether cars should be using ICE (internal combustion engines) versus switching over to EV (electrical vehicles). This is an area of significant discourse that ties into numerous other politically charged topics, such as environmental issues and climate change facets.

A lesser-known and yet related matter deals with the size of cars and their overall footprint in various respects. Should we have big-sized cars or only smaller-sized cars? Should we devise cars to discourage car use all-told, aiming to sway people to use mass transit and public transportation instead? And so on.

Here's something you likely didn't think about.

Some studies have examined whether the type of car owned is based on the political leanings of the car owner. Presumably, you might be able to find a statistical correlation between someone declared as being a Democrat as to the type of car purchased, and likewise find a statistical correlation between being a Republican and the type of car owned. I won't delve into those studies herein, though I would like to mention that you should interpret such studies and their results with a wary eye and a hefty dose of skepticism about the statistical validity involved.

Speaking of using statistics, there is another intriguing angle to political characteristics and cars. There are research efforts that seem to tie various *driving behaviors* of people to the political party affiliation of those drivers.

The questions often addressed include:

- Are drivers that get into car crashes or collisions more likely or less likely to be a Democrat or a Republican?
- Are drunk drivers more so likely to be liberals or conservatives?
- When those crazy road rage incidents occur, whereby drivers go berserk and strike out at each other, would those nutty raging lunatics tend to be liberals or conservatives?
- Who gets more traffic tickets and presumably drives more riskily, Democrats or Republicans?
- Etc.

Again, I am not going to dive into those research efforts herein. And, once again, please make sure to be on your toes when you read such studies or see blazing headlines about their results. All I will say is that the old line about statistics is still copiously true today, such that there are lies, darned lies, and statistics (I cleaned up that bit of salty wisdom for a more genteel audience).

We seem to therefore have ample evidence that the topic of cars is regrettably infused with political connotations.

I'll pick a different topic then, one that maybe will really be completely apolitical.

Ready this time?

Artificial Intelligence (AI).

Certainly, one would hope, AI must be apolitical, especially when it comes to the internal capacities of AI systems. You might of course suspect that there are politics *surrounding* whether AI ought to be used or not be used, but you would seemingly think that the internality of an AI system would be beyond any political fermentation per se.

Before we take a closer look at that prevalent assumption, it might be instructive to consider some other facets of AI that have recently caused many to rethink the feckless urge to produce and instinctively accept AI systems at the drop of a hat.

You see, in the rush toward the *AI For Good* excitement of the last several years, there has been a rising realization that not all AI is going to be necessarily good. We have come to see that there is also plenty of opportunity for the *AI For Bad* to arise. This can happen by the purposeful intent of those developing AI and can also happen by what some would stridently argue is a wholly irresponsible lack of proper oversight by AI developers and those promulgating AI systems.

Consider as an indicator of *AI For Bad* the matter of facial recognition.

Many thought that facial recognition was going to be the dandiest of AI technologies (and, in many ways, it is indeed a kind of *AI For Good*). It would be so easy to do banking at ATMs by simply having your face scanned for recognition rather than using a secret pin code and a banking card. It would be so convenient to walk into a grocery store and shop by merely using your face as a means to denote your online grocery account that could be charged for whatever items you select.

You know the drill.

The next thing you know, society began to discover that facial recognition is not all sweet-tasting candies and sweet-smelling roses. Some of the AI-based facial recognition algorithms did a lousy job of being able to discern people due to their race. Numerous other disconcerting and outright outrageous issues arose, including inherent biases related to gender and other factors.

The point overall is that there is a solid chance that any *AI For Good* is also going to carry associated baggage consisting of *AI For Bad.* There are some occasions whereby *AI For Bad* is entirely bad, and little redeeming qualities exist to suggest that there is a modicum of *AI For Good* within. All in all, though, usually an AI system is going to have a semblance of both *AI For Good* and *AI For Bad.* The former we would want to encourage, the latter we would want to prevent, curtail, mitigate, and when all else fails then catch and defang as soon as possible.

You might be thinking, yes, all of that makes sense and we ought to be mindfully scrutinizing AI for any kind of racial biases, gender biases, and any kinds of inequities. This would be the appropriate action and aid society in avoiding the bad and fruitfully garnering the good of AI.

Believe it or not, there is another factor that can be added to the list of surprising things wrapped into AI that many did not realize was in the AI motley stew.

Political leanings.

Recent studies showcase that AI systems can embody (as it were, though not anthropomorphically so), a plethora of political tendencies, opinions, preferences, and other such political-based attributes and infusions. This can in turn impact how the AI works, such as what the AI "decides" as based on the programming of the AI.

If you apply online for a loan and an AI-based algorithmic decision-making system is being used, you oftentimes have no clue as to what the AI programming consists of. Upon say getting turned down for the loan, you cannot be sure that the AI avoided using your race, gender, or other such factors in making the turndown choice.

Nor can you be sure that the AI didn't stifle your loan request due to its political biases.

When I state that in such stark terms, do not overinflate the notion by believing that the AI is sentient. As I will mention further in a moment, we do not have sentient AI today. Full stop, period. No matter what wild headlines you see, please know that there isn't anything close to being sentient AI today. We don't even know if reaching sentience with AI is possible. There is also no indication of when it will happen, or whether it will ever occur.

Back to the matter at hand.

Now that I've gotten onto the table that AI can contain political biases, we can take a closer look at how this happens and in what ways the political leanings can insidiously appear.

As an aside, if the notion that AI can embed political predilections causes you some horrendous gut-punching dismay or shock, chalk it up to yet another example of piercing the immaculate veil of AI. Society seems to have heretofore accepted a branding image of AI as incorporating the grand innocence and pristine aura of neutrality and balance.

We might have carried this over from other types of machines. Toasters do not seem to have inherent biases based on race, gender, and so on. We would similarly not expect a toaster to be politically minded, as it were. A toaster is a toaster. It is construed as just a machine.

The reason why the toaster perspective does not hold water when it comes to AI is that the AI system is programmed toward trying to carry on cognitive-like capacities. As such, this shoves the machine into the quandary of cognitive issues such as the embodying of biases and the like. I assure you, we will soon enough discover that AI-based toasters are rife with biases and problematic concerns.

A handy way to open the door toward understanding how AI can become politically imbued will be to take a gander at the use of AI in the advent of AI-based true self-driving cars. We can hit two birds with one stone and examine the generic and overarching topic of AI that contains political embodiment, and do so in the exemplar context of how this could arise in self-driving cars.

I do though want to clarify that AI political inoculation is a standalone topic that deserves to be given its own due. Do not mistakenly intertwine the AI of self-driving cars with the AI political dimensions. All AI will have politically inherent possibilities, and the depth and degree will depend upon how the AI is devised and fielded.

Here's then a noteworthy question that is worth pondering: *How will AI come to internally imbue political leanings, and can this even occur in the seemingly apolitical realm of the AI that is used for those emerging AI-based self-driving cars?*

Allow me a moment to unpack the question.

AI-Embedded Political Leanings

For Level 4 and Level 5 true self-driving vehicles, there won't be a human driver involved in the driving task. All occupants will be passengers. The AI is doing the driving.

Briefly put aside the self-driving car aspects and let's first explore the AI topic as to how it incorporates political leanings. The easiest way for AI to get politically minted is by the actions of the AI developers that craft the AI software. As humans, they could carry over their personal political leanings into what they program the software to do.

When AI systems first began to showcase various race and gender biases, there was a huge outcry that this must have been as a result of the AI developers that devised those systems. There were accusations that this was a purposeful act by AI developers. Others though suggested that the AI developers were lacking in diversity and ergo they carelessly or thoughtlessly allowed their existing biases to be carried over into their AI programming efforts.

For many AI teams, this sparked them to become more aware of assuring diversity amongst their fellow developers, including when new members were being added to their programming groups. In addition, special instructive educational courses were created to increase diversity awareness for AI developers. There are even AI development methodologies that encompass diversity aspects to explicitly guide AI projects toward watching out for inoculating biases and inequities into their systems.

Though almost no one is aware yet of the politically-embedded type of bias for AI, the odds are that it will eventually rise up in prominence and a vocal uproar will result. Once again, there will be close scrutiny of AI developers. Perhaps some are intentionally infusing their political leanings, while others might do so without a realization that they are doing so.

I dare say that the focus of assuming that the AI developers were the sole source of introducing biases into AI missed the totality of where the AI biases were arising from. A gradual awareness has been that the use of Machine Learning (ML) and Deep Learning (DL) became a notable contributor to the AI internal biasing aspects too.

Machine Learning and Deep Learning are computational patterns matching techniques and technologies.

You assemble data that you want to feed into the ML/DL, which computationally then seeks to find mathematical patterns in the provided dataset. Based on those calculated patterns, the ML/DL will be put to use, such as being able to do say facial recognition.

For facial recognition, we might feed in a bunch of pictures of people, and the ML/DL will calculate the notable characteristics of what makes faces recognizable, such as the shape and size of the nose, the shape and size of the mouth and lips, the shape and size of the forehead, and so on.

This computational approach would seem to be beyond any type of biasing influence. It is all just calculations.

Aha, but remember that we are feeding pictures (or whatever) into the ML/DL as part of the "training" or computational pattern matching. For facial recognition, if we were to feed primarily pictures showing people of one particular race, the odds are that the computational pattern matching would hone toward those facial aspects. Later on, supposing we put this facial recognition system into widespread use, those that used it and were of a different race might be less likely "recognized" mathematically because the ML/DL patterns are shaped around the race that was predominantly found in the training set.

So, you can plainly see how the otherwise "unbiased" mathematical approach of ML/DL can get skewed (there are other ways too, but I'm just mentioning this big one, herein). Did the AI developers purposely create a dataset that was racially imbalanced? I would suggest this is rarely an intentional act, though the lack of realization that they had done so is still not a sufficient excuse.

Nowadays, there is a strident push toward trying to get those using ML/DL to be more thoughtful about what data they use for training and what results this produces. Unfortunately, everyone has jumped onto the ML/DL bandwagon and many of these newbies or fly-by-nights that have taken up the ML/DL mantle are doing so without awareness of the biases being infused. There are possibly also bad actors that might intentionally do so, though let's hope they are few and far between.

I trust that the foregoing has gotten you up-to-speed on the AI Ethics aspects involving the infusing of biases into today's AI.

Go ahead and repeat the whole shebang, replacing the generic notion of biases with the specific indications of political-embedded leanings. I already mentioned that AI developers themselves might overtly or inadvertently carry their political leanings into what the programmed AI is doing. The other facet that I also brought up is that for the use of Machine Learning and Deep Learning there is a possibility of selecting training data that might purposely or accidentally carry across patterns that fit into a particular political dimension.

Well, I'm running a bit long on this column (oops, TLDR, some will acridly say), so I'll aim to briefly sketch an example of how AI for an AI-based self-driving car might get swept into these kinds of political leaning wormholes.

One well-known and oft-discussed potential equity issue about AI self-driving cars concerns the use of robo-taxis and who will have access to this new mobility-as-a-service option. Concerns are that only the wealthy will be able to afford to use robo-taxis, and thus those in lower-income brackets will be left out of the emerging era of driverless cars.

There is another twist parlaying from that qualm.

Envision that self-driving cars are roaming around a city and awaiting a ride request. A request comes in and a nearby robo-taxi self-driving car scoots over to pick up the rider. The rider indicates where they want to go, and the AI driving system plots out a path to get there. The AI driving system then proceeds to drive the autonomous vehicle to the desired destination.

All of that seems fine.

Here's a sobering trepidation that has been expressed.

Suppose the AI driving system opts to devise a path that avoids the more downtrodden neighborhoods. You might assume that the navigational plotting would only be based on the optimum path, such as the least distance, or maybe the shortest time. Maybe, maybe not.

Other factors could be the likelihood of the self-driving car going through what might be calculated as crime-ridden locales. It could be that the danger to the autonomous vehicle and the passengers is being taken into consideration of which path to take.

There is hand wringing that self-driving cars would almost always inextricably avoid the more impoverished or downtrodden communities. People riding in self-driving cars would never seem to realize that such places exist in their cities or towns. This in turn would presumably make them unaware of the needs of such communities. On top of this, those that live in those areas might rarely get an opportunity to use a self-driving car, even if affordable. There wouldn't be any robo-taxis roaming around in their midst, having by calculation kept themselves outside of those areas.

Would this bias come about due to intentional programming of the AI by the developers?

Could be, though not necessarily so.

Could this bias come from the use of Machine Learning and Deep Learning?

Sure, it is a considered possibility.

The AI driving system might be based on ML/DL that used data for training about where to proceed when mapping out a path. If that data was shaped around avoiding certain areas, the ML/DL would likely detect such a pattern and go forward with it. Over time, assuming that such data is further accumulated as the self-driving cars are out and about, the data subsequently used for updates and upkeep would further reinforce those same concocted patterns.

You could say that the patterns get compounded as the use of the prior pattern gets repeatedly set in place, a kind of snowball or ever-spiraling effect.

In a manner of speaking, you could construe that this seeming bias of where to drive is an example of how a potential AI political-embedded tendency could arise. One perspective would be to let the AI continue unabated in this predilection. Another would be to revise the AI to deliberately drive into those areas that were pattern-matched out of scope, which once again you could assert is a perhaps politically leaning posture being infused into the AI.

All told, the AI either *exhibits* a political leaning tendency or is at least perceived as doing so, regardless of whether it had any semblance (which it by sentience does not) about the politics of things.

Conclusion

There are lots of these kinds of examples that can be raised.

I'll stay with the self-driving car context and give you another quick example. Suppose a rider requests a lift by an AI self-driving car robo-taxi and does so to get to a political rally taking place at the downtown courthouse. The AI driving system refuses to take the rider there.

Why?

Imagine that prior data collected about political rallies as a destination point had indicated that the self-driving cars were getting caught in traffic snarls. Assume that this meant the self-driving cars were less able to make money off of the riders, due to the long wait times in traffic and charging a lesser rate for those wait times. An AI algorithm such as using ML/DL might computationally determine that going to political rallies is a sour money-making choice. Therefore, when requests for the robo-taxi arise to go to a political rally, the request is denied.

I think you can see how this might be seen as a politically motivated choice. Though the AI might not be directly using any kind of political motive in any manner of speaking, it, in any case, appears to be making a political choice.

You can bet your bottom dollar that we are going to soon enough confront a political backlash about the political leanings of AI. Mark my words!

Speaking of words, the famous Greek poet and playwright, Aristophanes, claimed that under every stone lurks a politician. In today's world, within every AI system, there is an indubitable chance of a lurking political-embedded leaning, whether you know of it or not.

Better start turning over those stones.

CHAPTER 21
AI ETHICS AND SOCIETAL WISH FULFILLMENT

Do you sometimes find yourself wishing upon a star?

I'm sure you do. We all do.

Such an act of wishing does not seem to matter who you are. There's always a distant chance of your dreams coming true whether they are near or are afar.

This has got to be one of the most longstanding poetic sing-song bents of humankind (expressed in many ways throughout time and history). You can pretty much assert that wish-fulfillment is a bedrock of the human spirit. We've wished before, we wish today, and by all accounts, we'll continue to be wishing in the future.

As you'll see in a moment, my focus for this discourse is going to be centered on *AI wish-fulfillment*.

This notion of AI wish-fulfillment turns out to be a quite sobering and contemplative matter, particularly by those that are versed in the realm of AI Ethics (also sometimes referred to as Ethical AI). The gist is that we as a society might be *blissfully* wishing for AI in a somewhat altruistic fashion, boding lamentably for a heavy falling out further down the road. You might say that the word "blissfully" should be construed as recklessly, mindlessly, and perilously.

Before we dive into the details of AI wish-fulfillment, it might be handy to do a wee bit more ruminating about the intrinsic nature of wishes and their impact on human behavior. This will suitably set the stage and get you primed for the beefy AI-specific part of this elucidation.

Open your mind to the fanciful world of wishes.

Imagine that you are dearly embracing a desirous wish that you'll attain an eagerly sought promotion at work. Meanwhile, suppose you are also clutching a heartfelt wish toward winning the mega-millions multi-state lottery.

Those are two quite illuminating sets of wishes.

First, in terms of garnering a promotion at work, I would earnestly suggest that your personal actions can demonstrably aid in bringing that wish to fruition. You might work night and day to showcase how hard a worker you are. You might gingerly nudge your supervisor or manager to remind them of a promotion that seems due or overdue. There are lots of everyday actions that you could take to try and steer that wish into reality.

Let's call that a practical kind of a wish and one that has a substantive probability of coming true. To clarify, there isn't any guarantee that this noteworthy wish is going to be ultimately achieved. Perhaps the company suddenly lays off a slew of employees and you are included in the bunch. Maybe the powers that be decide summarily you aren't suitable for a promotion. One never knows what might occur, though the point still is that your wish seems imminently practical and can be somewhat shaped by your wits and actions.

Consider next the wish to win the mega-millions multi-state lottery. I don't want to be the bearer of bad news but the odds of winning one of those massive pots are extraordinarily slim. Sorry if that seems gloomy. On top of the sour odds, there is really not much of any kind of personal effort or action that you can do to increase your chances of getting the winning ticket. You simply buy a lottery ticket and wait until the numbers are called.

Unless you can somehow hack your way into the lottery computers, you are stuck like the rest of us as being faced with incredibly high odds of not catching the enormous cache of dough. As an aside, a smarmy person would say that you could legally purchase thousands or millions of tickets to try and win the lottery, which though generally true, would seem rather unorthodox and not a viable strategy for anyone other than a handful of outrageously wealthy players. Let's put these outlier considerations aside.

The lottery administrators love to entice you by pointing out that if you don't buy a ticket you can't participate, so you have a zero chance of winning if you don't at least get into the game. Here are some of the most popular taglines by various lotteries:

- Dare to Dream
- Make the Impossible a Reality
- Give Yourself the Gift of a Dream
- Dreams for Sale
- Dream of the Impossible Dream
- Etc.

All told, and please prepare yourself to be potentially triggered, the wish to win the big lotteries is regrettably an impractical wish on the face of things. On the other hand, as earlier indicated, the wish to garner a promotion is reasonably plausible, usually, and ergo ranks in the category of practical wishes.

We should not though entirely discount wishes simply as a result of their practical or seemingly impractical nature.

It could be that wishing to win the lottery makes you happy. For a buck or whatever the lottery ticket costs, perhaps this gives you immense happiness for the days or weeks until the lottery numbers are announced. That's a snazzy deal. Low investment with a high return on happiness. You could argue that this is what the lottery organizers are betting on, namely that there will be a potential spillover from the impractical chances of winning into a "practical" semi-tangible result of your being momentarily happy (albeit lasting until you see the chosen numbers).

The essence is that wishes and the pangs of wish fulfillment can bring forth other consequential results beyond the target of the wish per se. You might say that sometimes a wish can have positive unintended consequences, while at other times a wish can have adverse unintended consequences. Wishes can drive us to do things that we might otherwise not have opted to do, both good and bad.

One other additional facet about wishes is that they can be of a personal or individualist caliber, or they can be of a group or collective quality. Your wish to get that promotion at work is presumably a personal or individualistic one. Others might have a similar wish at their jobs, though this is not especially connected to your particular wish.

The wish to win the lottery would certainly seem a widespread or collective wish. You can describe this as a societal-oriented wish based on how large-scale a wish it seems to be. This kind of wish is widely shared, aiding in shaping behavior across a vast spectrum of people and places in a very directly connectable way.

Now that we've got some handy wish-fulfillment axioms on the table, we can turn our attention to the intriguing matter of AI wish-fulfillment.

Are you ready?

Here's the deal.

AI ethicists point out that humankind at times has a societal wish-fulfillment regarding the advent of Artificial Intelligence (the venerated AI). Perhaps this is stoked by all those sci-fi movies and TV shows that we see. You could go back further in time and look at older books and dusty writings that have postulated a possibility of machines exhibiting human intelligence. This strident embodiment of wishes about AI is not a sudden revelation.

What makes it especially notable now is that we appear to be in a posture to devise and experience AI in a manner that heretofore was unable to construct or field. We'll come back to that in a moment.

One version of those AI wishes consists of a better world due to the emergence and use of AI. We might be able to use AI to solve world hunger and overcome other scourges that we all are collectively globally confronting. AI is the silver bullet if you will. A wonderful world will be the byproduct of our finally getting AI underway in a thankfully substantive sense.

Another version of those AI wishes is not quite so cheerful. If you were upset that I already mentioned that winning the lottery is lousy odds, you aren't going to like my noting that AI could be a real downer. Some highly vocal pundits have exhorted that AI is an existential risk. You know what they are talking about, such as that AI will be smarter than us (the so-called superintelligence) and will choose to kill us off. That hurts.

I'd ask that you push those dour AI wishes into the recesses of your mind for the purposes of this discussion, though do keep them at the ready. We don't want to let them get lost someplace. To make the dialogue here a bit cleaner, it will be easiest to focus on the happy face side of AI wishes. I assure you that we could readily expound upon the sad face (or the freaked-out face) version too (I'll likely cover this in a future column, don't you worry).

Assume that there is a wish about AI that consists of the upbeat side of things. Via AI, we are going to end up with a type of utopia. Again, as I just said, do not allow thoughts of a dystopia to creep into your mind for this particular chat. The world is going to be grandly happy with AI. Society will wonder how we ever got along without AI, to begin with.

Suppose that we entertain this happiness-inducing version of AI wish-fulfillment.

You might ask, can't we have our dreams?

As Cinderella told us, have faith in your dreams and someday that rainbow will come smiling on through and your wish will indubitably come true (that's a paraphing of the sage wisdom).

The problem with this AI wish-fulfillment is that when extended across and throughout society, it can engender questionable actions and endeavors associated with blindly pushing forward on AI that we might not really have wanted, or wanted in a different way or at a different time.

That might seem overly abstract, so let's recount what AI ethicists tend to highlight about the downbeats of the upbeat version of the AI wish-fulfillment phenomenon:

- We might ignore or undercut the real risks associated with AI
- We could overinflate the benefits of AI beyond what they really are
- We might proceed without caution on employing AI
- We could dangerously accept bogus exaggerations about AI
- We might reward fast-tracking of AI that leads to calamity
- We could focus on AI successes and ignore instructive AI failures
- We might allow groupthink to take us down the AI perils path
- And so on

In short, a society under the guise of AI wish-fulfillment could inadvertently be shooting our own collective foot (or is it those feet?). Whatsoever is untoward about AI will be swept under the rug. The collective wisdom of the crowd will be to tout the *AI For Good* and disregard the *AI For Bad.* Those that try to gain airtime to bring up *AI For Bad* are going to find no breathable space to do so.

It's going to be good times for AI and no turning back or even glancing over our fatigued shoulders.

In a recent research study published in the *AI And Ethics Journal* entitled "Socio-Cognitive Biases In Folk AI Ethics And Risk Discourse," the researchers ably ask how far this might go, namely that "from a strict utility maximization perspective, pursuing the scenario with infinite expected utility is the rational choice regardless of its probability. Similarly, any action which promotes the development of utopian AI would appear rational regardless of the probability of achieving the desired outcome, whatever the sacrifices" (article co-authored by Michael Laakasuo, Volo Herzon, Silva Perander, Marianna Drosinou, Jukka Sundvall, Jussi Palomaki, and Aku Visala).

Bottom-line, we might forsake all sorts of other important globe-saving tasks as we zealously pursue this AI wish-fulfillment. Thus, there is a double-whammy, whereby we perhaps craft and release AI that is riddled with *AI For Bad*, and meanwhile we might have been expending that energy and resources toward something else with a greater and more beneficial worldwide payoff. Make that a multi-whammy instead of merely a double-whammy.

Wishes can drive us to do some remarkably wild and crazy things.

Speaking of driving (yes, I snuck that in there), this allows me to shift into the topic of AI-based true self-driving cars, which will fit nicely into the AI wish-fulfillment theme.

You see, in my capacity as an expert on AI including the ethical and legal ramifications, I am frequently asked to identify realistic examples that showcase AI Ethics dilemmas so that the somewhat theoretical nature of the topic can be more readily grasped. One of the most evocative areas that vividly presents this ethical AI quandary is the advent of AI-based true self-driving cars. This will serve as a handy use case or exemplar for ample discussion on the topic.

Here's then a noteworthy question that is worth contemplating: *Does the advent of AI-based true self-driving cars contain AI wish-fulfillment considerations, and if so, should we be worried about it?*

Allow me a moment to unpack the question.

Those AI Wishes Coming True

For Level 4 and Level 5 true self-driving vehicles, there won't be a human driver involved in the driving task. All occupants will be passengers. The AI is doing the driving.

I will provide two prime examples of how some believe that AI wish-fulfillment is indeed alive and well within and around the emergence of AI self-driving cars. They decry these outsized, outstretched, and altogether ominous AI wishes.

The first example is one that I have already let the cat out of the bag by having mentioned just a moment ago, namely that we as a society are allowing tryouts of self-driving cars on our public roadways. Not everyone agrees that this is a wise thing to do.

A self-driving car coming along on your local street or highway might make a wrong move. The AI driving system is more so of an experimental nature than it is something fully vetted. Those outspoken pundits warn that we are allowing ourselves to be guinea pigs. Plus, they are usually quick to emphasize those self-driving cars should be first exhaustively and utterly tested via computer-based simulations and by use in specially prepared closed tracks and only after some form of governmental certification or verification has been undertaken should those autonomous vehicles be on our public roadways.

We have jumped the gun, they exclaim.

Why did we do so?

One answer is that we are mentally under the fog of AI wish-fulfillment.

We want with all our heart to have AI-based true self-driving cars that will seemingly reduce the number of annual injuries and fatalities due to car crashes (in the United States alone there are about 40,000 annual fatalities from car crashes and around 2.5 million injuries). We hope too that self-driving cars will enable widespread mobility-as-a-service. Those in society today who lack a car or are unable to afford a car will presumably have access to low-cost always-available robo-taxis.

The list of anticipated benefits arising from AI-based self-driving cars is lengthy and breathtaking. You would seem to have your head in the sand to not want to have self-driving cars. And want them now, not waiting until some later date. Each day that passes is another day of car crashes, injuries, fatalities, and inequities related to mobility.

Wait for a second, don't forget about the downsides of the upbeats of AI wish-fulfillment, some will vehemently yell at the top of their lungs. Let's reexamine the list and this time emphasize that rather than just any plain-old any kind of AI, we are now specifically discussing AI self-driving cars:

- We might ignore or undercut the real risks associated with AI self-driving cars
- We could overinflate the benefits of AI self-driving cars beyond what they really are
- We might proceed without caution on deploying AI self-driving cars
- We could dangerously accept bogus exaggerations about AI self-driving cars
- We might reward fast-tracking of AI self-driving cars that leads to calamity
- We could focus on AI self-driving car successes and ignore instructive AI self-driving car failures
- We might allow groupthink to take us down the AI self-driving cars perils path
- And so on

Yikes, is that what we are in the midst of doing?

While you are mulling over that example, let's add more fuel to the fire.

One aspect that very few are discussing is the incredibly massive privacy intrusion that AI self-driving cars are going to bring to our doorsteps, our neighborhoods, and the entirety of our lives. I have commented on this repeatedly, even anointing it as the veritable and proverbial "roving eye" that will soon be amongst us.

Allow me a moment to explain.

A self-driving car is driving down your street. It is on its way to picking up someone in your community. No big deal. The self-driving car is driving peacefully, legally, and abiding by all traffic laws. You barely even notice it as it passes your cherished home.

I realize that for those that are not yet familiar with seeing self-driving cars on the roads, you might find it hard to believe that you wouldn't stare, point, and gawk at a self-driving car that perchance went down your street. Well, I assure you, when you live in an area that has them aplenty, such as in Silicon Valley, it is the old line that when you've seen one, you've seen them all. Most people in the areas of the tryouts have already gotten used to seeing self-driving cars. Those autonomous vehicles are rampant. You encounter them frequently. More than you might think.

Nowadays, locals would tend to say that rather than being a standout as something exciting and futuristic, the self-driving cars roaming here and there is a mild nuisance due to driving extremely legally, such as making full stops at Stop signs and not willing to put the pedal to the floor. When you spot a self-driving car ahead of you, the reaction is to consider how to get around the thing or go a different way to avoid it. You might equate this to the annoyance you have when encountering a newbie teenage driver at the wheel (though, as clarification, the AI of today is not at all of a human proficiency).

Let's get back to the roving eye.

The self-driving car that went down your street was packed with various sensors, including possibly video cameras, radar, LIDAR, ultrasonic devices, thermal imagining units, and the like. You've undoubtedly seen pictures of self-driving cars that appear to have a rack on the rooftop and all kinds of gadgets jutting out from the exterior of the autonomous vehicle.

Those sensors are collecting data about the driving scene. The AI driving system computationally analyzes the data to try and figure out what kinds of driving actions are suitable. Where is the roadway headed? Are there cars parked on the street? Is a dog about to dart into the path of the self-driving car? These are all crucial to the driving actions and the AI adjusting the driving controls accordingly.

You might not have thought about something else that these sensors are doing. In the midst of detecting the roadway, they are also collecting data about anything else nearby. For example, suppose you are standing in front of your house and mowing the lawn. The self-driving car goes past your house. You don't think anything of it.

The next day, you receive a mailer that tells you that new lawnmowers are on sale. Why did you get this mailer? Because the video and other sensory data of the driving scene and surroundings went up into the cloud. The fleet operator or the maker of the self-driving car can examine that data. They might have a deal with other companies about how to mine the data. In this case, the fact that you were spotted mowing the lawn is handy. A company that makes or sells lawnmowers would pay to know that you have a lawnmower and that you use it. The data could be AI inspected to figure out which model you have and how old it is. All of this could be used to target you for a new lawnmower.

Realize too that the data would have your home address. This data could be paired with other demographic data and other databases to try and craft a deep profile about you. There are lots of other ways that this data could be utilized, many of them alarmingly nefarious.

Why in the heck would we let this self-driving car roving eye come into existence?

The answer by some is that we are under the happy-flavored aura of the AI wish-fulfillment phenomena.

Conclusion

Are we as a society taking too many chances about letting AI self-driving cars proceed apace?

Has the dreaminess of the AI wish-fulfillment overtaken our practical sensibilities?

These are important questions. AI ethicists are pounding away at trying to bring these crucial points to the collective consciousness of society. It is hard to poke through widespread communal dreams. An all-too-common response is that such "naysayers" are viewed as a spoilsport or disruptively a doom-and-gloom grouch.

One last remark for now.

Walt Disney was famously known for the sign that he placed above the entrance to Disneyland that said these immoral words: "Here you leave today and enter the world of yesterday, tomorrow, and fantasy." I ask you, with regard to today's AI self-driving cars, are we in the realm of down-to-earth pragmatics or are we slipping into a kind of fantasyland. The same question ought to be asked about all manner of AI that we are devising.

We are assuredly in for a dramatic journey (akin to *Mr. Toad's Wild Ride*), and as Walt was known for notably declaring, apparently we need to dream, believe, dare, do.

CHAPTER 22

RADICAL AI ETHICS

Has the prevailing tenor and attention of today's widely emerging semblance of AI Ethics gotten into a veritable rut?

Some seem to decidedly think so.

Let's unpack this.

You might generally be aware that there has been a rising tide of interest in the ethical ramifications of AI. This is often referred to as either AI Ethics or Ethical AI, which we'll consider herein those two monikers as predominantly equivalent and interchangeable (I suppose some might quibble about that assumption, but I'd like to suggest that we not get distracted by the potential differences, if any, for the purposes of this discussion).

Part of the reason that ethical and moral considerations have risen about AI is due to the gradually mounting spate of so-called *AI For Bad.* You see, originally the latest wave of AI was perceived as principally proffering *AI For Good.* This was the idea that AI could aid in solving many of the otherwise intractable problems that computing had heretofore not been able to aspire to aid. We might finally find ourselves leveraging AI to tackle many of the world's toughest issues.

Along that somewhat dreamy journey, the realization has hit home that there is the other side of the coin. That's the *AI For Bad.* For example, you might know about the brouhaha over AI-based facial recognition that has at times embodied racial biases and gender biases. Not good. There are now plenty of clearcut instances of AI systems that have a plethora of untoward inequities built into their algorithmic decision-making (ADM) functionality.

Some of the dour issues within AI are ethically borderline, while other issues are pretty much beyond any reasonable ethical boundaries. On top of that, you can count too that the AI might be ostensibly illegally acting or outright a no holds barred illegal performer. The two-step of getting hammered by the law and by ethical mores is aiming to slow down the *AI For Bad* and seek to prevent the ongoing onslaught of AI that by default might be fully riddled with egregiously immoral and unlawful elements.

One relatively common set of Ethical AI factors consists of paying attention to these characteristics of AI:

- Fairness
- Transparency
- Explainability
- Privacy
- Trustworthiness
- Dignity
- Beneficence
- Etc.

Those are the oft-cited social constructs that we ought to be mulling over when it comes to the crafting and fielding of today's AI. The odds are that if you perchance take a look at an article or blog post that covers AI Ethics, you will find that the theme of the piece is centered on one of those aforementioned factors or characteristics.

I believe that by and large those that are vocally calling for Ethical AI would agree that those factors are worthy of attention. Indeed, the real problem seems to be that those making AI and those promulgating AI don't appear to be getting the message. This has prodded those amid the AI Ethics movement to further expound on why these characteristics are so darned important. Regrettably, a lot of AI developers and firms leveraging AI either think this is nice to have, ergo merely optional, or they see the Ethical AI as more so an abstract academic exercise than something of everyday practical nature.

Per my predictions, a lot of those that have their head in the sand about Ethical AI is going to one day wake up and rudely discover that they are under the strident guise of society and also of the law. People will be quite upset upon discovering that the pervasive AI embedded into all manner of goods and services is peppered with inherent biases and inequities. Lawmakers are already pressing ahead with new laws to try and ensure that those promoting such AI are going to come under legally unambiguous rules, thus making it much harder for the AI builders and those that field AI to shrug off any adverse civil and prosecutorial criminal potentialities from their endeavors.

Without seeming to be flippant, the wheels of justice will inexorably grind their way toward those that are emitting and fostering untoward AI.

To clarify, the *AI For Bad* is not necessarily attributed solely to villainous actors. Turns out that the bulk of AI developers and those serving up the AI to the world at large are frequently unaware of what they've got on their hands. The sounding alarm about AI Ethics has apparently not yet reached their ears. You can have sympathy for those that are blissfully unaware, though this does not outrightly excuse them from their responsibility and ultimate duty of care.

I'd like to briefly mention that you should not fall for the insidious mental trap that the blame for the untoward AI lays at the feet of the AI itself. This is nearly laughable, though it keeps being used as an escape hatch and incredibly seems to work from time to time on those that aren't familiar with AI of today. You see, the AI of today is not sentient. Not even close. We don't know if AI sentience is possible. We don't know when sentient AI might be attained.

The bottom line is that the AI blame game of distracting everyone by pointing a finger at the AI as the responsible party is disingenuous if not altogether dishonest. Existing AI is programmed by human developers. Existing AI is released and made available by humans. The companies that build AI and the companies that license or buy the AI for purposes of using the AI within their goods and services are entirely based on humankind. Humans are the responsibility bearers, not AI (perhaps, in the future, we'll have AI of a different and more advanced semblance, and at that time we'll need to wrestle more closely with the distinction of where blame resides).

As a quick recap, we ought to be thankful that the Ethical AI vocalizers are stridently trying to get society clued in about the ethical implications of AI. Right now, it is almost akin to the Sisyphus act of rolling a boulder up a steep hill. Many that should be listening are not doing so. Those that listen are not always prompted into corrective action. Just as Sisyphus had the unenviable task of pushing that boulder up a hill for eternity, you can pretty much assume that the AI Ethics cacophony will by necessity need to be an eternal ruckus too.

That seems to settle the matter about AI Ethics and we can presumably move onto another topic.

But, wait, there's more.

You might be surprised or even shocked to learn that some assert that the existent body of Ethical AI considerations is remiss. The primary keystone of AI Ethics has gotten mired into a groupthink bailiwick, they exhort vociferously.

Here's the deal.

My earlier indicated list of AI Ethics factors is said to have become a stifling preoccupation by the Ethical AI crews. Everybody mindlessly accepts those factors and keeps pounding away at those same factors, over and over again. Similar to an echo chamber, the preponderance of AI ethicists is repeating the same song to themselves, relishing the sound of it.

Few are willing to break out of the pack. A herd mentality has overtaken Ethical AI (so it is claimed).

How did this conundrum arise? You can apparently explain this undesirable mainstreaming of Ethical AI as based on either happenstance or by design.

In the happenstance scenario, the key factors are exceedingly easy to focus on. You don't have to go outside the box, as it were. Furthermore, those that are within the Ethical AI camp are likely to be more interested in similar work or ideas, rather than searching out notions beyond the norm. Birds of a feather flock together. Inch by inch, the AI Ethics arena is said to have huddled into a cramped cluster and generally is fine with the familiarity and comfort that it inures.

I'm sure that will get the ire of many AI Ethics participants (keep in mind that I am just mentioning what others are contending and not affirming those allegations).

If you want to rachet up the ire, consider the suggestion that the phenomenon has arisen by design. In a somewhat perhaps conspiracy theorist realm, it is said that the AI technologists and the tech companies are either directly or subliminally contributing to the narrowing of Ethical AI considerations.

Why would they do so?

We'll ponder two possibilities.

One notion is that the AI technologists favor the existing set of Ethical AI considerations since those particular factors are somewhat amenable to being fixed via technology. For example, if you want explainability, AI technologists and AI researchers are working night and day to craft explainable AI (XAI) capabilities. The beauty then of the prevailing list of Ethical AI factors is that they fit within the purview of AI technology resolutions. Those that ascribe to that theory are apt to suggest that any other factors that aren't readily AI techno-solved aren't able to gain traction on the factors list.

You then have the other more nefarious variant. It is suggested that there are high-tech companies and others that want to provide essentially lip service to AI Ethics matters. In that sense, they relish a shorter list of technologically solvable concerns. Any attempt to add other concerns will make life harder for those tech companies. They want to minimize the investment needed to placate the Ethical AI proclamations.

I suppose that kind of allusion is bound to spur fisticuffs and go far beyond simple ire. Those that are tirelessly trying to abide by and contribute to Ethical AI are potentially being smeared by those claims, and you can readily imagine why they would be outraged at the seemingly unabashed and altogether brazen accusations.

Let's not get a brawl started and instead take a sober and reflective moment to see what else the Ethical AI camp is supposedly missing out on. The other camp that is pleading to extend and expand the viewpoint of contemporary Ethical AI is at times being referred to as *Radical Ethical AI*.

You might wonder whether the moniker of Radical Ethical AI is suitable or unwelcomed.

The connotation of something that is "radical" can be good or bad. One interpretation of Radical Ethical AI is that it is an attempt to shake up the status quo of AI ethics. The use of the "radical" showcases that we need to make a concerted dramatic turn and not just slightly adjust or weakly render a modicum of a swivel. You could argue that using "radical" will bring a shock to the existing approaches akin to using a defibrillator that otherwise via usual convention would not be attained.

Others would say that by attaching the word "radical" you are creating quite a mess. Some would interpret radicalism as being outlandish, slipping toward eccentric or oddball. Centrists might immediately reject the very notion of whether there is a groupthink due to the naming alone as an offending contrivance. Tone down the rhetoric, some would say, and you might get more serious attention and interest.

Notwithstanding the naming issue, you might be innately curious as to what it is that this other camp believes that the rest of us are missing. Set aside any visceral reaction to the whatchamacallit.

You might outwardly ask, where's the beef?

I'll try to represent some of the alluded to missing ingredients.

First, one claimed oversight is that the prevailing view of traditional (old-fashioned?) Ethical AI is a constraining hidden assumption that AI is inevitable. Thus, rather than examining whether AI should even be in the cards for particular kinds of uses and societal circumstances, the predominant position is that AI is coming and we need to get it into the best shape possible. You might smarmily say that this is akin to putting lipstick on a pig (i.e., it is still a pig, no matter what you do to make it seemingly look better).

If you take that to the extreme, the qualms about fairness, privacy, and the rest are perhaps said to be like moving chairs around on the deck of the Titanic. This ship is still going to sink, meaning that we assume AI is going to happen, no matter what. But, maybe we ought to be reconsidering whether sinking is the only option afoot.

I'll be getting back to this consideration in a moment.

Here quickly are some other claimed Ethical AI matters that are either not being given their due or that are squeezed out by the abundance of attention to other prevailing topics:

- Besides using AI to manage humans, such as increasing the use of AI to make hiring and firing decisions in companies, there is a likewise qualm about the use of AI to manage animals. There are efforts underway to utilize AI in farms, zoos, and generally any place that animals tend to be kept. How will AI impact animal welfare?

- There are times at which AI is seemingly being beta tested in especially vulnerable communities, doing so as a first try, and then the AI will, later on, be spread more widely. Keen ethical AI attention ought to be aimed at those practices.

- A lot of discussions appear to be taking place about replacing workers with AI, though there is less so attention to the impacts of AI as a monitoring tool used to oversee low-wage low-status workers.

- Insufficient attention would seem to be taking place regarding the ecological and environmental impacts of building and keeping the AI systems running.

- And so on.

There are some specialists in Ethical AI that will likely right away point out that those are in fact topics that can be found in the literature and discussions about AI ethics. They are not unheard of and nor are they breathtakingly new.

I believe that the perspective of the Radical Ethical AI purists is that they aren't claiming they have discovered completely untrodden ground. Instead, they are asserting that the existing focus of Ethical AI is choking out the breathable air of allowing other "outlier" topics from getting their due.

Perhaps a more palatable way to phrase this is that the prevailing AI Ethics attention has given less attention to other viably vital topics. You could suggest that there are blind spots and it would be handy to consider whether those can be brought further into the fold (this is likewise discussed in the *AI and Ethics Journal* in a recent paper entitled "Blind Spots in AI Ethics" by Thilo Hagendorff).

Now that we've covered the saga of whether Ethical AI is in a bit of a rut, which some would say is a preposterous contention and meanwhile others would insist that the rut is real and getting worse, perhaps we can take a moment to explore a use case to take a closer look at the matter.

In my capacity as an expert on AI including the ethical and legal ramifications, I am frequently asked to identify realistic examples that showcase the alignment dilemma so that the somewhat theoretical nature of the topic can be more readily grasped. One of the most evocative areas that vividly presents this ethical AI quandary is the advent of AI-based true self-driving cars. This will serve as a handy use case or exemplar for ample discussion on the topic.

Here's then a noteworthy question that is worth contemplating: *Does the advent of AI-based true self-driving cars present any outside-the-box Ethical AI considerations that are generally being unchallenged or insufficiently surfaced?*

Allow me a moment to unpack the question.

The Outliers Or Outcasts Of Ethical AI Considerations

For Level 4 and Level 5 true self-driving vehicles, there won't be a human driver involved in the driving task. All occupants will be passengers. The AI is doing the driving.

Let's focus on one particular matter that we can then dig into. Specifically, there is the overall charge that prevailing AI Ethics purportedly has a hidden assumption that AI is inevitable.

If we apply that keystone presumption to AI-based self-driving cars, it implies that the Ethical AI community is by-and-large assuming that self-driving cars will inevitably be devised and fielded. They are taking at face value that self-driving cars will emerge, whereas the counterclaim would be that they should <u>not</u> be making that hidden assumption and instead be chewing on that perhaps we ought to not have AI self-driving cars (or some variant such as only have them in special circumstances rather than on a widespread basis).

It's a great question.

To clarify and restate, the assertion than being that the predominant Ethical AI considerations about AI self-driving cars are missing the boat by apparently assuming that AI self-driving cars are inevitable. In that way of thinking, the expectation would be exhibited twofold:

1. Few if any cxaminations of whether we should even have AI self-driving cars would exist, or would be shunted to the side, or have no breath of air to get any shining light of attention, and
2. The likely focus on AI self-driving cars would instead be on the details surrounding the ethical AI ramifications of the traditional list of factors, such as explainability, fairness, privacy, etc., and altogether doing so under the general guise or silent presumption that we will decidedly have those vaunted autonomous vehicles (with no other option being widely entertained).

An interesting proposition.

Even a casual inspection of the general attention to such issues relating to AI self-driving cars would showcase that there is an assumption that AI self-driving cars are somewhat inevitable, though let's make sure that a huge caveat and double star footnoting cautionary indicator goes along with that sweeping statement.

Here's why.

We don't know as yet whether AI-based true self-driving cars will really be entirely possible.

Sure, there are narrowly devised public-roadway tryouts underway. These are absolutely not at Level 5. Nobody can reasonably argue to the contrary on that undeniable point. You can say that some of the proper tryouts are kind of veering into Level 4, but wobbly so and with relatively brittle ODDs (ODDs or Operation Design Domains are the stipulations of where a self-driving car maker states that their autonomous vehicle can safely operate).

That being said, the self-driving car arena is much further along than it was just a few years ago. There is reasonable cause for being upbeat about what will happen next. The biggest sticking point is the timetable of when this will play out. Previous predictions by the pundits have readily come and gone. You can expect the existing predictions to assuredly suffer the same fate.

In short, it would seem that you could informally say that there is a sufficient rationale for assuming that AI-based true self-driving cars are going to eventually arise. It would seem that we are heading toward Level 4 amidst very constrained ODDs. The next logical expansion would seem to involve having more ODDs, ones of greater variety and depth. At some juncture whereby we've conquered enough overlapping and somewhat exhaustive ODD spheres, this would seem to culminate into venturing gingerly into Level 5. That's at least the stepwise philosophy of anticipated progress (which not everyone embraces).

I mention those seemingly complex contortions because there is much confusion about what it means to proclaim that AI-based true self-driving cars exist or that we have arrived at the grand moment of their existence. What is your definition of AI-based true self-driving cars? If you say it is the moment you've edged teensy-weensy into Level 4, well, I guess you can start popping those champagne bottles. If you say it is once we've turned the corner on Level 4, you are going to need to put those champagne bottles in storage. If you say it is when we've mastered Level 5, those bottles are going into the back of the storage shelves and you should expect them to get dusty.

All in all, if society is in fact making an assumption that AI self-driving cars are inevitable, you could reasonably argue that this is an aboveboard assumption. Not everyone would agree to that contention, so for those of you that are upset at the alleged possibility, your vehement disagreement is so noted.

Are we potentially getting ourselves into trouble or dire straits by generally going along with that assumption of inevitability for AI self-driving cars?

There are intriguing twists and turns that this enigma brings to the surface.

For example, one already oft-discussed concern is that we might have AI-based self-driving cars that are exclusively available in some areas but not in others. The areas that will have self-driving cars are the "have's" while the areas that don't have them are the "have not's" that are essentially precluded from leveraging the benefits of self-driving cars.

This is the proclaimed *elitist* or i*nequity* phenomenological worry that many have expressed.

The idea is that AI self-driving cars will likely be operated in fleets. The fleet operators will choose where to deploy their self-driving cars. The presumed money-making place to use the self-driving cars is in the wealthier parts of a town or city. Those living in the poor or impoverished parts of a town or city won't have ready access to self-driving cars.

The same logic is extrapolated to contend that countries will similarly find themselves also in the same predicament. Wealthier nations will experience the use of self-driving cars, while poorer nations will not. The have's will have more access and use of autonomous vehicles, the have not's will not.

You might be wondering what the have's are getting that the have not's are not getting. A frequent indication is that there is an expectation that AI driverless cars will have many fewer car crashes and car collisions. The belief is that the number of consequent human injuries and fatalities due to car crashes will diminish dramatically. As such, the wealthier parts of a town or city, or the wealthier nations, will be able to curtail their car-related injuries and fatalities, while the human-driven regions that don't have the option or replacement via AI-based self-driving cars will not see any such commensurate reduction.

Please know that there are other touted benefits of AI self-driving cars that would similarly be accrued in the have's and not be incurred in the have not's.

The gist here is that you can stretch the "are self-driving cars inevitable" by pointing out that Ethical AI is already handwringing about self-driving cars only being selectively available. I know it might seem like a pretzel of logic. What this is saying is that we are already notably concerned about AI not being available in some societal segments. In that stretch of thinking, this instantiation of AI is not inevitable with respect to those contexts per se (if you get the drift).

Conclusion

You are undoubtedly familiar with the cleverly devised sage advice that what you don't know can harm you, while what you don't know that you don't know can really wipe you out.

One viewpoint about the Radical Ethical AI posture is that despite any naming-related consternation, we should at least hear what it is believed that we are missing out on. Maybe there is a groupthink taking place and so-called conventional Ethical AI or old-fashioned AI Ethics has managed to become stagnant and stuck on particular considerations. If so, a kick in the posterior might aid in getting the engines running again and moving toward a widened scope.

Or, it could be that Ethical AI and AI Ethics are doing fine, thank you very much, and this offshoot is just trying to be a fly in the ointment. The downside doesn't seem especially disruptive or disconcerting. When or if things get somehow out of hand, a devout and concerted reassessment of the realm might be of insightful merit.

Continuous improvement is a laudable aspiration. And, you can nearly inarguably state that when it comes to the advent of AI, we don't want to belatedly discover that we didn't know what we didn't know, and that we should have known to be on top of the aspects that we didn't know (or, that we knew them, somewhat, and inadvertently suppressed them).

APPENDIX

APPENDIX A
TEACHING WITH THIS MATERIAL

The material in this book can be readily used either as a supplemental to other content for a class, or it can also be used as a core set of textbook material for a specialized class. Classes where this material is most likely used include any classes at the college or university level that want to augment the class by offering thought provoking and educational essays about AI.

In particular, here are some aspects for class use:

- Computer Science. Studying AI, ethics, etc.
- Business. Exploring technology and ethical adoption for business.
- Sociology. Ethical views on the adoption and advancement of technology.

Specialized classes at the undergraduate and graduate level can also make use of this material.

For each chapter, consider whether you think the chapter provides material relevant to your course topic. There is plenty of opportunity to get the students thinking about the topic and force them to decide whether they agree or disagree with the points offered and positions taken. I would also encourage you to have the students do additional research beyond the chapter material presented (I provide next some suggested assignments they can do).

RESEARCH ASSIGNMENTS ON THESE TOPICS

Your students can find background material on these topics, doing so in various business and technical publications. I list below the top ranked AI related journals. For business publications, I would suggest the usual culprits such as the Harvard Business Review, Forbes, Fortune, WSJ, and the like.

Here are some suggestions of homework or projects that you could assign to students:

a) Assignment for foundational AI research topic: Research and prepare a paper and a presentation on a specific aspect of Deep AI, Machine Learning, ANN, etc. The paper should cite at least 3 reputable sources. Compare and contrast to what has been stated in this book.

b) Assignment for the Ethics topic: Research and prepare a paper and ethics. Cite at least 3 reputable sources and analyze the characterizations. Compare and contrast to what has been stated in this book.

c) Assignment for a Business topic: Research and prepare a paper and a presentation on businesses and advanced technology. What is hot, and what is not? Cite at least 3 reputable sources. Compare and contrast to the depictions in this book.

d) Assignment to do a Startup: Have the students prepare a paper about how they might startup a business in this realm. They must submit a sound Business Plan for the startup. They could also be asked to present their Business Plan and so should also have a presentation deck to coincide with it.

You can certainly adjust the aforementioned assignments to fit to your particular needs and the class structure. You'll notice that I ask for 3 reputable cited sources for the paper writing based assignments. I usually steer students toward "reputable" publications, since otherwise they will cite some oddball source that has no credentials other than that they happened to write something and post it onto the Internet. You can define "reputable" in whatever way you prefer, for example some faculty think Wikipedia is not reputable while others believe it is reputable and allow students to cite it.

The reason that I usually ask for at least 3 citations is that if the student only does one or two citations they usually settle on whatever they happened to find the fastest. By requiring three citations, it usually seems to force them to look around, explore, and end-up probably finding five or more, and then whittling it down to 3 that they will actually use.

I have not specified the length of their papers, and leave that to you to tell the students what you prefer. For each of those assignments, you could end-up with a short one to two pager, or you could do a dissertation length paper. Base the length on whatever best fits for your class, and the credit amount of the assignment within the context of the other grading metrics you'll be using for the class.

I mention in the assignments that they are to do a paper and prepare a presentation. I usually try to get students to present their work. This is a good practice for what they will do in the business world. Most of the time, they will be required to prepare an analysis and present it. If you don't have the class time or inclination to have the students present, then you can of course cut out the aspect of them putting together a presentation.

If you want to point students toward highly ranked journals in AI, here's a list of the top journals as reported by *various citation counts sources* (this list changes year to year):

- Communications of the ACM
- Artificial Intelligence
- Cognitive Science
- IEEE Transactions on Pattern Analysis and Machine Intelligence
- Foundations and Trends in Machine Learning
- Journal of Memory and Language
- Cognitive Psychology
- Neural Networks
- IEEE Transactions on Neural Networks and Learning Systems
- IEEE Intelligent Systems
- Knowledge-based Systems

GUIDE TO USING THE CHAPTERS

For each of the chapters, I provide next some various ways to use the chapter material. You can assign the tasks as individual homework assignments, or the tasks can be used with team projects for the class. You can easily layout a series of assignments, such as indicating that the students are to do item "a" below for say Chapter 1, then "b" for the next chapter of the book, and so on.

a) What is the main point of the chapter and describe in your own words the significance of the topic,

b) Identify at least two aspects in the chapter that you agree with, and support your concurrence by providing at least one other outside researched item as support; make sure to explain your basis for disagreeing with the aspects,

c) Identify at least two aspects in the chapter that you disagree with, and support your disagreement by providing at least one other outside researched item as support; make sure to explain your basis for disagreeing with the aspects,

d) Find an aspect that was not covered in the chapter, doing so by conducting outside research, and then explain how that aspect ties into the chapter and what significance it brings to the topic,

e) Interview a specialist in industry about the topic of the chapter, collect from them their thoughts and opinions, and readdress the chapter by citing your source and how they compared and contrasted to the material,

f) Interview a relevant academic professor or researcher in a college or university about the topic of the chapter, collect from them their thoughts and opinions, and readdress the chapter by citing your source and how they compared and contrasted to the material,

g) Try to update a chapter by finding out the latest on the topic, and ascertain whether the issue or topic has now been solved or whether it is still being addressed, explain what you come up with.

The above are all ways in which you can get the students of your class involved in considering the material of a given chapter. You could mix things up by having one of those above assignments per each week, covering the chapters over the course of the semester or quarter. As a reminder, here are the chapters of the book and you can select whichever chapters you find most valued for your particular class:

<u>Chapter Title</u>

1 Introduction To AI Ethics

2 AI Ethics And AI Values Alignment

3 AI Ethics And The AI Control Problem

4 AI Ethics Precepts Of The Vatican

5 AI Ethics Principles Of The US DoD

6 AI Ethics And The Trolley Problem

7 AI Ethics Self-Learned By AI

8 Ethical AI Monitoring Of Unethical AI

9 AI Ethics Leadership Empowerment

10 AI Ethics Of Humans Feuding With AI

11 AI Ethics Self-Awareness By AI

12 AI Ethics And AI Criminal Accountability

13 AI Ethics And Legal Personhood

14 AI Ethics And The Uncanny Valley

15 AI Ethics And Distributing Harm

16 AI Ethics And Humans Mistreating AI

17 AI Ethics And AI Racial Biases

18 AI Ethics And AI Blame Assignment

19 AI Ethics And Societal Panopticons

20 AI Ethics And AI Political Biases

21 AI Ethics And Societal Wish Fulfillment

22 Radical AI Ethics

ABOUT THE AUTHOR

Dr. Lance B. Eliot, Ph.D., MBA is a Stanford Fellow and a globally recognized AI expert and thought leader, an experienced executive and leader, a successful serial entrepreneur, and a noted scholar on AI, including that his Forbes and AI Trends columns have amassed over 5.8+ million views, his books on AI are frequently ranked in the Top 10 of all-time AI books, his articles are widely cited, and he has developed dozens of advanced AI systems.

He currently serves as the CEO of Techbruim, Inc. and has over twenty years of industry experience including serving as a corporate officer in billion-dollar sized firms and was a partner in a major consulting firm. He is also a successful entrepreneur having founded, ran, and sold several high-tech firms.

Dr. Eliot previously hosted the popular radio show *Technotrends* that was also available on American Airlines flights via their in-flight audio program, he has made appearances on CNN, has been a frequent speaker at industry conferences, and his podcasts have been downloaded over 100,000 times.

A former professor at the University of Southern California (USC), he founded and led an innovative research lab on Artificial Intelligence. He also previously served on the faculty of the University of California Los Angeles (UCLA) and was a visiting professor at other major universities. He was elected to the International Board of the Society for Information Management (SIM), a prestigious association of over 3,000 high-tech executives worldwide.

He has performed extensive community service, including serving as Senior Science Adviser to the Congressional Vice-Chair of the Congressional Committee on Science & Technology. He has served on the Board of the OC Science & Engineering Fair (OCSEF), where he is also has been a Grand Sweepstakes judge, and likewise served as a judge for the Intel International SEF (ISEF). He served as the Vice-Chair of the Association for Computing Machinery (ACM) Chapter, a prestigious association of computer scientists. Dr. Eliot has been a shark tank judge for the USC Mark Stevens Center for Innovation on start-up pitch competitions and served as a mentor for several incubators and accelerators in Silicon Valley and in Silicon Beach.

Dr. Eliot holds a Ph.D. from USC, MBA, and Bachelor's in Computer Science, and earned the CDP, CCP, CSP, CDE, and CISA certifications.

ADDENDUM

Latest Trends In AI Ethics

Practical Advances in Artificial Intelligence (AI) and Machine Learning

By
Dr. Lance B. Eliot, MBA, PhD

For special orders of this book, contact:

LBE Press Publishing

Email: LBE.Press.Publishing@gmail.com

Made in United States
Orlando, FL
04 November 2026

90206769R00203